JOSEPH ARCH

Joseph Arch at the time of the formation of the National Agricultural
Labourers' Union in 1872.

(*By permission from Cole Collection, Nuffield College, Oxford.*)

Joseph Arch

(1826-1919)
The Farm Workers' Leader

Pamela Horn
Ph.D., B.Sc.(Econ.)

Kineton: The Roundwood Press
1971

Set in 'Monotype' Times, series 327 and printed by Gordon Norwood at
The Roundwood Press, Kineton, in the County of Warwick.
Plates made by The Process Engraving Company Limited, Coventry.
Bound by Eric Neal, Welford, Rugby, Warwickshire.

Made and printed in Great Britain

Contents

Appendices

Illustrations

No man, having put his hand to the plough, and looking back, is fit for the Kingdom of God. LUKE IX; 62

Preface

IT IS A TRUISM to say that life in rural England today is very different from what it was a hundred and more years ago. No longer is agriculture the major industry, as was once the case, while the number of workers employed on the land has dwindled dramatically. English society is now predominantly urban and it is difficult to remember that it was not always so. Yet, when Joseph Arch was born in the South Warwickshire village of Barford in 1826, the countryman was still the typical Englishman — despite the growth of the new Northern industrial towns and of the factory system. When he died in 1919 the world he had known as a child had disappeared for ever.

This is the first full-length biography attempted of Arch, a man whose roots lay deep in the English countryside of the nineteenth century. It seeks to trace his career as leader of the farm workers, his efforts to improve their often miserable lot in life, and his entry into Parliament as an M.P. — the first agricultural labourer ever to obtain that honour. Nowadays his name is little known but to many Victorians it was, for a time, a household word. The biography attempts to explain his rise to fame and also to describe the village society from which he sprang and to which he remained closely linked throughout his long life.

In writing this book I have found Joseph Arch's autobiography, *The Story of His Life Told by Himself* (first published in 1898) a valuable — although not always reliable — source. In addition, I have received help and information from many people. I should like to thank all of them. In particular, however, I wish to express my gratitude to Mrs M. A. Fabyan of Massachusetts, U.S.A., one of Arch's surviving grandchildren; to Miss J. Swinyard of Wiltshire County Library; to Mr R. Moore of Snitterfield for the loan of manuscript material relating to Arch; to Mrs C. M. Barker of Oxford; to Mr D. Rudd of Barford; to the Staff of the Museum of English Rural Life at Reading University; and to the Staff of the British Museum Newspaper Library at Colindale. Mr Richard Hemmings and Mr George Worrall of Barford have kindly given information on Arch's later life in retirement at Barford, and to them, too, my warm thanks are due.

I owe an especial debt of gratitude to Mr A. G. Davies of Barford, who has tirelessly provided me with much information on the village and who has permitted me to inspect Joseph Arch's cottage — happily little changed from the days when he knew it.

Finally, on a more personal note, I should like to thank my parents for their encouragement to me over the years and my husband for his constant help and advice. He has cheerfully spent long hours reading chapter drafts and discussing 'Arch' topics with me; without his inspiration and assistance this biography would never have been written.

PAMELA L. R. HORN

PART ONE
1826-71

CHAPTER ONE

Early Life: 1826–46

THE PLACID South Warwickshire village of Barford lies on the left bank of the Avon, clinging snugly to a curve of the river, which forms its western boundary. The northern end of the parish is largely occupied by Barford Wood, which now forms part of Warwick Castle estate, and about two or three miles distant is the county town of Warwick itself. Stratford-on-Avon is only about seven miles away, and so Barford can be said to be well and truly in 'Shakespeare country'. It was here that Joseph Arch was born on 10th November, 1826.

At the time of Joseph's birth the village bore the peaceful outward appearance of many largely agricultural communities — and agriculture was indeed the major industry. At the time of the 1831 Census of Population, of the 167 families into which the inhabitants were divided, 85 families were engaged 'chiefly in agriculture,' as opposed to 41 engaged in 'retail trade or handicraft' (including those, like blacksmiths, who chiefly served the agriculturists), and 41 engaged in other, more varied occupations. And of the 192 males aged 20 years of age or more living in the village at that date, fifteen were farmers and no less than seventy-eight, agricultural labourers.[1]

Barford had probably changed little over the centuries, and many of its houses and cottages dated back to an earlier period. There were several seventeenth century timber framed cottages, with 'peaked gables and projecting frames and eaves of darkened wood', most still with their thatched roofs, like the one in which Joseph himself was born, and there were also solid old brick cottages built at about the same period. (Unfortunately, despite their attractive outer appearance a number of them suffered from that hidden hazard of village life — bad drainage — and only in the 1860's, after an outbreak of fever, were steps taken to remedy this.) A fine eighteenth century stone bridge spanned the 'willow fringed' Avon at this point, while in the centre of the village stood (and stands) the parish Church of St. Peter.

The tower of the Church dates from the end of the fourteenth century, but the rest of the building was reconstructed in 1844, during Joseph's own lifetime, in the style of that period. It has ashlar stone walls and slate roofs, and the Arch cottage stands almost directly opposite to it.

As we have seen, agriculture provided the most important single occupation for the inhabitants of Barford, and since the soil was quite fertile, it was a relatively prosperous industry, at least for the farmers and landowners, if not for the labourers. James Caird in his mid-nineteenth century survey of English agriculture noted in particular that: 'The red, deep, sandy loam in the centre of (Warwickshire), especially from Stratford by Wellesbourne to Warwick and Coventry, is the most valuable tract of soil, as it is equally adapted to turnip and bean culture. It lets at from 35s. to 45s. an acre . . .'[2]

Joseph Arch himself fitted well into this rural background. Both of his grandfathers had been agricultural labourers, and his own father followed in the same tradition. However, on neither side of the family was the connection with Barford of very long standing. Joseph's father had been born at the nearby village of Rowington, and his mother's parents, Joseph and Mary Pace, had only settled at Barford in the year 1794, when their daughter, Hannah (Joseph's mother), was about eleven years of age. Joseph Pace had been employed as a skilled hedger and ditcher on the Earl of Warwick's estate and it was whilst he was living in a lodge belonging to the estate that he and his wife had succeeded in saving up sufficient money to buy the freehold cottage at Barford — something which very few of their fellows were able to achieve at that time. The cottage and garden were purchased for £35 from a Warwick maltster by the name of John Aston.[3]

Hannah Pace probably lived in the Barford cottage for only a short time before she left home to obtain work as a servant at Warwick Castle. She later married a coachman, named John Sharrard, and it was following his death in 1816 that she married John Arch, as her second husband. This wedding took place on 12th October, 1818; Hannah was almost ten years her husband's senior, and at the time of their marriage was aged about thirty-five.

Within a fortnight of the wedding, Hannah's father died,[4] and so the couple settled down at Barford to live with his widow, Mary Pace, in the family cottage. It was there that their first child, a daughter, was born in the autumn of the following year. Altogether there were to be four children. The two eldest, both girls, were Mary, born in 1819, and Ann, born in 1821. Not until January, 1824, was the first son, John, born but he died less than eighteen months later, in April, 1825, and more than a year then elapsed before Joseph arrived in November, 1826.

From the beginning Joseph seems to have been his mother's

favourite, perhaps because he was the only surviving boy, and he obviously returned her devotion, As he later wrote: '. . . if ever a man truly loved and admired his mother, I did!'[5] Hannah was a strong, sturdily built, determined woman, very different from her quiet and unassuming husband. It was from her that Joseph inherited both his early interest in religious Nonconformity and his independent attitude.

And all of Hannah's determination and resourcefulness were needed in those difficult days of the 1820's and 1830's. Her husband was 'a sober, industrious agricultural labourer, steady as old Time, a plodding man, and a good all-round worker . . .' but for all his conscientiousness, his wages never rose above 1s. 8d. a day, or 10s. a week. Sometimes they fell below that figure, especially during the winter months, when work was often in short supply and a full week's employment (and consequently pay) not always available. Furthermore, even he could rebel on occasion. According to his son, in 1835 he refused to sign a petition in favour of the Corn Laws, i.e. in favour of that continued protection of home-grown wheat to which most agriculturists were at the time passionately wedded. For this action he was thrown out of work for four months, and it was Hannah, working as a laundress, who then largely supported the family with her earnings.[6]

Yet, even without unemployment, the lot of the labourer was a hard one. Average basic cash wages were low, and although wheat and barley (and consequently bread) had fallen in price from the heights reached at the beginning of the century, during the Napoleonic wars,[7] they were still expensive — wheat in the Barford area averaging 8s. 6d. per Winchester bushel in the period 1829–31.[8] The price of beef and mutton, at an estimated 6d. or 7d. per lb., was normally well outside the budget of the average labourer and his family,[9] and for many 'even a morsel of bacon was considered a luxury'. Frequently, poor people were forced to steal turnips from the fields and to poach, or else to rely on charity soup and food (perhaps provided by the local clergyman or squire) in order to satisfy the pangs of hunger.[10] During the difficult winter months, too, many labourers were forced to rely for their subsistence on poor relief, paid out of the local rates; in the year ending 25th March, 1827, for example, Barford poor law expenditure amounted to the large sum of £535 13s. — and this for a total population of around 750 only. Although in the succeeding years the parish overseers managed to keep below that peak, even in 1834 the expenditure was £314 17s. — an indication of the considerable number of people who had to rely on the pitifully few shillings per week allowed as poor relief when all other income had failed. Following the passage of the Poor Law (Amendment) Act of 1834, which was designed to tighten up the distribution of out relief, Barford's poor rate expenditure fell further. Yet even for the year ending 25th March, 1837, it amounted to the not inconsiderable sum of £294, of which £195 had been expended directly on 'relief of the poor'. At the time of the Census of Population held in June, 1841, the parish had fourteen people officially classed as paupers; of these thirteen were women and one was an old man.[11]

Nevertheless, it seems reasonable to assume that the determined paring down of expenditure which these figures reveal did cause great difficulties for some at least of Barford's poorer inhabitants. This appears especially so since the village's population continued to grow steadily for some years to come, only reaching its peak (according to the Censuses of Population) in 1851 — when it stood at 872.

Joseph's own family, saved the outlay of perhaps £3 per annum for rent, which many Barford cottagers had to pay, and with the advantage of a large garden, were able to avoid some of the worst of the hardships suffered by their less fortunate fellows. In any case, Hannah Arch's proud spirit prevented her from availing herself of even minor charitable aids, like the soup provided by the rector, Francis Mills, and his wife. Joseph later recalled how: 'Numbers of people used to go to the rectory for soup but not a drop of it did we touch. I have stood at our door with my mother, and . . . seen her face look sad as she watched the little children toddle past, carrying the tin cans, and their toes coming out of their boots . . . I never went to the rectory for soup.'[12] Yet, even for *his* family, life was difficult, and bread too often the staple diet.

From the age of about six until nine, Joseph attended the local village school, receiving an education in the three 'R's' of which he later spoke with some approval. Although the school was then accommodated in a new building, completed only in 1822, Barford was one of those fortunate villages which had long had educational facilities for its poorer inhabitants. As early as 1677, the then rector, the Rev. Thomas Dugard, had bequeathed '£5 forever issuing out of certain lands . . . £4 for such person as should teach fourteen poor boys and the other £1 to teach two poor girls.' During the next one hundred and fifty years and more, this small endowment was supplemented by other gifts, so that by the 1830's the school could provide for sixty children. Joseph's schoolmaster, Richard Sabin, was a conscientious man and a good teacher; he was clearly trusted by the Arch family, too, for in 1826 he had been chosen by them to act as an executor in connection with the Will made by Hannah's mother, Mary Pace.[13] Joseph's own admiration for him as 'sensible and practical above the common,' and with the 'true interests of his scholars at heart', only serves to bear this out.

Unfortunately, much as the boy may have benefited from his

education, in 1835 all this had to be put behind him. Money was short and, like most other nine-year-old Barford boys, he must start work, bird scaring for the meagre wage of 4d. for a twelve-hour day![14] Clad in smock frock and old, heavy hobnailed boots, he went to his lonely, monotonous task of shouting and shaking a rattle to scare the greedy birds from the growing corn. Like many another bird scarer, he discovered that the birds quickly learnt to disregard the noise and to calculate the exact distance that his young arm could throw a stone. When they were eventually driven away from one end of a field, they would descend, with mocking cries and an increased appetite upon the other.

Sometimes Joseph got so bored with his work that he decided to risk the consequences by seeking diversions in bird-nesting, or climbing trees, or trespassing on nearby land.[15] But woe betide him should his master discover him idling. A sharp cut or two with a stick was soon administered to teach him to behave differently in the future!

After about a year of this (during which time he was employed by several local farmers), Joseph next obtained work as a ploughboy, for a wage of 3s. per week — a rate which was, incidentally, still current in Barford for ploughboys thirty years later! The head carter was a strict disciplinarian, a 'cruel flogger', as Arch called him, and he has provided a graphic picture of this period of his life, in his autobiography: 'Many a time and oft in the dark and early hours of the morning has little Joseph Arch, the ploughboy, trudged up the lane, 'creeping like snail unwillingly to work', with his satchel on his shoulder, containing not books, but his food for the day. This would be a hunch of barley bread, with occasionally an apple baked in paste of coarse wheat-meal. Apple-dumpling day was a red one in my boy's calender . . .'[16]

Despite the harshness of his working conditions, however, Joseph persevered and by the time he was aged 12 or 13 his wage had risen to 8d. per day. It was at about this period in his life that he moved to a new employer — Edward Greaves of Avon Side House, Barford — who was one of the principal landowners in the parish, along with the Earl of Warwick and the Ryland family.

Avon Side, a large rambling property backing on to the river, was very conveniently for Joseph, situated in Church Street, only about a hundred yards away from the Arch cottage. Mr Greaves, its owner, was a banker and justice of the peace as well as a landowner, and on his relatively small home farm of 80 acres he employed about nine men. Joseph's first task for him was to drive horses to the plough just as he had done for his previous employer, but quite soon Greaves perceived that he was a lad with some initiative and he 'promoted' him to stable boy — with a welcome rise in pay to 8s. per week. Joseph was to remain at Avon Side for a number of years, only leaving when he was about 16 or 17.

But while Arch's career was developing and he himself was growing up, certain changes were apparent in his own immediate family circle. His grandmother, Mary Pace, had died (she had in fact died, aged 86, in August, 1833, before he started work), and the younger of his two sisters, Ann, had left home. At the time of the Census of Population in June, 1841, therefore, only Joseph and his elder sister, Mary, were still living at home with their parents. A few months later, in November, 1841, Ann Arch married John Cogbill, a local blacksmith, at Barford Parish Church. Both were under twenty-one years of age and soon after their marriage they appear to have left Barford.

Within the village itself, however, life flowed on along its accustomed channels. Joseph continued his simple education at home, with his mother's help and encouragement, and spent much of his free time in reading his books — including of course the Bible (and Shakespeare). Unfortunately for him, there was no formal evening school held at Barford in those days, unlike the position in the 1860's for example, when classes for young people were held regularly on two evenings per week for sixteen weeks during the winter months. Self-help was thus his only recourse.

At that period there were indeed few outside diversions to occupy Joseph's precious leisure moments. As he himself pointed out: 'There was not much in the way of amusement going on in the village to distract my attention . . . The village lad had two kinds of recreation open to him. He could take his choice between lounging and boozing in the public house, or playing bowls in the bowling alley' — neither of which appealed to Joseph[17]. He did, however, join the village friendly society (established in 1832) and presumably he also attended its meetings. These were held first at the George Inn, then in the school room, and finally, from the late 1870's (when membership was about 74) at the Red Lion.[18] Like the other members, he probably also attended the society's annual feast day, held every Whit Tuesday, when the members paraded the village in holiday mood before attending at the Parish Church for a service conducted by the rector. After this, they repaired to their clubroom to celebrate and also to elect new officers for the coming year; but they were careful not to allow the festivities to get out of hand. According to the Rule Book, any member who left the 'club room for the purpose of gaming or acting disorderly' was to be fined one shilling or 'suspended from benefit for six months'. This was no doubt a suitably sobering prospect for most of them![19] Arch, for his part, continued to belong to the society at least until the end of the nineteenth century and possibly to the time of his death.[20]

7

In addition to his educational and friendly society activities, these years in the early 1840's saw the development of two further interests, which were to be of great significance in Joseph's later life. The first was his growing concern with politics. From as early as 1844/45, he spent precious pennies — earned in running errands or doing odd jobs — on the purchase of old newspapers, so that he might read the speeches of Gladstone and Bright. From these he formed his life-long political opinions.

The second interest was in regard to religion. Although John Arch had always attended Church regularly, his wife proved less orthodox. She was frequently impatient with the influence exerted by the rector and his wife over the lives of the Barford labourers and their children, and it was her influence which was to prove decisive for her son. When, in about 1840, some Methodist preachers — 'rough and ready men' devoted to their religion — came over from nearby Wellesbourne to hold meetings in a barn at Barford, Joseph and his mother were among those who attended. Later in the decade, the boy's interest was to find direct expression when he himself became a Primitive Methodist local preacher.

In this fashion therefore the months and the years ran uneventfully by until suddenly, in September, 1845, the peaceful family life was shattered, with the death of Hannah Arch, at the age of 62. As Joseph's autobiography reveals, the bereavement was a very great blow: 'It was an irretrievable loss, a terrible grief to me.'[21] The mainspring of the household had gone.

However, Hannah's death carried with it legal repercussions as well. Under the terms of her mother's Will (made in February, 1826, seven years before she died) provision was made that after Mrs Pace's death the family cottage was to pass to Hannah for her lifetime only and was then to descend to her two daughters, Mary and Ann, 'as tenants in common and not as joint tenants.'[22] This provision, deliberately excluding John Arch as it did, might have caused some discord in the family circle, but, in practice, both John and later his son, appear to have ignored its implications. Both certainly claimed the Parliamentary franchise under the freeholder clause, on the basis of cottage in 'own occupation,'[23] and neither Mary nor Ann seems to have laid any claim to the property.

Shortly after his mother's death, Joseph was given two opportunities to leave Barford. He was offered 'a good situation in the army, as officer's attendant,' and was also 'pressed to emigrate to America under very favourable auspices.' Perhaps fortunately for the development of agricultural trade unionism, he rejected both offers, in deference to his father's wishes.[24] He thus continued to live at home with his father and, for a time, his elder sister, Mary, who kept house for them, until she, too, obtained employment elsewhere (like her sister before her). The two men were then left to cater for themselves, and both of them, of course, continued working. Joseph was employed on several local farms and was acquiring increasing proficiency in the various agricultural skills which were later to stand him in such good stead.

Nevertheless, despite this, the home life of father and son remained unsatisfactory, and in the circumstances Joseph's next step is scarcely surprising. On 3rd February, 1847, just under eighteen months after his mother died, he married, at Barford Church. He was aged twenty years and three months and his bride was Mary Ann Mills, a domestic servant and the daughter of Isaac Mills, a carpenter from the nearby village of Wellesbourne Mountford.[25] A new phase in his life — as husband and later father — was about to begin.

[1] *Population of Great Britain,* 1831 *Census* — Parliamentary Papers, 1833, Vol. XXXVII, p. 672.

[2] James Caird — *English Agriculture in* 1850–51 (London, 1968 edn.), p. 221.

[3] Abstract of Title to The Cottage, Barford. The present owner of The Cottage has kindly given permission for me to quote from the Abstract and I am grateful for his generous help It is perhaps interesting to note that at the time of purchase in 1794, Joseph Pace nominated Edward Page of Barford, schoolmaster, to act as Trustee on his behalf; presumably he felt the need for the assistance of a person of some education.

[4] Barford Burial Records at Warwickshire County Record Office, D.R. 207/4.

[5] Joseph Arch — *The Story of His Life told by Himself* (London, 1898), pp. 8–9.

[6] *Ibid.,* p. 10.

[7] At its highest point during the Napoleonic Wars, in 1812, wheat was averaging 29s. 6d. per cwt. and barley, in the same year, 18s. 8d. per cwt. By 1836, wheat averaged 11s. 4d. per cwt. and barley 9s. 2d. — See *A Century of Agricultural Statistics* (H.M.S.O. 1968), p. 81. At around this time the ordinary wheaten 4 lb. loaf cost perhaps 8d. or 9d. — John Burnett — *A History of the Cost of Living* (London, 1969), pp. 262–263.

[8] *Royal Commission on the Poor Laws* — Appendix A, Part II — Parliamentary Papers, 1834, Vol. XXIX, p. 75a.

[9] *Ibid.* Evidence of Mr W. Handley, a Barford farmer, agent and surveyor.

[10] Joseph Arch, *op. cit.* pp. 12–15.

[11] 1841 Census of Population for Barford — Public Record Office, H.O. 107.1134. Details of Barford's poor law expenditure can be found in: *Account of money expended for Maintenance and Relief of the Poor for the five years ending 25th March* 1825–29 — Parliamentary Papers, 1830–31, Vol. XI, and *Account of money expended for Maintenance and Relief of the Poor for the five years ending 25th March* 1830–34 — Parliamentary Papers, 1835 — Vol. XLVII. Also *Third Report of Poor Law Commissioners for year ending 25th March* 1837 — Parliamentary Papers, 1837, Vol. XXXI. For a comparative study of poor relief expenditure in two Kentish villages prior to 1834, see — James P. Huzel — 'Malthus, the Poor Law, and Population in Early Nineteenth-Century England' — in *Economic History Review,* 2nd Series, Vol. XXII, No. 3, December, 1969.

[12] Joseph Arch, *op. cit.,* p.15.

[13] See Abstract of Title to the Cottage, Barford.

[14] More than thirty years later the Barford bird scarer's wage was still the same. Second Report of *Royal Commission on Employment of Children, Young Persons and Women in Agriculture,* Parliamentary Papers, 1868–69, Vol. XIII, Pt. II, Appendix A, p.222 Joseph's own eldest son was, incidentally, kept at school until the age of 12 — perhaps

the father had learnt from his own experience. — See 1861 Census of Population for Barford — Public Record Office, R.G.9.2219.

[15] Joseph Arch, *op.cit.*, p.28.

[16] *Ibid.*, p.32.

[17] *Ibid.*, p.34.

[18] It was, incidentally, the Red Lion public house which was re-named the Joseph Arch, in a ceremony held in April, 1960. The George Inn, the original friendly society venue, was situated in Bridge Street, almost opposite to the Red Lion. It was sold for £250 in 1871, and was then delicensed; it is now used as a butcher's shop. The friendly society moved from there to the school room in 1868, and a few years later established itself at the Red Lion. I am indebted to Mr. A G Davies of Barford for his help in locating the George Inn and also to Mr Hadley of Barford. For other information on the George Inn see Kelly's Directory of Birmingham, Staffordshire, Warwickshire and Worcestershire, 1868, and 1851 Census Return for Barford — H.O.107.2072. For details of the Friendly Society at the end of the 1870's — See Parliamentary Papers, 1883, Vol. LXVIII — Return of Friendly Societies.

[19] Barford Friendly Society Records at Public Record Office — F.S.3/383. The Society according to its 1845 rules, allowed sick members 8s. per week during illness; at death £2 10s. was allowed for funeral expenses for all members of two years' standing or more, plus a second £2 10s. to be paid to the widow or next of kin within the following twelve months. At the death of a member's wife the member was allowed £1 towards her funeral expenses. A further and more detailed Rule Book was issued in 1868, when somewhat higher benefits became available.

[20] Joseph Arch, *op.cit.*, p.34.

[21] Joseph Arch, op.cit., p.38. In his autobiography, however, Arch unaccountably dates this event as 1842. Barford parish records show it to be September, 1845 — Warwickshire County Record Office, DR.207/4.

[22] See Abstract of Title to the Cottage, Barford.

[23] See Copies of the Registers of Voters for the South Division of Warwickshire at Warwickshire County Record Office. John Arch did not appear as a voter in 1832–33 (before the death of Mary Pace), but appears every year thereafter, until his death. Joseph's name appears from that date. The cottage only legally came into Joseph's ownership in 1909. See Abstract of Title and also information kindly provided for the author by Professor Grove of Naunton, Gloucestershire.

[24] Rev. F S Attenborough — *Joseph Arch* (Leamington, 1872), p.30.

[25] Barford Marriage Registers at Warwickshire County Record Office, DR.207/3. As a matter of interest, like John Arch and Hannah, Isaac Mills, Joseph's father-in-law, was several years younger than his wife, Charlotte. At the time of the 1861 Census of Population he was aged 55 and she was 63. Both were still living at Wellesbourne, just as they had been when Joseph married. — See 1861 Census of population for Wellesbourne — Public Record Office, R.G.9.2229.

CHAPTER TWO

Years of Apprenticeship: 1847-71

FTER THEIR WEDDING, Joseph and Mary Ann Arch returned to the family cottage at Barford, where the remainder of their married life was to be spent — save for the periods when Joseph was travelling away from home in connection with his work. Mary Ann was about a year older than her husband and, with her training as a domestic servant, she soon proved to be a competent housewife, well able to look after both her husband and her father-in-law. In appearance, she was 'the very picture of health, cleanliness, and respectability; and in conversation (she displayed) a force of mind and character, which (might) be termed surprising . . .' Allied to this were deep and sincere religious convictions.[1] However, her educational attainments were not all that her husband might have desired, and in later life, when his own career had progressed beyond the rather narrow confines of village life, he felt this limitation particularly severely. Somewhat unfairly he tended to blame Mary Ann herself for it, rather than the society in which she had grown up: 'My wife was not the woman my mother was . . . She was no scholar and . . . she was no companion in my aspirations.'[2] Nevertheless, if she had no scholastic ambitions of her own, she certainly encouraged her husband to add to his knowledge, and to his stock of books. 'He used, in fact, often to sit up late at night reading any books that he could get, whilst smoking his pipe by (the) kitchen fire', after his wife had gone to bed.[3]

The young couple's first child, a daughter named Hannah, was born towards the end of 1847, and in November of the following year came the birth of their first son, John. Altogether there were to be seven children (four boys and three girls), the last of them, Thomas, being born in May, 1864. The youngest of the girls, Elizabeth, was the only one not to survive childhood. She died on 12th March, 1859, at the age of five.

For Mrs Arch this increase in family presented growing household problems. Although her father-in-law was still working as a labourer

II

and Joseph himself was earning about 11s. a week (but sometimes less), she found it extremely hard to make ends meet. Then, too, from her previous employment as a domestic servant she knew that in the houses of the well-to-do 'better food was given to the cats and dogs' than she could afford to buy with her few shillings to feed her children. This bred feelings of bitterness and frustration. Consequently, after the birth of her second child she told her husband that she could no longer manage on their small income; either he must ask for a rise in pay or she would go out to work herself. This latter suggestion hurt Joseph's pride, and he resolved to ask for an increase without further delay. As he had half feared, the request was turned down and so he decided to leave and see if he could fare better on his own account as a jobbing labourer.

This decision proved to be a major turning point in his life — the first real expression of his independence. His first position was digging gravel at Warwick, and every day he set off from Barford at the crack of dawn so as to arrive ready to start work at 5 a.m. From that he moved to another job, woodcutting at the nearby village of Bishop's Tachbrook and followed this up with drainage contracting. In this way, therefore, he embarked on his career as a free-lance. Soon he began hedge-cutting on a considerable scale (he had first experimented in this whilst still working for Mr Greaves, the banker), and it was in this sphere that he was to show particular proficiency. By the 1850's he had so perfected his hedging skills that he was beginning to win prizes in local competitions. His first reported success came in the year 1857, when he obtained a third prize of 10s. in the 'ordinary hedging class' of the Wellesbourne Ploughing Society's Show. There were altogether sixteen competitors and he was entered for the event by a local farmer, Thomas Horley of Fosse Farm.[4] (The Wellesbourne Ploughing Society had in fact been offering prizes for hedgecutting since 1840).

This proved to be the beginning of more than a decade of prize winning for Arch. In October of the following year he won the Warwickshire Agricultural Society's second prize of £1 15s. for 'hedging and ditching,' and further successes followed, to a greater or lesser extent, until in 1869 he won the Society's sixth prize of 15s. for this event. He did not compete in the 1870 and 1871 Shows.

Quite soon, in view of his undoubted aptitude, Joseph was able to command wages of perhaps 2s. 6d. to 3s. 6d. per day — well above the basic 11s. or 12s. per week earned by many of his less enterprising fellows. He was now travelling all over his own county and into many others as well, carrying out hedge-cutting, drainage, ploughing and mowing contracts. On at least one occasion, in 1860, he and another Barford hedge-cutter earned an average of 4s. 6d. per day for twelve days whilst they were performing a fencing contract on the Arkwright family's Hampton Court estate, near Leominster in Herefordshire.[5] In addition, Mr Arkwright paid their travelling expenses from Dinmore in Herefordshire to Stratford-on-Avon — involving a further outlay of 16s. 2d. for each man. The rate paid to the two Warwickshire men for this fencing contract was well in excess of the average normally given for that type of work in Herefordshire, but the quality of workmanship was such that Arkwright did not object. Indeed, when he wrote on the subject many years later, he declared: 'The pay was fair and the work well done. At that date, fourteen years ago, our own hedgers could not have done the same amount of work . . .'[6]

Among other areas visited by Joseph at this time were South Wales and Gloucestershire. In the latter he worked mainly around the village of Welford-on-Avon, where he stayed in a small cottage with a friend who was also an agricultural contractor.[7] Altogether Joseph went into Gloucestershire for ten years in succession, sometimes remaining in the county for only three weeks, but on other occasions for as long as six, depending on the amount of work available.

Whilst on his travels he was not, of course, always as fortunately placed as he appears to have been in Herefordshire and Gloucestershire. As he later noted: 'Hard work, good wages, rough quarters, strange companions, long journeys and long absences — such was the programme.' On occasion, in order to economise on his expenditure, he slept on straw in barns and even under hedges. During some of his visits to Wales, however, he was invited to preach in the chapels, and he noted with particular gratitude the kindness shown to him by many Welsh cotters during his visits to their country.

Naturally Arch was also employed by local agriculturalists as well, and one Warwickshire farmer for whom he worked on more than one occasion was John Canning, of Sherborne. Another was Edward Greaves, for whom he had worked in his youth, and who was a major Barford landowner. Greaves was a strong Conservative, being for some years M.P. for Warwick, but this difference of political opinion with the Radical Joseph did not prevent him from sponsoring the latter's entry for the hedging and ditching competition of the Warwickshire Agricultural Society's Show in 1868. Although, according to Arch's own account in his autobiography, he tried to persuade the hedge-cutter to vote Tory at the General Election held a month or two later, he apparently bore no ill-will when Joseph refused.

(Ten years earlier, in June, 1858, Mr Greaves had, no doubt, won the hearts of young Hannah, John and Annie Arch when he provided tea and plumcake for all the Barford school children on the occasion of Queen Victoria's visit to Warwick Castle. 'After tea they were amused by a balloon ascent, various games, and by a good supply of oranges, with showers of nuts and cakes, and their hilarity was kept

13

up until about eight o'clock . . .,' according to an account in the *Warwick Advertiser*).[8]

However, apart from his skill in agricultural work, Joseph was fortunate in being able to turn his hand to other activities. In particular, he was employed by a local carpenter and builder to do roofing work and woodwork, but his versatility was such that coffin-making, hurdle making and gate hanging all came within his scope. It is significant that after his father's death in 1862, he was skilful enough to replace the old thatched roof of the cottage with the existing slate one and was also able to add some windows and a small greenhouse.[9] Upstairs he strengthened the floor of one of the bedrooms and built a narrow staircase in place of the wooden ladder which had formerly given access to the upper rooms. More than a hundred years later evidence of his work is still preserved at the cottage. It was, of course, this ability to carry out a variety of tasks which helped to develop his self-confidence and spirit of independence and which enabled him to raise his earnings above those of many of his fellow labourers at that time. 'Being a good all-round man (he) was never at a loss for a job.'

In addition to the development of Arch's agricultural skills and his obvious self-reliance, however, these years provided two further important pointers for the future. Soon after his marriage he had become a Primitive Methodist local preacher, and by that means he served his apprenticeship in the difficult art of public speaking. In this connection, in March, 1849, he was involved in the purchase of land at Barford for the erection of a Methodist Chapel. In his capacity as a preacher, too, he became known over a wide area. Mention has already been made of the fact that he was in the habit of preaching whilst he was working in South Wales, but he also travelled extensively in the nearby Warwickshire villages and towns, in order to fulfil his preaching commitments. In later life, his third son, Edward, could remember, for example, walking on Sundays to Stratford-on-Avon when his father had preaching duties in the town.[10] And coupled with this work was a staunch belief in teetotallism. Joseph lost no opportunity in urging temperance principles upon his fellow labourers, for too often he saw how drunkenness led many of them into serious debt.

Alongside his continuing interest in religious Nonconformity, however, there was equally an ever-stronger political feeling in favour of the Liberal Party. Arch had begun to read political speeches and to take notice of political discussions while still a teenager, and his enthusiasm for politics certainly did not diminish with the years. Following the death of his father in October, 1862, at the age of 70, Joseph became a registered voter for the South Warwickshire constituency, under the 40s. freeholder franchise. At a time when most agricultural labourers were without the vote, since they were merely tenants and not owners of their cottages, this in itself was a valuable status symbol. But to Joseph it was more than that. Although he did not take the opportunity to vote in the 1865 Election (in his autobiography he rather gives the impression that he did), in the 1868 contest he played a full part. During the campaign he stumped the countryside in the Liberal cause and voted for both of that Party's candidates on polling day — an action requiring some courage in itself, in those days of open voting, when many of the farmers and landowners — his future employers — would be supporting the opposite side. But despite all the efforts made, neither of the Liberal candidates (Lord Hyde and Sir R. N. C. Hamilton, Bart.) was, in fact, successful. The Conservatives retained both seats — albeit by a very narrow margin, the second Tory only scraping home by 29 votes over his nearest Liberal rival.[11]

Although this result must have been a disappointment for Arch, it seems that at least one benefit accrued to him as a result of his campaigning — he made contact with leading Liberals in the area and became known as a political activist. Certainly, it was claimed many years later that Arch's work in the 1868 General Election had encouraged the *Royal Leamington Chronicle* to pay early attention to the agricultural trade union movement which he came to lead in 1872. It was through the columns of that newspaper that the movement secured its first vital publicity. The proprietor of the *Chronicle*, J. E. Matthew Vincent, was himself a Liberal of the 'advanced' school.[12]

By the end of the 1860's, therefore, Arch's personal life was entering upon a more secure phase. Earlier in the decade the prolonged illness of his father (who had been confined to the house for ten months before he died) had provided a considerable drain on the son's slender financial resources. Mrs Arch had been forced to give up her small part-time earnings of 2s. a week as a charwoman so that she could nurse the old man, and in view of their plight, Joseph decided to apply to the Warwick Board of Guardians for a grant of poor relief at the rate of 1s. 6d. per week to compensate for his wife's loss of earnings and to meet some of the inevitable nursing expenses. This moderate demand was rejected by the Board, however, and Joseph was informed that his father must either enter the workhouse, or be nursed at home at his son's expense. Since the workhouse was almost universally hated and feared by old people because of its harsh and unsympathetic institutional atmosphere, Joseph had no choice but to take on the responsibility himself. Although John Arch had stuck to work as long as ever he could, going to the fields 'until the doctor said he would die in them if he went again', the total of his savings was 4s. 6d. — quite inadequate to pay even the doctor's bills! In this way, physically helpless and financially quite dependent on his son, he lingered for

15

eight months until eventually the Board of Guardians relented. 'Against Arch's will, but with the consent of his wife', they agreed to allow the old man 1s. 6d. a week and a loaf as out relief.[13] He continued to receive this tiny sum for the remaining two months of his life. Joseph's opposition to the receipt of the relief was, of course, grounded on his bitter resentment at the brusque treatment afforded to him at the time of his original request.

After the cost of his father's funeral and the doctor's bills had been met, Arch found himself £10 in debt. By dint of hard work the debt was paid off. Then on 15th May, 1864, his seventh and last child, Thomas, was born. By this time the two eldest children were working — Hannah being employed as a domestic servant and John as a farm labourer. Soon, they were joined by Annie, the second daughter, who became a dressmaker.

But by the end of the decade the position had changed again. Hannah had married and left home, and on 6th September, 1869, John joined the Army, enlisting in the 2/23 Foot, later the Royal Welsh Fusiliers. His original engagement was for twelve years' service, but, in fact, he was to remain in the Army for just over twenty-one years. He was by now a slim young man of twenty, of medium height and with light brown hair and hazel eyes. Once enlisted, his first promotions came fairly rapidly. He was made a corporal on 28th October, 1871, and a sergeant about two years later.[14] Not surprisingly, this progress was a matter of considerable pride to his father.

Although Annie, the third child, continued to live at home, she, too, was busy with her dressmaking and sewing. In particular, she helped Mrs Purser, wife of the landlord of the Guernsey Temperance Hotel, Leamington, 'with her large family's making and mending,'[15] but she also worked in a number of other homes in the district, including that of Mr Vincent, the proprietor of the *Royal Leamington Chronicle*.[16] Annie was probably the most like her father of all the children. She had the same strong face and sturdy frame, and she, too, became an enthusiastic Primitive Methodist. At the age of nineteen (i.e. in about 1870), she was appointed a local preacher in the Leamington circuit and carried out many preaching engagements in the area. Later on she was to speak at some of her father's trade union meetings and to preach at services held especially for the labourers.

Of the remaining children, Joseph, the second son — like his elder brother — worked for a time as a farm labourer, although by the mid-1870's he had left the land to join the railways as a clerk/porter. The other two surviving children, Edward and Thomas, were still at school.

Such, therefore, was the situation of the family in 1870. In a material sense they were obviously much better off than had been the case when most of the children were young and dependent; now only two were still at school. In addition, the Arches, unlike most other labouring families, enjoyed the great advantage of security of tenure of their small four-roomed cottage, and they were free, too, from the burden of rent. Inside, the house was kept scrupulously clean and the rooms were simply but comfortably furnished. A contemporary sketch of the low-ceilinged, oak-beamed living room, which was published in the *Illustrated London News* of 13th April, 1872, enables one to gain some idea of its contents. The main articles of furniture obviously comprised two wooden tables and several inexpensive wooden windsor chairs, but on the high mantelpiece stood some of the chimney ornaments beloved by most Victorian cottagers — including a pair of the ubiquitous Staffordshire pottery dogs sometimes known as 'comforters'. In a corner stood an eight-day grandfather clock which John and Hannah Arch had brought from Leamington more than thirty years before. (Joseph later recalled in his autobiography how his father had 'carried home the case over his shoulder, and (his) mother (had) trudged at his side with the works in her market basket.'[17]) By the hearth was placed a simple wooden arm chair, which was nearly one hundred years old and had once belonged to Joseph's grandmother, and on the walls, significantly, were a number of religious prints and a few well-filled book shelves; one of the tables, too, was piled high with books and newspapers — a tribute to Joseph's literary and political interests. His religious interests were, of course, equally confirmed, not only by the prints on the walls but also by a Primitive Methodist local Preacher's plan which hung behind the inner door.[18]

And if the inside of the house were well maintained, the same could be said of the exterior. 'The garden was choke full of fruit and vegetables in their season . . .' and they, of course, provided a valuable supplement to the family diet.

Outside the home Joseph's growing status as a skilful free-lance worker not only gave him considerable influence and authority with his fellows, but it also brought him into contact with an increasing circle of brother labourers. He did not hesitate to use this opportunity, where possible, to speak out against the hardships of their lives and to press for change. And with his sturdy, thick-set figure and strong bearded face, he was a man to be taken notice of — the epitome of dogged determination. His constant harping on the need for change gradually began to awaken a response in the minds of his listeners.

Joseph had been dissatisfied with his low wages and conditions of employment even in the early 1850's. Twenty years later many others were coming to share his feelings — and justifiably so. In certain instances they responded to the situation by a reversion to the old-fashioned methods of arson. For example, at Carlton Curlieu and Kibworth in Leicestershire, in 1870, there was an outbreak of rick burning, and tied to the hedge near to the scenes of the fires were discovered threatening letters. One letter found at Kibworth warned the farmer victim of the attack: 'If you don't raise wages this week, you won't have a chance next. If there is any Irish left here after this week they will have to have a fresh gaffer. This is the last week of low wages . . .' Despite the offering of rewards, the perpetrators of these acts were never discovered.[19]

Nevertheless, the number of stack fires caused by malevolence rather than accident was not great in this period and, in general, dissatisfied labourers preferred to register their discontent by voting with their feet and leaving the land altogether. In this way they were following in the footsteps of their dissatisfied predecessors of earlier generations, who had sought employment in the docks and factories and on the railways of industrial England.

Yet, by the end of the 1860's some few dissatisfied labourers could be found to whom neither of the above solutions seemed acceptable. Instead, for almost the first time, they decided to imitate the urban workers and to try to form trade unions.[20]

As early as 1866 a short-lived agricultural union (the Agricultural Labourers' Protection Association) had been established in Kent, while in June of the same year a similar attempt was made around the village of Great Glen, near Leicester. Here the workers in this and nearby villages formed a union and demanded an increase of 2s. in their basic weekly wage of about 10s. The employers responded by evicting all of the strikers living in tied cottages, and in the face of their opposition, the combination soon seems to have died a natural death.[21] In 1867, a further attempt was made to set up a union, this time centred on the town of Buckingham and seeking to organise workers in both Buckinghamshire and Northamptonshire. The strike of labourers in the Buckinghamshire village of Gawcott, which was called in connection with this union, even aroused the attention of the national press. Various newspapers (including *The Times*) contained reports of it, and it evoked a response from labourers in a number of other Buckinghamshire villages; thus an Agricultural Labourers' Protection Union was established at Great Missenden, and at Ivinghoe on 20th May, two hundred labourers and others met in a field opposite to the new Wesleyan Chapel 'to form a committee, choose a secretary, and discuss the subject of wages . . .'[22] Yet, once again, the opposition was too great and the movement faded away.[23]

Next, in the spring of 1868, came the first attempt to establish a National Union. On this occasion, however, the impetus came not from the labourers themselves but rather from middle-class well-wishers, including Canon Girdlestone, the incumbent of the Devonshire parish of Halberton, who had already won considerable fame for his efforts to improve the lot of his poorer parishioners. Girdlestone and his friends called a conference at Willis's Rooms, London on 28th March, 1868, to discuss the 'cause of the unsatisfactory condition of the agricultural labourer', and to consider the best means of improving that condition. The urban trade union leaders, Robert Applegarth and George Potter, were also invited to attend the gathering, along with a number of other Radicals like the Hon. Auberon Herbert and Professor Thorold Rogers. In the event, however, the labourers' response proved too weak and these well-meaning efforts all came to naught.[24]

Such, then, was the rather unpromising history of the rural union movement up to the end of the 1860's. Tentative attempts had been made to form agricultural trade unions but through lack of leadership and effective organisation, they had rapidly disappeared in the face of determined opposition from the farmers. However, fresh energy was given to the whole cause in 1871, with the passage of the Trade Union Act of that year; this legislation explicitly legalised registered trade unions and provided full security for their funds. The publicity which attended the passage of the Act, coupled with the success of a contemporaneous movement among the engineers and builders for a nine-hour day, underlined the advantages which could be gained from combination. It was in this atmosphere of renewed hope, therefore, that the next serious attempt was made to establish an agricultural union — in Herefordshire, in 1871.

The Herefordshire Union, more properly entitled the North Herefordshire and South Shropshire Agricultural Labourers' Improvement Society, was established largely through the initiative of Thomas Strange, a Primitive Methodist school teacher from the parish of Leintwardine, where the first meeting of the Society was held. It soon secured a considerable measure of support — Arch himself later estimated that it recruited members in six different counties and eventually obtained a membership of about 30,000. But it was an essentially peaceful organisation, its watchword being, 'Emigration, Migration but not Strikes'. As a result of this type of approach therefore one of its main achievements was the sending of 'surplus' labour from Herefordshire to employment in Yorkshire, Lancashire and Staffordshire, where wages averaging 16s. and 17s. per week could be obtained, instead of the 10s. or 11s. basic rate earned in Herefordshire.[25] Some men also emigrated to America and even to Queensland, under the auspices of the Union, and the movement began to gain recognition from a number of Liberal and Radical politicians, including George Dixon, M.P., of Birmingham.[26] Indeed, early in December, 1871, Dixon chaired a union meeting at Brampton Bryan, and 'in response to a vote of thanks . . . promised liberal aid to a fund which it (was) proposed to raise to enable some of the men to emigrate'.[27]

Soon the Herefordshire example was being followed elsewhere, so that during the winter of 1871/72 a small union, called the Staffordshire Agricultural Labourers' Protection Society, was set up in the North Warwickshire/Staffordshire border area, centring around Perry Bar, and tentative steps were being taken to establish a county union in Leicestershire;[28] in Lincolnshire villages, too, union agitation became apparent around the same time, largely under the direction of William Banks, a Boston journalist.[29] The North Warwickshire/Staffordshire Union was in fact started as the result of a meeting held at the Fox Tavern in Perry Bar, early in January, 1872. It received the encouragement of the landlord of the public house and its prime aim was to alleviate the distress which every winter brought to many labourers in the form of unemployment or underemployment — with reduced wages. However, there was a more specific reason for this first meeting as well; it had been called to consider the plight of a local waggoner who, having become too ill to work, had been dismissed by his employer early in December. After a short time, 'houseless, penniless and well-nigh starving' he had died, and his family had been reduced to utter destitution.[30] The case naturally aroused bitter indignation, but the unionists had other grievances as well. In particular, they sought to bring about some reduction in the long working day. Among the first demands put forward were those for a nine-hour day and for farm workers living in tied cottages to have written agreements which ensured them at least six months' notice if they were required to quit their home. For one of the hardships of the labourer living in this type of accommodation was that if, like the Perry Bar waggoner, he lost his job, he also lost his home and if he could not obtain a new situation quickly, he and his family might be reluctantly forced into a mere hovel or into the workhouse because they could obtain no other shelter. Furthermore — as the Leicestershire strike of 1866 clearly demonstrated — the powers of farmers to evict workers from tied cottages, should they resort to industrial action, was obviously a very strong bargaining counter and one extremely difficult for the worker to combat.

Such, then, were the early attempts at solidarity among the farm labourers. It is important to appreciate that there *was* this upsurge of bitter feeling and discontent even before Joseph Arch and his union officially appeared on the scene. Unfortunately for their long-term success, these efforts lacked both cohesion and the essential qualities, of leadership which Arch was so well able to provide. Nevertheless in his autobiography he, perhaps naturally, tends to underestimate the value of all that had gone before and implies that the union movement was created by his labours alone.

20

As might be expected, in the circumstances of growing unrest Joseph certainly lost no opportunity of making his own views known. As he later wrote in his autobiography, 'I would speak a few words to this man and a few to that, trying to stir them all up, and make them see where the only remedy for their misery lay; in season and out of season I was at them, dropping the good seed of manly discontent; and I made sure, too, that most of it was not cast on to stony ground.'[31]

Yet, concentration on the outward signs of dissatisfaction displayed by the active few should not blind anyone to the apathy of the majority of labourers at this time and to their extremely low status in society. To his better-off compatriots in mid-Victorian England, the farm labourer was one of the most backward members of the community. He was classed as dull and stupid — a 'Johnny Raw,' a 'chaw bacon,' and a 'clodhopper'.[32] Indeed, there is little doubt that the *Illustrated London News* of 13th April, 1872, expressed the view of many when it declared: 'The farm labourers (have been) hitherto looked upon as the lowermost stratum of the industrial classes . . . (They) are for the most part segregated into small neighbourhoods. Their opportunities for the interchange of views and sentiments are few and far between. Their intellectual condition is low . . .'

It was just this apparently unpromising section of the work force that Joseph had to try to lead in unified protest against the harshness of their daily living conditions. However, before the circumstances of that revolt and of Joseph Arch's role in it are examined, it is perhaps worthwhile to digress and to consider how the English agricultural labourer of the early 1870's actually *did* live. Although Arch's own life gives some indication of the reasons for dissatisfaction, it is essential to examine the broader problems, which extend beyond the compass of any one man's life.

[1] Rev. F S Attenborough, op.cit., p.42.
[2] Joseph Arch, op.cit., p.46–47. However, Mary Ann's signature in the Barford marriage register is in a neat hand and certainly does not appear illiterate.
[3] F G Heath — *The English Peasantry* (London, 1874), p.180.
[4] *Warwick Advertiser* — 31st October, 1857
[5] Frederick Clifford — 'The Labour Bill in Farming' in *Journal of the Royal Agricultural Society of England*, 2nd Series, Vol.XI, (1875), pp.108–109. John Ivens, Joseph's fellow worker on this occasion, was also a prize-winning hedge-cutter. In October, 1861, he won seventh prize in the Warwickshire Agricultural Society's 'hedging and ditching' competition, and in October, 1866, a third prize in the same event.
[6] Frederick Clifford, loc. cit., pp. 108–109.
[7] Pamphlet on *Joseph Arch* written by John Evans of Stamford Hill (n.d., probably 1886) — British Museum 08285. ee.14.
[8] *Warwick Advertiser* — 19th June, 1858.
[9] Joseph Arch, op.cit., pp.4 and 57.
[10] Information kindly provided by Edward Arch's eldest daughter, Mrs Marian Arch Fabyan, who lives in Massachusetts, U.S.A.

[11] See 1865 and 1868 Poll Books for South Warwickshire constituency and the Warwick Advertiser — 28th November, 1868. Once again, Arch's memory played him false when he came to write his autobiography, for he states: 'We ran our men in by twenty-seven votes'. — Joseph Arch, op.cit., p.58.

[12] *Leamington Chronicle* — 20th March, 1919. J E M Vincent was originally editor of the *County Herald and Free Press* of Coventry. He remained in this position until 1865, when he moved to Leamington to publish the *Leamington Chronicle,* in conjunction with a Mr. T E Jones. In October, 1866, the partnership was dissolved by agreement, and Vincent became the sole proprietor of this newapaper.

[13] Rev. F S Attenborough, op.cit., p.38. Arch in his autobiography, however, denies that any help was in fact received at all. The Minute Books of the Warwick Board of Guardians reveal that this type of treatment was by no means unique. For example, in November, 1859, Charlotte Lunnon of Barford, unable to obtain any help from the Warwick Board, wrote to the Poor Law Board in London to ask for assistance. She stated that she was 'a Widow in (her) fifty-seventh year unable from Bodily Infirmity to work for (her) living residing in the same house with (her) son a labourer but twenty years old and not able to support (her) from his earnings . . .' She claimed that she had brought up twelve children and that five of her sons had joined the Armed Forces. The letter was referred by London to the Warwick Guardians, but the latter firmly rejected the claim, stating that they considered she had 'sufficient means for her subsistence'. — Meeting of the Guardians, 3rd December, 1859. — C.R.51 — Warwickshire County Record Office.

[14] John Arch rose ultimately to the rank of Company Sergeant Major in 1888, whilst with the Royal Monmouth Engineering Militia. He finally left the Army in February, 1891. — See Records of Service of John Arch in Soldiers' Documents, W.O.97/2207 — P.R.O. He eventually died at Porth, South Wales, at the age of 86 (in about 1934). — Information kindly provided by Mrs. M A Fabyan.

[15] See letter from Mr. J C Purser, dated 3rd February, 1931, in Cole Collection, Nuffield College, Oxford.

[16] *Labourers' Union Chronicle* — 7th August, 1875.

[17] Joseph Arch, op.cit., pp.401–402.

[18] A Clayden — *The Revolt of the Field* (London, 1874), p.6.

[19] *Leicester Chronicle and Leicester Mercury United* — 23rd July and 10th September, 1870.

[20] Of course, a well-known early attempt to form an agricultural union was that at Tolpuddle, Dorset, in 1833. For their pains, the leaders of this small organisation were transported to Australia — See, for example, O J Dunlop — *The Farm Labourer* (London 1913), pp. 124–126. And *The Martyrs of Tolpuddle* published by the Trades Union Congress General Council (London, 1934).

[21] P L R Horn — *The Leicester and Leicestershire Agricultural Labourers' Society 1872 –73 in The Leicestershire Historian,* Vol. 1, No. 5 (1969), p.152.

[22] *Midland Free Press* — 11th May, 1867 and *Buckingham Express* — 1st June, 1867.

[23] P L R Horn — 'The Evenley Strike of 1867' in *Northamptonshire Past and Present,* Vol. IV, No. 1, 1966/67, p.47. See also E L Jones — 'The Agricultural Market in England 1793–1872' in *Economic History Review,* 2nd Series, Vol. XVII, No. 2, December, 1964, for further examples of early unions.

[24] For details of this abortive attempt to form a National Union for farm workers see P L R Horn — *Agricultural Labourers' Trade Unionism in Four Midland Counties,* 1860–1900 (unpublished Leicester Ph. D. thesis, 1968), pp. 27–28.

[25] Joseph Arch, op.cit., p.110.

[26] *Loughborough Advertiser* — 14th December, 1871. George Dixon was an 'advanced' Liberal and an enthusiast campaigner in the cause of popular education.

[27] *Loughborough Advertiser* — 14th December, 1871.

[28] See P L R Horn — 'The Leicester and Leicestershire Agricultural Labourers' Society 1872–73', loc. cit. for information on the efforts made in Leicestershire.

[29] Rex C Russell — *The Revolt of the Field in Lincs.* (Louth, Lincs., 1956), Chapter II.

[30] *Loughborough Advertiser* — 18th January, 1872. *Birmingham Daily Post* — 11th January, 1872.

[31] Joseph Arch, op.cit., p.66.

[32] *Midland Free Press* — 23rd March, 1872.

CHAPTER THREE

Joseph's Brethren: the Farm Workers at the end of the 'Sixties

'The gentry owned the land, the farmers rented it, the labourers worked it. This was the normal pattern of English agriculture under Victoria . . .'   W. J. READER
Life in Victorian England (London, 1964), p. 38

IN 1870, agriculture was still employing — as it had always done — more male workers than any other single industry within the country. Most numerous among them were, of course, the agricultural labourers, shepherds and farm servants who, at the time of the 1871 Census of Population, comprised some 922,024 persons in all. In addition, there were 33,513 female labourers and 24,599 female farm servants, while roughly one-tenth of the male workers (96,715) and about one-thirteenth of the females (4,197) were under the age of 15. But although agriculture still employed the formidable total of nearly one million male and female labourers, there had been a considerable decline in numbers as compared with the middle of the century. In the case of male workers the reduction amounted to nearly 200,000 from the all-time peak reached in 1851.

Several factors accounted for this fall in numbers. The third quarter of the nineteenth century was, in the main, a period of prosperity and expansion for the manufacturing and service sectors of the economy, and with that expansion came naturally a demand for increased labour. At a time when agricultural wages were still low, the promise of higher earnings in the towns provided a powerful magnet which many labourers were unable to resist. Then, too, this period witnessed the greater use of farm machinery, and an ever-growing trend towards pastoral farming, at the expense of arable, both of which factors reduced the demand for labour in the agricultural areas. In some instances, of course, the greater use of machinery had itself been made necessary by a local shortage of labour, especially during the busy harvest season[1] — but this was by no means always the case. And it is important to remember, too, that despite the large exodus of workers, in a number of villages there were still significant pockets of rural unemployment, or underemployment, especially during the winter months, when work was in short supply.

Nevertheless, it seems that the reduction in the overall size of the national agricultural work force, coupled with rising prices and the generally profitable condition of agriculture, was sufficient to bring about *some* increase in basic wages during the 1860's, even if farm wages still remained on average only about 46 per cent of industrial ones.[2]

Of course, the actual wages earned by individual farm workers varied quite considerably according to each man's age, skill and experience, and to the type of work he performed — so that carters and shepherds were normally paid more than the general labourer, for example. In addition, the wage rates of each category of worker differed very considerably from district to district, according to the existence, or otherwise, of more highly paid alternative employment in the neighbourhood. It comes as no surprise to discover, for instance, that agricultural wages in the industrial North of England were well in excess of those in the rural south. One estimate for the period 1869–70 gives an 'average' weekly wage in Durham for day labourers of 16s. 2d., in Northumberland of 15s. 8d. and in Lancashire of 14s. 8d., while in Dorset, the figure was 9s. 4d. and in Norfolk about 10s. 5d.[3] Although such 'average' figures have a number of serious weaknesses — since they hide the fact that the actual wages paid varied very much according to the individual's own capabilities and age — nevertheless they do serve the useful purpose of highlighting the fact that labourers in the mining and industrial districts fared very much better than their fellows elsewhere.

Another important difference between the northern and the southern counties was the tendency for northern farmers to hire their labourers on an annual basis, rather than from week to week. In this way the Northumberland labourer, for example, was ensured a guaranteed annual wage and was normally paid even when he was sick or unable to work because of bad weather. In Northumberland indeed it was quite usual for the entire family to be hired in this way, and most Northumberland hinds were expected to provide female labour; despite this, however, their lot was very much more comfortable than that of many of their brother workers, and it is significant that when agricultural trade unionism developed during the 1870's it made little headway in Northumberland — or indeed in the North of England generally.[4]

Compared with the relatively secure life of the annually hired Northumberland worker, the position of the day labourer in the purely agricultural areas of the south was very different — especially if he lived in a district where there was a 'surplus of labour', with consequent winter unemployment or underemployment. While the man with initiative might in such a situation take the plunge and move to better-paid employment elsewhere, for many ill-educated, impoverished farm labourers such a step was almost unthinkable. Far too few of Joseph's brethren possessed his willingness to travel and his admirable qualities of determination and independence.

The sad details of many workers' irregularity of employment were revealed towards the end of the 1860's by the Reports of the Royal Commission on the Employment of Children, Young Persons and Women in Agriculture 1867–69, and a few examples taken from the pages of these Reports brings home just what it meant in human terms.

The first extract concerns John Quincey, labourer of Spalding in Lincolnshire. Quincey informed the Assistant Commissioner who interviewed him that he normally worked with machinery as a 'machine man': 'I get 3s. a day, but I've not had a full week's work since harvest. I'm out of work now (November 21). I shan't get anything to do, except odd days, there's lots more like me. The farmers here employ very few men in the winter . . . It costs us 14d. a day for bread.'[5] This interview took place in the winter of 1867.

In Oxfordshire, in the late autumn of 1868, a similar story was told in respect of the village of Westcot Barton. Here one young labourer, aged 21, declared that he had 'done no work for five weeks . . . 27 of us this morning out of work.' And the wife of another labourer in the same village noted that her husband was 'out of work, and (had) only done a month since harvest if it were all put together, it's almost starvation.'[6] The population of Westcot Barton in 1871 was 284.

Finally, at Spratton in Northamptonshire, Mrs Balderson, a labourer's wife, confessed that although her husband was in employment at the time interviewed, he had been 'out of work for five or six weeks before that'; and in Wiltshire, the Assistant Commissioner himself concluded that, 'the labour market in (the county) has of late years been, and is now, overstocked . . .'[7]

These are but random cases to illustrate the incidence of local unemployment or underemployment, and many other similar ones could, unfortunately, be quoted.

Sometimes, through the initiative of better-off members of the community certain otherwise timid labourers might be encouraged to move away and leave their miserable conditions behind them. Thus, through the work of the incumbent, Canon Girdlestone, about four to five hundred men, many of them with families, were migrated from

Arch family circa 1873.

From left to right;

Standing - Annie; John;
Joseph jnr.;
Hannah;

Seated - Joseph senr;
Mrs Arch;
Edward;
Thomas.

*(By courtesy of Mr D. Rudd
of Barford.)*

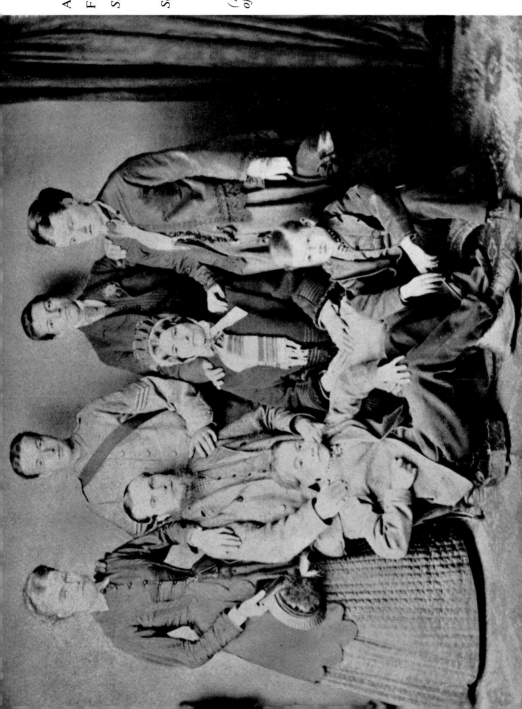

Sketch of the interior of the Arch cottage at Barford in 1872.

the low wage parish of Halberton in Devonshire to better-paid employment in Lancashire, Yorkshire, Durham, Kent, Sussex and other counties. A number were sent to the Manchester and the West Riding Police Forces, and all of the migrants secured a rise of from 5s. to 14s. per week on their old basic weekly wages of 7s. or 8s. It will be remembered that in 1868 Canon Girdlestone also unsuccessfully sought to establish a national union for the agricultural workers.

However, although Canon Girdlestone's work in Devonshire was widely praised by outside observers, it had comparatively few imitators. And the Canon himself noted the uncertainty of the labourers when first confronted with the idea of leaving their homes. 'Almost everything had to be done for them, their luggage addressed, their railway tickets taken, and full and plain directions given to the simple travellers. The plan adopted when the labourers were leaving for their new homes, was to give them . . . plain directions written on a piece of paper in a large and legible hand. These were shown to the officials on the several lines of railway, who soon getting to hear of Canon Girdlestone's system of migration, rendered him all the assistance in their power by readily helping the labourers out of their travelling difficulties . . . Many of the peasants of North Devon were so ignorant of the whereabouts of the places to which they were about to be sent, that they often asked whether they were going 'over the water'.' (F. G. Heath — *The English Peasantry* (London, 1874), p. 155). It was these very characteristics of timidity and ignorance of the outside world which were later to strike Joseph Arch when he attempted to organise the farm workers into a union.

So far, attention has been principally turned to the question of *basic* wages, but many labourers would hope to add to their basic income either by work such as hedging, ditching and mowing, which was paid at piecework rates, or by the extra earnings obtained during the busy haymaking and harvest seasons. In addition, both shepherds and carters were normally given annual hiring fees, and for the shepherds there were frequently special payments at such times as lambing or shearing. Upon the higher wages earned during the harvest season, in particular, depended many families for the purchase of their clothing and for the settlement of debts they may have run up during the difficult winter period. These harvest earnings could make a considerable difference to income during the six or seven weeks in the year when they were available. For example, whereas in parts of Leicestershire able-bodied labourers usually received from 11s. to 13s. per week as their basic wage, with 1s. a week extra for Sunday work, during harvest time they might obtain from 20s. to 30s. a week. In Northamptonshire, Mr Albert Pell, M.P., of Haselbeach, estimated that although his ordinary day workers normally earned 12s. per week for six days'

27

labour, during harvest, wages would be '25s. to 27s. a week, and the hours of labour indefinite and dependent on the weather; this (would) last for four weeks, to be followed by a fortnight's labour at about 21s.; but during the harvest work a labourer (would) require 5s. to 6s. worth of beer weekly, which he (would) have to pay for.' In addition, Mr Pell estimated that during the year opportunities for task work, such as hoeing, ditching, spreading dung, etc. were such that an average of 3s. per week might be earned through the year, and he considered that in practice, an average weekly income of as much as 15s. 10d. might be obtained by the man whose ostensible basic wage rate was 12s.[8]

Similarly, in Norfolk, where 'the weekly wage . . . was 12s. it was estimated that the total annual earnings of an able-bodied labourer, including his piecework, would range from £37 to £40 . . . the annual earnings of a farm labourer, who loses no time and gets his fair allowance of piecework would give an average throughout the year of about 2s. per week in excess of the current weekly wage . . .'[9] Clearly then piecework in its varied forms could provide a valuable addition to the basic weekly wage, where it was available — and for whom! Not all men were able to share in it, either because of lack of skill or lack of opportunity, and, of course, the effects of unemployment for a week or two in the winter could cancel out most of the benefits of these 'extra' earnings.

As well as the additional cash earnings, the labourer's income might also be supplemented in other ways, through allowances in kind — perquisites. In many cases an allowance of beer was made to the men whilst they were working, particularly at harvest time, while in other instances potato ground might be supplied free or at a reduced rent in the farmer's own field, fuel would be hauled without charge, and on occasion, meals were provided in the farmhouse. Stockmen were normally supplied with a cottage rent free — but, of course, this perquisite possessed all the disadvantages of tied accommodation, with, too frequently, insecurity of tenure. In the Northern and Midland counties, the labourer very often had the benefit of an allotment of grass land which enabled him to keep a cow, and to obtain milk for his children, while in Northumberland and parts of Scotland the farmer himself might keep a cow for each of his men.[10] In Northumberland indeed payment in kind was an accepted and valued part of the labourer's income.

Unfortunately, the perquisites question had its less attractive side as well. First of all, like piecework, by no means all workers shared in it; a great deal depended on the individual farmer and on the relationship which existed between him and his men. Secondly, not all perquisites were of equal value. John Dent, a contemporary agricultural observer and a Member of Parliament, pinpointed this in 1871, when he wrote: 'Perhaps one of the greatest evils which affect the condition of the labourer in the Southern, Western and South Midland Counties, is the practice of giving beer or cider to the men in lieu of wages. This custom not only prevents a fair share of the wages going for the support of the family, but generates that love of drink, which . . . (is) the curse of the labourer.'[11] Significantly, one of the demands of Arch's union, when it became established, was for the payment of all wages in cash and not partly in cash and partly in kind. The practice of paying wages partly in alcoholic liquor was only finally made illegal under the Truck Act of 1887.

Apart from piecework earnings and perquisites, the family income of many labourers was further augmented by the earnings of their wives and children. Although the total of women working on a permanent basis was declining, a large number of them went to help at least at harvest time, while the 1871 Census showed that there were still over 33,000 female labourers in full-time employment — including 3,407 in Northumberland (where the farmers frequently hired the female members of the family along with the male) and 2,959 in Wiltshire. Arch's own county of Warwickshire, on the other hand, had only about 460 in this category.

For those women who were employed in the fields, tasks included weeding, stone picking, hoeing and spudding thistles, as well as helping at haymaking and harvest. Wage rates for women tended to vary between 6d. and 1s. per day, according to the nature of the work and the availability (or otherwise) of alternative non-agricultural employment; in some places a slightly higher amount than 1s. might be earned during the harvest season.

Of course, one significant cause of the reduction in the number of permanent women labourers which occurred during the 1860's was undoubtedly the passage of the Gangs Act of 1867. Prior to this legislation large public gangs of women and girls, as well as some boys and youths, were often employed by farmers to carry out the tasks of weeding, potato picking, etc. on their land; the gangs were supervised by an overseer and they usually operated on the large arable farms of the Eastern Counties. The lack of cottage accommodation in these areas meant that the local labour supply was often insufficient, and the system suited the farmer very well, since he paid for his labour only when he required it. When the gang had finished at one farm it was immediately free to move to another, where its services were required. Some of the gangs were quite large. In Binbrook, Lincolnshire, for example, it was estimated that 203 people went out with the gang, and as many as 380 from Spalding, while at March in Cambridgeshire the figure was 388 and at Chatteris in the same county, 260. At Yaxley, in Huntingdonshire, which had a population of 1,411, there were 161 members of the public gangs working in May, 1866 — and it was noted that membership had been even higher during the previous year. The Yaxley workers were divided into four separate gangs, the major portion of them being between the ages of 7 and 18, but there were five children under the age of 7, and sixty-four of the total were women and girls. The local vicar called the gang system 'the most ruinous that ever could have been adopted; detrimental to all morality, virtue, and sense of religious feelings (the language of the greater number of them being of the most offensive nature) . . .'12 The situation was especially bad where the gang travelled such long distances to their place of work that a daily journey to it was impossible, and they were lodged together in barns upon the farms, with the sexes mixed indiscriminately.

The 'iniquities' of the public gangs were exposed by the Sixth Report of the Children's Employment Commission in 1866, and it was as a result of the Commission's findings that the Gangs Act became law in August, 1867. It restricted the age of children allowed to work in public gangs to 8 years or over, and prohibited gangs of mixed sex. All gang masters had to be duly licensed by a justice of the peace at petty sessions. It is significant that following the passage of this legislation the number of public gangs dwindled rapidly, but even after they had virtually disappeared some of the reported evils of immorality and coarse behaviour, which had characterised them, still persisted. The Rector of Rotherwell in Lincolnshire was quite clear that 'the only way to strike at the evils of field work (was) to forbid all female labour in the fields . . .'13 Mrs Grocock, a labourer's wife from Billingborough in the same county seems to have shared his sentiments when she declared: 'I don't believe in girls going out at all to work. I'd sooner let mine go on "taters and salt".'14

Of course, in the non-ganging areas of the country there seems little doubt that many of the women who worked in the fields were quite respectable. They merely wanted to supplement the family income or, perhaps, like Mrs Austin of Harbury in Warwickshire, they went out to work because they had little to occupy them at home. Mrs Austin had no children and she told the Assistant Commissioner in connection with the Royal Commission on the Employment of Children, Young Persons and Women in Agriculture, during the winter of 1868 that she only went to work 'from April until harvest' in each year and during that period she earned about 8d. a day.

One of the greatest problems faced by all of these women was, of course, that of keeping their often shabby clothing dry; the long skirts frequently became sodden and muddy when they worked out in wet weather, and many resorted to old sacks to protect both skirts and shoulders. Few were as well equipped as the regular women labourers of Northumberland. They wore a pair of stout boots, 'a very short thick woollen petticoat, warm stockings, a jacket, &c.; over all a washing pinafore with sleeves, . . . which preserves their dress from the dirt.'[15]

The demands of agriculture frequently interfered not only with a wife's role in the home but also with the education of her children; in many cases — like the young Joseph Arch — boys, in particular, had to start work at a very early age. Not until the introduction in 1880 of compulsory education for all children, at least up to the age of 10, was this problem in any way solved. The Rev. James Fraser, later Bishop of Manchester, noted in 1867 that: 'In agricultural districts it has become a rare thing to find a labourer's son in the schools above the age of ten. Many of the schools are filled with babies . . . nearly two-thirds (of the children) . . . pass out of school to work with less of elementary knowledge than Standard IV denotes . . .,' i.e. less than the extremely modest minimum level of education which a child was expected to attain by the Committee of Council on Education![16]

Interviews carried out in the rural areas all too often bore out this gloomy picture. At the village of Redenhall, in Norfolk, for example, an eleven-year-old boy, William Butcher, who was keeping sheep in the churchyard, admitted that he had been at school for one year only; he 'could never write his name, (had) forgotten nearly all his reading. . . (had) another brother, who is 13, (who) cannot read any better than he can, and cannot write. Thinks a sovereign is five shillings; (afterwards changed it to 10 shillings); . . .'[17]

In the very North of England, the level of education was rather higher than in the south. Whereas in the mid-1860's it was noted that in Bedfordshire, 34 per cent of the women getting married could not sign their name, and in Cornwall, 42 per cent, in Northumberland: 'No greater stigma (could) attach to parents than that of leaving their children without the means of ordinary education, every nerve (was) strained to procure it.' Almost every village in the county had its school where the children were thoroughly grounded in their three R's (reading, writing and arithmetic).[18] It was concluded that for Northumberland as a whole, 'there was an absence of that gross ignorance which (was) said to prevail in other less favoured counties.'[19]

But if the wage rates and educational facilities of agricultural workers were frequently of a poor standard only, the same must unfortunately be said of other aspects of their life. This applied not only to food, but also to such things as fuel — especially in the southern counties. In the north, cheap fuel was normally available to provide heat for cooking and also for the drying out of wet clothes; in the purely rural areas of the south and west, however, labourers were frequently unable to afford to buy coal and might not be allowed to pick up wood, unless it lay on common land. In these circumstances, during wet weather they had frequently to put on in the morning still damp clothes they had taken off the night before. It was generally agreed that the inability to obtain dry clothing was a major cause of ill-health and a contributor to the rheumatism to which most agricultural labourers became martyrs in their old age.

Food was equally unsatisfactory. Too often it comprised bread, burnt crust tea, skim milk and cheese. Although some might hope to supplement this with bacon from a pig they had reared and killed themselves, it was by no means always possible for them to keep such an animal. In Halberton, in Devonshire, for example, the men were forbidden to keep pigs or hens 'in case they stole food' from the farmer to feed them. Similar prohibitions regarding the keeping of pigs also existed in the South Oxfordshire village of Mapledurham and in numerous other places.

Often by the cultivation of allotments or, as with the Arches, of a good-sized garden, vegetables could be grown to supplement the diet of bread and burnt crust tea, or tea-kettle broth as it was called, on which many farm workers subsisted. Nevertheless, at least one contemporary writer on the subject considered that in the low-wage districts, although 'the food available (was) sufficient for men in normal health, . . . there is certain medical evidence to show that if there was a disposition to disease, then the quality was found to be defective. Further, as the husband had necessarily to have the largest share of the food, and also the strengthening diet, . . . the woman and children frequently suffered from insufficient nourishment . . . the principal diet of the agricultural labourers was wheaten bread or other food made from flour. Barley bread was, however, frequently eaten in the western counties; . . . In some counties nearly half a man's weekly wages appears to have been spent on bread for his family . . . The high price of tea prohibited much being drunk . . . Fresh meat (beef or mutton) was seldom eaten, except in some of the northern and north midland counties (chiefly on Sundays) . . . In the low wage counties the monotony of the bread diet was relieved by eating it soaked in broth or spread with dripping or lard . . . Bacon or pork was, as a rule, eaten on Sundays only; and, at times, when this could not be obtained for the Sunday dinner, potatoes were eaten with melted butter or grease'.[20] In the Newent area of Gloucestershire it was reported that 'many families (had) nothing but bread from one week's end to another . . .'[21]

And if the provision of food was an ever-present problem, so was the purchase of clothing. By this time the old smock frock was being worn less and less by agricultural workers, and many of them were substituting for it clothes made of hard-wearing cord. In a number of villages local charities or clothing clubs might help to clothe a family, while those who had slightly better off relatives working in the towns or in domestic service could expect to receive occasional cast off garments from time to time. In other cases, harvest earnings might suffice to satisfy the family's needs or else clothing and shoes would be purchased on an instalment plan; every month the bagman clothier would call to collect contributions and sometimes the payments were extended over such a long period that the articles were worn out before they were paid for; a similar policy might be adopted to pay for shoes.[22] Indeed, for most labourers and their families, the biggest problem *was* to obtain boots and shoes. The Roman Catholic priest of Louth, Lincolnshire, even informed the Assistant Commissioner for the Royal Commission on the Employment of Children, Young Persons and Women in Agriculture at the end of the 1860's that he thought one of the greatest difficulties preventing children from going to school was the lack of proper clothing 'and especially of shoes'.[23]

The footwear problem was equally recognised by employers. One landowner from Playford, near Ipswich, a Mr Biddell, complacently suggested that 'instead of raising the little boy's wages . . . an expenditure of 4s. or 6s. in shoes and leather buskins ensures dry feet to the boy during the winter months, when tending stock in wet yards . . .' This well-to-do 'philanthropist' also went on to suggest that: 'A worn-out waggon cloth on two poles will easily make a shade from a March wind while cleaning roots for sheep in the open field. Attention to little matters like these will in every case make the employment of boys in agriculture perfectly harmless at whatever early age they may be sent to work . . .'[24]

After wages and regularity of employment, there is no doubt that the next most vital factor affecting the comfort and well-being of the labourer and his family was the adequacy, or otherwise, of their cottage accommodation. Here, too, many of Joseph's brethren were very much worse off than he was himself. Normally those who lived in cottages attached to large estates, or in closed parishes (i.e. parishes where the ownership of the land was concentrated in the hands of one or two large landowners only) were likely to have housing of a reasonable quality. The worst cottages were often the mud ones erected by the labourers themselves on common land — often mere hovels — or the small cottages owned by local tradesmen. These bad cottages were frequently situated in 'open' villages, where land ownership was widely dispersed. Indeed, in Oxfordshire, the Assistant Commissioner remarked in connection with the 1867–69 Royal Commission on the Employment of Children, etc. in Agriculture: 'I don't think I visited any open village in which there were not some very bad cottages'. In Leicestershire, the cottages were described as 'generally bad,' and the Assistant Commissioner observed with regard to the county as a whole, that: 'One peculiarity of the villages is the absence of gardens. Allotments, however, are almost universal.'

Many of the cottages were unfortunately not only poor in construction and maintenance but also extremely small in size. At Barlestone in Leicestershire, for example, some had no back door and consisted of one room up and one down. At the village of Stathern in the same county, it was claimed by the incumbent that because of the small size of the cottages 'as many as three generations' slept in one room.[25]

These were no isolated instances, as further investigation shows. In the parish of Hillborough, in Norfolk, where the population numbered 252, there were 53 cottages — 22 of them with one bedroom and one living room only. Not surprisingly it was noted that 'the bedrooms (were) overcrowded with no proper separation of the sexes.' One even had eleven people sleeping in what the relieving officer called 'a very small room!' At Narborough, in the same county, where there was a population of 261, 21 of the 58 cottages in the parish had one bedroom only. Significantly, the worst affected parishes in Norfolk were also 'open' ones.

The rents of the cottages usually ranged between 1s. and 2s. a week, but where the accommodation was very poor or very small the level might fall as low as 6d. or 9d. It was indeed this very fact of lowness of rent which prevented any real effort to improve the rural housing position; labourers' wages were too small to enable them to pay an 'economic rent', and building speculators therefore had no incentive to try to cater for their needs. Of course, some landlords, like Sir C. Isham and Mr A. Pell in Northamptonshire, or Lord Wantage (then Colonel Loyd-Lindsay) in Berkshire might build good cottages for workers on their estates, but this was usually done on moral and philanthropic grounds rather than on economic ones; they were unlikely to see any direct profit on the transaction.

Some slight improvement in the cottage position was brought about by the passage of the Union Chargeability Act of 1865. This led to the replacement of the parish by the Poor Law Union as a basis for assessing poor law rates, and it meant that landowners no longer had any incentive to keep the population of their own 'closed' parishes down to a low level so as to avoid liability for inhabitants' support should they become eligible for poor relief. With the widening of the area of chargeability the landlord became equally responsible for the payment of his share of the rates to relieve those living in nearby 'open' parishes. In these circumstances he no longer sought to keep his own cottage accommodation down to a minimum.

Nevertheless, despite the passage of this legislation and the efforts of paternalistic landlords, the cottage accommodation available at the end of the 1860's was often extremely bad. It was, in fact, possible for the Rev. James Fraser (who visited 300 villages in Norfolk, Essex, Sussex, Gloucester and parts of Suffolk in connection with the 1867/69 Agricultural Employment Commission) to declare that according to his investigations in only *two parishes* out of the three hundred had the 'cottage provision appeared to be both admirable in quality and sufficient in quantity; . . . ' His indictment was severe. 'The majority of the cottages that exist in rural parishes are deficient in almost every requisite that should constitute a home for a Christian family in a civilised community . . . Physically, a ruinous, ill-drained cottage, 'cribbed, cabin'd, confined,' and over-crowded, generates any amount of disease — fevers of every type, catarrh, rheumatism — as well as intensifies to the utmost that tendency to scrofula and phthisis which, from their frequent intermarriages and their low diet, abounds so largely among the poor . . .'[26] And even with those cottages which possessed an attractive outer appearance, there was the insidious problem of inadequate drainage, with its disastrous effect in spreading disease and contaminating the water supply!

This, then, was the position of the mid-Victorian agricultural labourer, for whom low wages, poor food and inferior cottage accommodation were too often the only rewards for long days spent in continuous toil. However, these hardships were not the only difficulties which he had to face. In his brushes with the law the agricultural labourer was very often equally at a disadvantage. Until the passage of the Master and Servant Act of 1867, for example, it was possible for an annually hired labourer or farm servant to be imprisoned should he break his contract of employment — although his master, for a similar breach, faced a fine only. Thus, John Whittaker of Hose, Leicestershire, was sentenced to fourteen days' hard labour for absconding from his employment in January, 1867, just prior to the passage of the legislation.

The standard of obedience demanded from workers was also sometimes excessive, although much depended on the whim of the individual farmer. For example, in a case involving two young farm labourers from Great Ashby, Leicestershire, in August, 1869, their employer charged them 'with going out at night for a short time, after they had done work for the day. The complainant said the lads were good servants, and he had no other fault to find with them; . . .' The case was heard before Lutterworth petty sessions on 12th August and the magistrates asked the young men to apologise and to pay the costs of 7s. each. At the same time an order was made out that unless the money was paid within a month, the defendants were to be committed to gaol for fourteen days![27] Somewhat earlier than this, two Cornish labourers had likewise suffered from their employer's excessive zeal for discipline; for 'refusing to obey their master's lawful command to attend Church on Sunday' they had been sent to prison![28]

Nevertheless, it was perhaps in regard to poaching that the most resented brushes between the labourers and the law took place. Poaching offences were fairly frequent in rural areas, particularly when unemployment was high and food in short supply or expensive. In her *Joseph Ashby of Tysoe*, for example, Miss M. K. Ashby notes that Joseph's grandfather was an experienced poacher; and petty sessional court records abound with cases involving others who followed his example.[29] The Poaching Prevention Act of 1862, which gave the rural police the right to search any person whom they suspected of poaching was, in particular, deeply resented by the labourers. Even Joseph Arch's own brother-in-law, Thomas Colledge, was stopped one Saturday evening whilst returning from Warwick to Barford 'with his week's groceries in his pocket . . .' A policeman met him and asked him what he had got in his pockets, but accepted the explanation that they were filled with groceries without a formal search. (Colledge was a local blacksmith and was perhaps more articulate or more deter-mined than most labourers.)[30] Others were less fortunate, and as Joseph himself said, it was very difficult for labourers to believe that 'hares and rabbits belong(ed) to any individual,'[31] and could not be killed, especially when they had been eating precious greenstuff from the labourer's garden or allotment.

Penalties for poaching offences often seemed disproportionately severe, in view of the relatively trivial nature of many offences. For example, a young man charged with trespassing in search of game at Bagworth, in Leicestershire, in October, 1867, was fined £5 and called upon to meet costs of £1 0s. 6d. — or in default to face three months' hard labour.[32] Since very few labourers would have £6 0s. 6d. in hand to meet such a claim, he was, in effect, being sentenced to three months' hard labour for the offence. Joseph Arch himself quoted a case in-volving two married women from his own village who were charged under the 1862 Act with stealing turnips from a field where they had been working; they were found guilty and were fined.[33] And, similarly, on 15th February, 1872, Ann Whitehead, a widow with two children, was stopped by the local policeman at Whitnash, Warwickshire; he discovered that she was concealing turnip tops to the value of 6d., and since she could not give a satisfactory explanation of how she had obtained them, she was charged with theft. She pleaded guilty at Leamington Petty Sessions and had to pay 5s. costs![34]

Indeed, as the last cases indicate, the powers of search authorised by the Poaching Prevention Act could be used by the police to detect cases of petty theft, or to stop women carrying away turnips from the fields — which many of them regarded as a rightful perquisite if they had been turnip cleaning for their employer.

Cases of minor theft were, of course, as severely dealt with as poaching offences. Thus, Henry Roby, a labourer of Ashby in Leicestershire, was found guilty of stealing twenty pieces of wood, value 1s., and was sentenced to eighteen months' hard labour, in July, 1864![35] And Mary Hales of Stoke Albany in the same county, a charwoman, was sentenced to six weeks' hard labour, in May, 1867, for stealing '8 ounces of bacon, value 5d.'[36] Small wonder that in the face of possible penalties like these the spirit of most labourers was crushed, or that many of them — too many — drowned their sorrows in drink.

Furthermore, if the labourer's working years were often ones of hardship and deprivation, the prospect of retirement was normally an even more unhappy one. Very few labourers indeed received a pension from their employer or from a friendly society to which they had contributed during earlier years. For the majority, old age meant reliance on poor relief or on the financial support of children (who could ill-afford this outlay from their own small wages). The usual outdoor poor relief payment was about 3s. per week per person, but in some poor law unions, such as the Bicester Union in Oxfordshire, even smaller sums might be given; 2s. and 2 loaves was a frequent form of relief for the aged pauper in the Bletchingdon district of that Union during the period 1870–71 and 1s. and 1 loaf was certainly not unknown.[37]

Case studies show, too, that the income of an unmarried son or daughter living at home could lead either to a refusal of out relief to the parent or to its severe reduction. Yet the need to rely upon children was often seen as degrading by a man who had worked hard and honestly all his life. Flora Thompson, discussing this problem in *Lark Rise to Candleford* wrote: 'It was a common thing to hear ageing people say that they hoped God would be pleased to take them before they got past work and became a trouble to anybody.'[38] Such was the attitude of the old people in Mrs Thompson's North Oxfordshire hamlet of Juniper Hill.

Of course, certain of the more fortunate old people might be able to support themselves by regularly earning a little money at some light employment, perhaps given on charitable grounds by a farmer for whom they had formerly worked, and the anxiety of labourers to obtain work in old age is demonstrated by the relatively large numbers who continued in employment after the age of sixty-five. At the time of the 1881 Census of Population, about one-twelfth of the entire male agricultural labouring work-force was aged 65 or above — over 72,000 persons in all.[39]

Not until the passage of the Old Age Pensions Act in 1908 was the position in any way eased, and it is not difficult to understand the gratitude of old people when the scheme came into operation. To modern eyes the first pensions seem extremely modest. The full weekly sum of 5s., payable to men and women aged 70 or over, was only available to those who had an income of £21 or less from other sources. Of course, since most agricultural workers had *no* income from any other source, this restriction did not worry them. However, for the aged labourers in the 1860's no such help was available. Like Joseph's father, John Arch, most could only expect to end their days completely dependent on their children, or upon the tiny sums grudgingly given as poor relief by the local Board of Guardians.

Yet, if life in rural England at the beginning of the 1870's was often harsh, there were some bright spots as well. At Christmas time, for example, the local gentry or the farmers frequently provided gifts of meat, clothing or coal for their workers; the local newspapers abound with examples of villagers gratefully acknowledging these gifts by the insertion of a notice in the relevant column of the paper. Harvest time was, again, another period of celebration, when a substantial harvest supper would normally be provided, the beer would flow freely and singing and jollifications would last into the night.

Many labourers, like Joseph Arch, also joined a local friendly or sick benefit society, and every month or every fortnight they would meet together and talk over their common problems. Each year, too, such societies would have their annual feast day, when the members paraded the village with banners flying and perhaps a local band playing. After the parade and, usually, a Church service for the members, would come the feast itself. This would normally be an occasion for heavy eating, drinking and dancing — a red letter day in the life of most labourers, even if they spent most of their meagre savings in one fell swoop and perhaps suffered from a hangover the next day!

Both landowners and farmers frequently sought to encourage their workers to join the benefit societies — not, of course, for the drinking and feasting they provoked on their anniversary day, but rather because they inculcated attitudes of thriftiness, when every week or month a small sum had to be paid towards the society's funds. Prizes were even offered at the various agricultural shows for those men who had longest been members of a benefit society. Employers felt that the thrifty man would tend to be a more careful worker (and, no doubt, one less likely to be a burden on the poor rates).

Through friendly societies men got to know one another and could discuss matters of common interest. Nonconformist chapels and co-operative retail stores were two other, albeit very different, ways in which labourers could learn to work together. It is significant that many of the leaders of the agricultural trade union movement were

38

local preachers, particularly for the Primitive Methodists — like Joseph Arch himself. Through their preaching activities they learnt to make contact with their fellow workers and to express their opinions clearly and persuasively. (And by this time most villages would possess at least one Nonconformist Chapel[40]).

Co-operative stores were by no means universal in the 1860's and early 1870's, but the Assistant Commissioner of the 1867/69 Royal Commission on the Employment of Children, etc. in Agriculture, reporting on Northamptonshire, remarked that in the Market Harborough area of Leicestershire and Northamptonshire they were well established. He stated that they had done 'an immense deal to raise the character of the labourer'.[41] The great advantage to be derived from co-operative stores was, of course, the freedom from debt of their members. Cash payments had to be made for goods purchased, and benefit was derived from the distribution of profits earned by the societies in the form of dividends. After the establishment of the agricultural trade unions in the 1870's many local branches sought to set up co-operative stores in their area for the benefit of members; Joseph Arch's surviving account book/diary for 1876–77 contains several entries to the effect that he had himself sent 'co-op. rules' to various villages, like Hinton, near Wimborne, in Dorset.[42]

Such, then, were the hardships and the compensations of the life of the average mid-Victorian English agricultural labourer. To a casual observer he seemed reconciled to his humble lot — content to endure, as he had always endured in the past, the petty oppressions and the difficulties of his daily life and yet ready to savour to the full any simple pleasures which came his way. It appeared part of the natural order of things that he should have little or no say in the running of the community in which he spent his life; that nobody should consult him about the distribution of the local charities, for example, in which he might have a deep personal interest; and that he should not even possess the Parliamentary franchise, which had been granted to the urban householder in 1867.

But beneath the apparently calm exterior, there were growing signs of revolt. Efforts were being made, with increasing success, as we have seen, to form agricultural unions, while demands were being pressed for higher wages (despite the improvements which had already been secured during the 1860's) and for shorter hours. Franchise extension, too, was becoming a matter of growing interest. Furthermore, through the increasing numbers of cheap local newspapers in circulation, labourers might learn something of what was going on in the towns — and even if all labourers were not able to read, there were invariably some who could, and who would read to the rest. Consequently, as 'the tide of social betterment (began) to flow strongly in the towns, . . .

it agitated even the stagnant backwaters of remote agricultural districts. The peasant, ignorant and illiterate though he was, could hardly remain insensible to the fact that, while the condition of workmen in other industries was improving, his remained the same . . . The labourers were crying for a man to lead them, to organise them, to voice their needs. The time was ripe and the man came; . . .'[43] That man was Joseph Arch.

[1] E L Jones — 'The Agricultural Labour Market in England 1793–1872' in *Economic History Review,* 2nd Series, Vol. XVII, No. 2 December, 1964, p.333. However as late as 1871 it has been suggested that 'barely one-quarter of the British corn area was mechanized'. — E J T Collins — 'Harvest Technology and Labour Supply in Britain 1790–1870' in *Economic History Review,* 2nd Series, Vol. XXII, No. 3, December, 1969, p.455.

[2] E L Jones, loc. cit., p.328. By 1871, the commerce and finance groupings and domestic service were, incidentally, employing more workers overall than agriculture, but in domestic service the role of women was, of course, pre-eminent.

[3] W Hasbach — *A History of the English Agricultural Labourer* (London, 1966 edn.),p.284.

[4]. J P Dunbabin — 'The Incidence and Organisation of Agricultural Trades Unionism in the 1870's in *Agricultural History Review,* Vol. 16, Part II, 1968 p.118. The existence of a prosperous coal-mining industry within their county borders must have helped the labourers of both Northumberland and Durham.

[5] Quoted in Rex Russell, op.cit. p.11.

[6] *Royal Commission on the Employment of Children, Young Persons and Women in Agriculture,* Second Report by Mr. Culley on Oxfordshire, Appendix B, Parliamentary Papers 1868–69, Vol. XIII, p.340.

[7] *Royal Commission on the Employment of Children, etc. in Agriculture,* First Report, by Mr. Norman on Northamptonshire, Parliamentary Papers 1867–68, Vol. XVII, p.455, and Second Report by Mr. Norman on Wiltshire, Parliamentary Papers 1868–69 Vol. XIII, p.53. E J T Collins, loc.cit., notes in connection with the supply of agricultural labour and the swings of the trade cycle that: 'The relative over-supply position in slumps was much enhanced if during the previous phase of labour scarcity, farmers had switched permanently into faster methods.' p.468.

[8] *Royal Commission on the Employment of Children, etc in Agriculture,* First Report by Mr. Norman on Northamptonshire, Parliamentary Papers 1867–68, Vol. XVII, p.427.

[9] *Royal Commission on the Employment of Children, etc. in Agriculture.* First Report by the Rev. James Fraser on Norfolk, Parliamentary Papers 1867–68, Vol. XVII, p.23.

[10] John D Dent, M.P. — 'The Present Condition of the English Agricultural Labourer' in *Journal of the Royal Agricultural Society of England,* 1871, p.351.

[11] Ibid., p.352.

[12] *Children's Employment Commission* — Sixth Report — Report on the Agricultural Gangs, 1866, pp.viii and 44.

[13] R Russell, op.cit., p.8.

[14] Ibid., p.12.

[15] *Royal Commission on the Employment of Children, etc. in Agriculture* — First Report by Mr. Henley on Northumberland, Parliamentary Papers, 1867–68, Vol. XVII, p.54.

[16] *Royal Commission on the Employment of Children, etc. in Agriculture* — First Report by the Rev. James Fraser, M.A. on Norfolk, Essex, Sussex, Gloucester and parts of Suffolk, Parliamentary Papers 1867–68, Vol. XVII, pp.18–19.

[17] Ibid. p.197 (Evidence).

[18] O J Dunlop — *The Farm Labourer* (London, pp.128 and 130.

[19] *Royal Commission on the Employment of Children, etc. in Agriculture* — First Report

by Mr. Henley on Northumberland, Parliamentary Papers 1867–68, Vol. XVII, p.71.

[20] A Wilson Fox 'Agricultural Wages in England and Wales during the Last Half Century' in *Essays in Agrarian History* (Newton Abbot, 1966). The article was first published in 1903.

[21] *Royal Commission on the Employment of Children etc. in Agriculture* — First Report by the Rev. James Fraser, M.A. on Norfolk, Essex, Sussex, Gloucester and parts of Suffolk — Parliamentary Papers, 1867–68, Vol. XVII, p.215 (Evidence).

[22] Rev. J Y Stratton — 'Farm Labourers, their Friendly Societies, and the Poor Law' in *Journal of the Royal Agricultural Society of England,* 1870, p.91.

[23] Rex Russell, op.cit., p.9.

[24] *Royal Commission on the Employment of Children etc. in Agriculture* — First Report by the Rev. James Fraser, M.A. on Norfolk, Essex, Sussex, Gloucester and parts of Suffolk, Parliamentary Papers 1867–68, Vol. XVII, p.185 (Evidence).

[25] P L R Horn — *Agricultural Labourers' Trade Unionism in Four Midland Counties,* 1860–1900 (unpublished Leicester Ph.D. thesis, 1968), p.13.

[26] *Royal Commission on the Employment of Children etc. in Agriculture* — First Report by the Rev. James Fraser, M.A., Parliamentary Papers 1867–68, Vol. XVII, p.35.

[27] *Leicester Chronicle and Leicester Mercury United* — 14th August, 1869.

[28] H J Keefe — *A Century of Print,* p.60, quoting from *Punch* of 5th March and 11th November, 1864.

[29] M K Ashby — *Joseph Ashby of Tysoe* (Cambridge, 1961), pp.3–4.

[30] *Select Committee on the Game Laws* — Evidence from Joseph Arch on 2nd May, 1873, Q.8117–8119. Colledge had married Joseph's sister, Mary at the end of the 1840's He was five years younger than his wife and was born in the village of Claverdon, but after the marriage the couple went to live in Church Street, Barford, not very far from the Arch cottage. — See 1861 Census Return for Barford at Public Record Office, R.G. 9.2219 and also MS. note by the Rev. Douglas Long, a former Barford curate, among documents now in the possession of Mr. R Moore, who has kindly permitted me to use them.

[31] *Select Committee on the Game Laws* — Evidence from Joseph Arch on 2nd May, 1873, Q.8161.

[32] *Leicester Chronicle and Leicester Mercury United* — 12th October, 1867.

[33] *Select Committee on the Game Laws* — Evidence from Joseph Arch, Q.8088.

[34] *Warwick Advertiser* — 24th Februrary, 1872.

[35] *Leicester Chronicle* — 16th July, 1864.

[36] *Leicester Chronicle and Leicester Mercury United* — 18th May, 1867.

[37] Bletchingdon District of Bicester poor Law Union — Relieving Officer's Application. and Report Book at Oxfordshire County Record Office

[38] F Thompson — *Lark Rise to Candleford* (Oxford, 1963 edn.), p.70.

[39] 1881 Census of Population — Occupations, Parliamentary Papers 1883, Vol. LXXX.

[40] In some 'closed' parishes, however, the opposition of the landowner might be sufficent to prevent the erection of a Chapel. Thus in Berkshire, in the paternalistic Colonel Loyd-Lindsay's model villages of Ardington and Lockinge 'no Dissenting chapels could be built . . .but a small building, now a shed in the garden of West Ginge lower farm, was sometimes used as a meeting house. Dissenting Chapels, however, existed in Wantage and West Hendred, the neighbouring parishes on either side . . .' — M A Havinden — *Estate Villages* (London for University of Reading, 1966), p.70.

[41] *Royal Commission on the Employment of Children etc. in Agriculture* — First Report by Mr. Norman on Northamptonshire, Parliamentary Papers 1867–68, Vol. XVII, p.121.

[42] Account Book/Diary of Joseph Arch for 1876–77 now preserved at the Museum of English Rural Life, University of Reading.

[43] Joseph Arch, op.cit. p.67.

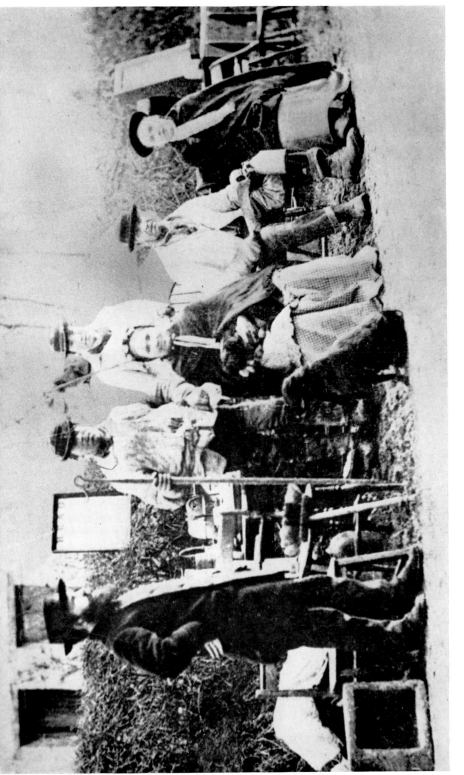

Eviction of a unionist family at Cherhill, Wiltshire, on 10th February, 1876.

(By permission from Cole Collection, Nuffield College, Oxford)

"SMALL BY DEGREES."

Suffolk Farmer. "Two Shill'n's a Week more?! Never! That'll never do!—out o' the Question!"

Suffolk Ploughman. "You're right there, Mas'r Wuzzles, sart'n sure! It 'on't dew. Our Sal sahy there'll be Eight Shill'n' and Threepence for Bread, Three-and-Sixpence for Rent and Coal, and Half-a-Craown for Club, Clothes, Botes, and Shoes for the owd 'Oman, five Kids, and me. No, that 'on't dew—that, that 'on't, bum by. But it'll be enow to

PART TWO
1872-73

43

CHAPTER FOUR

The Revolt: 1872

'When Arch beneath the Wellesbourne tree
His glorious work began,
A thrill of hope and energy
Through all the country ran; . . .'

(Opening lines of *'The Wesllesbourne Tree'* —
a favourite union ballad of the 1870's; it was
sung to the tune of *'Auld Lang Syne'*)

BY THE BEGINNING of January, 1872, the agricultural trade union movement had already become established — to some degree at least — in a number of counties in southern and central England, including, in particular, Herefordshire, North Warwickshire, Lincolnshire and Leicestershire. Now it was to be the turn of South Warwickshire.

Interestingly enough, despite Arch's later pre-eminence in the agricultural union field, the first move here came not from him but rather from labourers in the village of Harbury — or 'Hungry Harbury', as it was known locally. A meeting was held on 29th January at the New Inn, Chapel Street, in that parish and, according to the *Royal Leamington Chronicle*, it was attended by 'the agricultural labourers of the village and neighbourhood, to consider the step of asking for a general advance in the rate of wages'.[1] Presumably the chief local influence behind this was Edwin Russell, a Harbury tradesman and Methodist lay preacher, who was later to play an active part in the creation of the Warwickshire Union. But beyond this it seems likely that the gathering was primarily inspired by knowledge of trade union agitation elsewhere. The *Warwick Advertiser*, for example, as early as 6th January, 1872, was giving information on the North Warwickshire/ Staffordshire organisation (the Staffordshire Agricultural Labourers' Protection Society) and was reporting its demands for higher wages,

44

while the work of the Herefordshire Union had also received some coverage in the local press.

The first Harbury meeting ended without any clear decision being taken, other than to hold a second similar gathering on the 26th February. Yet, although so little had apparently been achieved, the mere calling of the meeting was an undoubted indication of the growing dissatisfaction of South Warwickshire labourers with their conditions of employment. It is significant that shortly afterwards a fresh effort at organisation was made, and this time it involved Joseph Arch himself.

Wednesday, 7th February, 1872, was a wet and miserable day, and Joseph was at home making a box for the use of his soldier son, John, when suddenly there came a knock at the door. Mrs Arch opened it and standing on the threshold were two labourers from nearby Wellesbourne, Henry Perks and John Harris, who had been sent over by their fellows to ask Joseph if he would help them to form a Union.[2] Mrs Arch listened to their request with some surprise, but she quickly invited them inside and soon they told Joseph what they had in mind. They said they had come to ask him to conduct a meeting at Welles-bourne that evening; they were looking for someone to guide them — a man of character and determination, who could inspire them with confidence. Joseph, with his reputation for plain-speaking and inde-pendence of mind, appeared just the leader they were seeking. (And, in addition, since he lived in his own cottage, he had the great advan-tage that he could not be evicted for espousing an unpopular cause — unlike many of his less fortunate brethren.)

After some hesitation, Arch accepted the invitation — his hesita-tion being due to his anxiety that it should not be a 'sort of hole-and-corner movement, which would come to nothing . . .' He told the men to book the club room at the Stag's Head Inn, Wellesbourne, for the meeting, and declared bluntly that provided they were firmly resolved to combine, he was prepared 'to run all risk and come over (to) help (them)'.[3] This latter was no idle statement. There *were* risks involved for him, since if his name were associated with an unsuccessful trade union agitation, he could expect to receive short shrift from the farmers and might have great difficulty in getting any employment locally in the future.

With rather mixed feelings, therefore, he set off early that evening from Barford to cover the few miles to the meeting place. He was dressed in his ordinary working attire — a pair of cord trousers, a cord vest and an old flannel jacket, which he later kept as a souvenir of the (to him) historic occasion. As he marched along the wet, muddy road to Wellesbourne, he turned over in his mind the possibilities of the success — or failure — of the enterprise he was undertaking. Through lack of education, lowness of wages and the scattered nature of their employment, farm workers would not be an easy group to organise into an effective trade union.

However, when Arch arrived at Wellesbourne, he felt most of his worries melt away. Although it had been intended to hold the meeting in the club room at the Stag's Head Inn, in fact there were so many people present that the room had become grossly overcrowded. It had therefore been necessary to move them all outside and to hold the meeting on the green in front of the Inn, beneath the branches of the massive chestnut tree which grew there. The entire neighbourhood was full of excited onlookers, 'as lively as a swarm of bees in June,' and in his autobiography Joseph claims that there were nearly 2,000 labourers present. The *Warwick Advertiser* gives a more conservative, and probably more accurate estimate, of 'between 500 and 600 men,' but there is no doubt that despite the shortness of the notice, a very large crowd had assembled, from Wellesbourne and neighbouring villages.[4] (Since there had been too little time to prepare any formal advertisements or handbills, information about the meeting had been passed on by word of mouth from one labourer to another, as they met during the course of their work. The waggoners were particularly important in this, and 'as they tramped alongside their teams they told every man they met in smock or fustian of the meeting to be held, and urged them thither. By the village inns the teams that day halted something longer than usual, while their drivers, over a mug of beer, told mine host, and all who were tasting the quality of his tap, of the new Union and of its approaching assembly.'[5])

It had by this time become pitch dark, and the problems of holding an outdoor meeting were aggravated by the action of a local opponent, who had arranged for the gas street lamps around the green to be switched off. But this did not discourage the men. They 'hung lanterns on the tree, and mounted lights on various sorts of bean sticks', so that the meeting could go on.[6] Although a thirty-four-year-old local labourer, Thomas Parker, had been chosen to act as chairman, it was Joseph Arch whom the men had chiefly come to hear. It was an unforgettable scene as, by the flickering light of the lanterns, he mounted an old pig-killing stool from which he was to address the crowd. Once secure on his perch, he looked down on the 'earnest upturned faces' of his audience — 'faces gaunt with hunger and pinched with want,' and he was filled with a deep desire to improve the lot of these poor, oppressed and often half-starved fellow workers, come what may! In his autobiography he has compared them to 'the children of Israel waiting for someone to lead them out of the land of Egypt' — and he obviously saw himself in the role of Moses.[6a]

The main theme of Joseph's speech was the need for the establishment of a union so that the men could fight for better conditions, higher wages and improved housing for themselves, and consequently greater comfort for their wives and families. He emphasized that the labourers 'ought to obtain an increase of 6d. per day on the present rate of wages (about 10s. a week) and a reduction of the number of hours (per day) to nine'.[7] The vigour and self-confidence displayed in his speech aroused his listeners' enthusiasm, and by the end of the meeting a decision had been taken in favour of combination. It was agreed to form 'a committee and deputation to wait upon employers and learn their views', with regard to the proposals on wages and hours, and then to hold a further meeting a week later.

Thus was the first step taken. It was followed on 12th February by a meeting of labourers at the village of Leek Wootton, which was not attended by Arch, and by a second and even larger gathering, attended by about a thousand labourers, at the green at Wellesbourne, on 14th February. On this occasion, the meeting was chaired by Benjamin Herring, a forty-year-old gardener's labourer who lived near to Joseph in Church Street, Barford, but, as before, Arch was the principal speaker. Once again, he called for the formation of a union, to secure a daily wage of 3s. and a working day of nine hours, but, in addition, he pressed for wider aims as well. The Union must support members on strike and give assistance to them in sickness and infirmity, so that they could avoid reliance on the grudging aid of the poor law. With typical energy he warned that some masters were offering a rise of 2s. per week to stop their men from joining the Union, 'but this was simply to prostrate the movement, and if they were thus bribed out of the union, and the movement failed, the masters would punish them by reducing their wages again, or turning them off on the first opportunity'.[8]

His listeners seem to have heeded these words, for immediately large numbers of them — perhaps 200 or 300 — presented themselves for membership of the Union, and recruitment began there and then in the open air, and later in the cottage of John Lewis, one of the local Wellesbourne leaders. All of the early committee meetings were in fact held in Lewis's humble stone-flagged cottage, and the union funds were collected in two large tea cups belonging to him.

This was but the beginning. Night after night, in face of opposition from farmers and landowners, often in pouring rain during that wet spring, Arch tramped from village to village addressing meetings. During the course of February he gave up all other employment in order to devote himself more fully to the work of propaganda and agitation; yet, despite the hardness of his task, he was content. He was convinced that a beacon had been lit, 'which would prove a rallying point for the agricultural labourers throughout the country.' In his speeches he emphasized time and time again the benefits which union membership could bestow — but this was not his only theme. He also drew attention to the question of the parliamentary franchise, and stressed the need for the vote to be given to the rural householder, as it had been given to the urban one in 1867. As in the case of a meeting held at the village of Bishop's Tachbrook on the Monday following the second successful Wellesbourne meeting, he linked this political demand to the higher wages the unionists were seeking:' . . . in the country the labourer was deprived of the political rights extended to the working classes in towns and was likely to be unless the labouring class got 3s. a day, which would be a lever to raise them politically, socially, religiously . . .'[9]

At the same time, he allayed any fears about the financial or legal position of the movement by pointing out that the recent Trade Union Act of 1871 had given them 'complete control over their officers and security for their funds'.

Of course, although Arch was the main inspiration behind the movement, others, too, were encouraging its spread. Thus at Harbury, Ratley, Napton, Leek Wootton and Flecknoe, as well as other Warwickshire villages, meetings were held quite independently to discuss the demands for higher wages and to consider the possibility of strike action if these demands were not met. Non-labourers of a Radical turn of mind were also active, like Mr William Taunton, an auctioneer from Coventry, who attended a meeting at Stoneleigh to urge the labourers to form a union. And, similarly, at Whitnash, early in March, Henry Duckett and Henry Taylor, two enthusiastic members of Leamington Trades Council, addressed a pro-union meeting of about five hundred labourers. Taylor, a spare, energetic young man of about twenty-eight, was at that time employed as a carpenter in Leamington but he was later to become the first general secretary of the National Agricultural Labourers' Union, after its establishment at the end of May, 1872. Despite Joseph's somewhat ungracious attitude towards the assistance rendered by these urban unionists — in his autobiography he declared that he had 'made up (his) mind to keep clear of them all; . . . our movement was well supported before they took any notice of us' — there is no doubt that they did provide valuable guidance as to the form and character which the agricultural movement ought to assume.[10]

Equally necessary for the success of the union cause was the publicity given by the local press. Through the columns of the newspapers, labourers in every village could discover what was happening in other parts of the county, and, at the same time, the attention and sympathy of the general public could be aroused. The Radical proprietor of the *Royal Leamington Chronicle*, J. E. Matthew Vincent, was an early friend of the labourers and his newspaper contained extremely detailed accounts of their first meetings.

Yet, despite the progress being made, the new movement was still a very tentative organisation. Time for consolidation was badly needed. But that was just what the unionists were not prepared to allow. Having once combined, they were anxious to achieve some positive benefits as quickly as possible, and as early as the third week of February, labourers on the Earl of Jersey's estate at Ratley had come out on strike (probably under the leadership of Edward Haynes, a Primitive Methodist lay preacher, who was a local activist), while at Bishop's Tachbrook, too, a few labourers had also struck. At Ratley, indeed, there was some violence, as attempts were made to remove by force non-strikers from one of the farms where a dispute was in progress.[11] Nevertheless, these were only small-scale affairs, and it was appreciated by Joseph and the other members of the Executive Committee of the Wellesbourne union that something more was needed.

In these circumstances, it was decided to put forward specific and clear demands for an increase in wages and a reduction in the number of hours of work. The original minimum of 3s. per day basic rate was dropped in favour of a daily rate of 2s. 8d., while the hours of work were to be 'from six to five and to close at three on Saturday,' with '4d. per hour overtime.' (The request for payment for overtime was, of course, a relatively new departure.) All of these proposals were incorporated in a circular letter which was sent out, with Arch's approval, by men in the Wellesbourne area to the local farmers (principally those on the estates of Sir Charles Mordaunt and Mr Spencer Lucy), early in March. The letter was modestly subsibed, 'Your Humble Servants,' but there was a mailed fist inside the velvet glove, in so far as notice was given that if negotiations were refused, the men would come out on strike after Saturday, 9th March, the date when their notice was due to expire.

The employers, for their part, were quite confident in their own power over their workers and they contemptuously ignored the letter. Their confidence was rudely shattered therefore when on 11th March the men were as good as their word and a strike was seen to be in progress. Unlike the previous small disputes at Ratley and Bishop's Tachbrook, about two hundred workers were involved on this occasion, from Wellesbourne and the nearby villages of Moreton Morrell, Hampton Lucy, Charlecote, and Loxley. At Hampton Lucy and Charlecote, however, several of the labourers who occupied tied cottages, decided not to make a stand when they realised that they would be evicted if they did. They remained at work and received 'a slight increase of wages' in return for this 'loyalty' to their employers.

For the strikers themselves it was a momentous occasion; 'there was hardly a labourer in Wellesbourne who went to work as usual. Men who for forty and fifty years had never known what it was to have a free day, hung about idle, and did not know what to do with themselves. Many a man and woman that Monday morning felt that there was a grim struggle before them; that they and their children might have to suffer pangs of hunger even worse than those they had endured in the past; . . .'[12] It was an act of faith in themselves — and in their leader, Joseph Arch.

Soon this unexpected display of solidarity and determination on the part of Arch and the South Warwickshire labourers was attracting the attention not only of the local press, but also of the Birmingham papers and, most important, of *The Times*. The first mention of the Wellesbourne strike appeared in *The Times* of 14th March. The report significantly pointed out that the dispute was causing 'much' inconvenience to farmers whose spring work had already been 'greatly delayed by continuous rain,' and who wanted to take advantage 'of the present fine weather . . .' From the weather angle, the strike was obviously well-timed so as to exert maximum pressure on the employers.

It was also reported that labourers in villages not affected by the major dispute (like Bishop's Tachbrook and Snitterfield) were agreeing to pay a weekly levy of 1s. to the strike fund, while at Barford and Cubbington, the members had agreed to contribute 'as far as their means would allow.' This display of spirit by the humble farm worker began to arouse the interest of the general public even further. As the *Royal Leamington Chronicle* of 16th March declared in an editorial: 'The degraded position of the English labourers in the present day, when all other classes of people are enjoying the advantages of an unexampled commercial prosperity — is a scandal to the country, and now that the labourers have had the intelligence to make a movement on their own behalf, they will find friends and practical sympathisers by the thousand . . .' And certainly 'practical' sympathy was urgently needed, if the strike were not to collapse through lack of money. The *Chronicle* informed its readers that a local committee had been appointed in Leamington to receive contributions for the labourers on strike.

That this support was essential can be understood when it is realised that at the beginning of the dispute the union 'had only five shillings in hand and that was in copper, pennies and half-pennies contributed by some of the labourers; most of them had not a farthing to their name'.[13] Worse than that indeed many were in debt, for 'owing to the miserable wages paid the men they were nearly always in debt to the shop a week a-head — this system of dealing was called 'one week under another,' and it meant that the greater part, if not the whole, of the labourer's wages were spent each week before they were earned.'[14] As Arch declared, they had staked their all — their 'widow's mite' — on the Union, and 'it was fight or fall'; there was no alternative!

Particularly active in collecting funds in connection with the newly established Leamington Relief Committee were members of the Leamington Trades Council, among whom Henry Taylor, Henry Duckett and Thomas Wager, a painter who was later to become the third general secretary of the agricultural labourers' union, were especially prominent. Altogether the Leamington Trades Council collected £40 towards the strike relief.[15] However, in addition to this, in Barford and certain other villages tradesmen gave help by becoming honorary members of the Union, and support from farther afield came flowing in as press publicity began to have its effect. The Leamington Relief Committee as a whole in fact managed to collect £242 13s. 4d., while the *Leamington Chronicle* organised the collection of a further £336 5s., and in all, by the 23rd March, 1872, the considerable total of £838 3s. 6¼d. had been secured from the various voluntary subscriptions. They came from as far away as Bournemouth and Worthing in the south and Jarrow and Manchester in the north, while there were even donations from Scotland.[16]

Nevertheless, although money began to flow into the union's reserves from quite early on, it was only after the appearance of a series of sympathetic articles on the strike written by Archibald Forbes, the well-known correspondent of the Liberal *Daily News*, that the greatest impact was made. The first of these appeared in the edition of 27th March and it described in graphic detail the poor living conditions and low income of the labourers concerned. Arch himself recalled with particular gratitude the debt owed by the Union to Forbes for writing these articles.[16a]

Meanwhile, Joseph was, of course, extremely busy, holding meetings wherever he could 'get men together.' Most of the meetings were held out-of-doors — partly because of their large size and partly because of the difficulty of getting accommodation in communities where the most influential inhabitants were hostile to the Union. As Joseph later recalled: 'Sometimes we gathered under a tree, sometimes in a field; now it would be in an orchard, and the next might be by the roadside. We met by sunlight and moonlight and starlight and lantern light — the sun in the sky or the farthing dip — it was all one to the Union man at that time.' The meetings usually commenced with the energetic singing of one of the union songs, and then continued with a series of vigorous encouraging speeches. Arch himself seemed tireless: 'I felt as if there was a living fire in me . . . There was a strength and a power in me which had been pent up and had been growing, and now it flowed forth'. As it flowed, it swept many a rural audience along with it, until men and women forgot their fears of landowner and farmer and declared instead for the Union!

But what was the reaction of the farmers to all this activity on the part of Joseph and his friends? Early in March, Sir Charles Mordaunt (one of the two most affected landowners in the 'strike' area) and about two hundred farmers had held a meeting at which they had strongly condemned the Union. Threats were made to discharge *all* workers who became unionists and although most of the farmers failed, in practice, to abide by this decision, a few did adhere to a policy of determined opposition. Consequently, some lock-outs inevitably occurred, as, for example, at Tysoe, Claverdon and Wasperton, and charges of breach of contract were also brought against workers who failed to give adequate notice before coming out on strike. Thus, Thomas Chambers, a waggoner of Moreton Morrell, was fined 5s. 6d. and had to pay 14s. compensation and 10s. 6d. costs, when he appeared before Warwick County Bench at the end of March, charged with this type of breach of contract.[17] Other employers followed the same policy.[18] Again, at Radford and Wellesbourne, certain of the men were evicted from their cottages and at Harbury and Snitterfield they were dismissed from work on account of their union membership. Efforts were even made to replace the striking labourers with Irishmen, although not until April were any apparently secured for this purpose. During that month, however, two large parties came over.[19]

The Warwickshire labourers were nevertheless fortunate in so far as within the county lay the great Radical centre of Birmingham. Help for their struggle was readily forthcoming from this source, both from politicians and from the urban workers. In particular, Jesse Collings, a Radical businessman and a close associate of Joseph Chamberlain, George Dixon, the Birmingham Liberal M.P. who had earlier been associated with the Herefordshire movement and Mr J. S. Wright, a businessman and chairman of the Birmingham Liberal Association all provided encouragement — as did the dynamic Joseph Chamberlain himself. In his biography of Chamberlain indeed J. L. Garvin has stated that the Warwickshire trade union movement 'was under Chamberlain's eye from the first . . . Within twelve days after it began Chamberlain addressed a meeting at the Temperance Hall, Birmingham, and in an impassioned . . . speech he championed the rural revolt . . .'[20] However, he showed his help in a more practical fashion as well. At a meeting held on 3rd April, at Birmingham Town Hall, in support of the labourers (and presided over by Mr Wright) it was announced that Chamberlain had already given £20 to the Union funds and had promised to provide a further £5 a week for ten or twelve weeks; Wright announced that he was willing to subscribe £3 per week for a similar period.[21]

Among the trade unionists, the Birmingham Boat Builders can be noted as expressing 'hearty sympathy' with the labourers, while the Birmingham Trades Council, at a meeting held on 6th April, decided to form a sub-committee for the purpose of 'collecting and forwarding any funds to the South Warwickshire Agricultural Labourers' Society'. This did not prove a very fruitful source in practice, however — partly because the strike ended early in April — and only about £4 was actually collected.[22]

Elsewhere in the country, unionist interest was likewise aroused. The London Trades Council formed a committee to help the movement, and William Allan of the Amalgamated Society of Engineers was appointed treasurer of the fund established for that same purpose. At a meeting on 9th April, the Council agreed to make a collection, and a total of £245 5s. 1d. was realised — £168 12s. being contributed by the Executive Council of the Boiler Makers' and Iron Ship Builders' Society. The Amalgamated Society of Engineers provided a further £300 from their own funds.[23] Many other unions contributed in a similar (although rather less generous) manner.

In London, also, the interest of members of the Land Tenure Reform Association was secured. Although this Society aimed primarily at a reform of the land laws, support for the labourers was given because it was felt that they were particular sufferers from the land law system. Among the members of the Association who rallied to the labourers' cause were Howard Evans, a journalist who later spoke at many agricultural union meetings, and the Hon. Auberon Herbert, M.P. for Nottingham, who had been briefly associated with Canon Girdlestone's abortive attempt to establish a national farm workers' union in 1868. Herbert and his wife in fact came to Warwickshire and spoke at a number of the meetings held by Arch and the labourers towards the end of March, 1872. They even tried to turn to good account the labourers' idle hours, whilst they were on strike, by distributing 'reading books, writing slates, copy books &c. among the men' in the Wellesbourne area. John Lewis, by now secretary of the Wellesbourne branch of the Union, was appointed to go round the cottages to help the members with their 'lessons'![24]

For Joseph Arch, of course, these weeks were exhausting ones. He was fully engaged in addressing meetings in the villages and in arranging for the distribution of the strike benefit of 9s. per week which could now be paid to the men still out. When Archibald Forbes came to the county, Arch was involved in escorting him around the countryside. He gave himself no rest, but despite his weariness, he had the satisfaction of seeing the movement spread not only through South Warwickshire, but also into other nearby counties, including Oxfordshire, Northamptonshire and Buckinghamshire, where several independent unions — as well as branches of the Warwickshire movement — were being set up. And there is no doubt that for the labourers Arch remained the focus of attention. Although it is true that the help of others was needed to make the Union a viable proposition, without him it is unlikely that it could ever have captured the imagination of the labourers in the way it did. This fact was, for example, recognised in many of the union songs, such as 'We'll All be Union Men,' the chorus of which began: 'Joe Arch he raised his voice, 'Twas for the working men, . . .' The words of 'The Wellesbourne Tree' quoted at the beginning of this Chapter make a similar point. The emphasis was all on the part which Joseph had played — and was continuing to play. (See Appendix 6 for further songs with this theme.)

However, although increasing interest in the Union was obviously apparent among the farm labourers, this, on its own, was scarcely enough. Clearly a more formal organisation was needed if permanent success were to be secured, and even while the South Warwickshire strike was still in progress, it was decided to hold a massive demonstration towards this end on Good Friday, 29th March, 1872, at the Portland Street public hall in Leamington. The demonstration was to affirm faith in the Union and to draw up rules for the merging of all the Warwickshire branches into one society, to be known as the Warwickshire Agricultural Labourers' Union.

To help them to achieve their aim the unionists had sought advice from a number of outside well-wishers, including Canon Girdlestone and George Potter, the founder of the influential trade union newspaper, *The Beehive*, who was a native of nearby Kenilworth. On the basis of the advice thus received the labourers could then put forward their own plans and proposals.[25] However, they were obviously a little dampened by Canon Girdlestone's reaction in so far as he 'wrote in a friendly spirit advising compromise and conciliation. He said the Warwickshire labourer was already better off than many of his kind.'[26] Whilst this may have been true — he was certainly better off than his fellows in North Devon, for example — Arch and his supporters felt that far too many injustices remained for them to accept the situation with any complacency. As Arch declared: 'We did not dispute the fact that the bulk of the labourers in Devonshire got only eight shillings a week, that few or none got more than nine shillings, and that bad cottages and high rents were the rule there. It was all too true; but to our thinking, this only showed that the sooner they had the Union all through Devonshire and such benighted regions the better for Hodge.' ('Hodge' was the nineteenth century nick-name for the farm labourer.)

The day appointed for the Leamington demonstration dawned wet and miserable, but this did not deter the labourers. Men and women came tramping into the town in considerable numbers, in some cases marching in large groups, dressed in their best clothes and headed by the village fife and drum bands. John Lewis, for example, collected a large number of supporters together at Wellesbourne — they met under the famous chestnut tree at 8.30 in the morning — and they marched proudly in procession to Leamington, singing as they went.

Joseph was to be the main Union speaker at the meeting, but apart from him there were several non-labourers present, including Auberon Herbert, who took the chair, Jesse Collings, and Edward Jenkins, a barrister of the Middle Temple, who had earlier written a well-known contemporary 'tear-jerking' novel of working-class life, called *Ginx's Baby*. In addition, once the meeting had got under way, letters were read from other politicians, who were not able to be present but who signified support for the Union. These included A. J. Mundella, Radical M.P. for Sheffield, and George Dixon, M.P. for Birmingham, while a dramatic message was read from an anonymous 'friend' counselling moderation but saying that the 'right of combination must be fought for to the death;' with the message came the welcome donation of £100! Not surprisingly the labourers present greeted both the message and the money with loud cheers.[27]

After this rather unexpected introduction, the formal business of the meeting commenced. Rules were discussed and adopted, laying down the conditions of membership, and an executive committee of eight was appointed — with Joseph Arch as its chairman. Among the objects of the Union mentioned in the rules, apart from those relating to the raising of wages and the reduction of the hours of work, were three of particular significance: 'to improve the habitations of the labourers; to provide them with gardens or allotments, and to assist deserving and suitable labourers to migrate or emigrate.' (Although Joseph himself was not at that time in favour of emigration—which he felt robbed the country of some of its most enterprising workers—the emigration agents of both the Ontario and the Brazilian Governments had already been active in the South Warwickshire area during the strike, and they had succeeded in securing some labourer emigrants.[28])

However, Arch *was* more favourably disposed to the question of migration and at the Good Friday meeting he announced that he had offers of employment for '50 men in Yorkshire,' at 18s. a week, and '20 in Newcastle at £1.' Any men still involved in the Wellesbourne dispute were advised to take advantage of these offers or of any similar ones which might arise later.

The formal business of the meeting ended with the fixing of the contributions to the new Union at sixpence entrance fee, and twopence per week subscription. The Warwickshire Agricultural Labourers' Union was now in business.

Nevertheless, given the limited size of the hall in which the meeting had been held, by no means all of those who wished to attend had been able to squeeze into the room. They had overflowed into the street and so, in the evening, when the discussions inside had been completed, Joseph and Archibald Forbes went outside to address them. Joseph's own feelings can be imagined. From the obscure beginnings of a local gathering one wet Wednesday evening in February had come, within less than two months, this massive demonstration. In his autobiography he has described the scene:

'When I stood up in my moleskins, I faced such a crowd of my fellow creatures as I had never before set eyes on. It was a floodtide of humanity which swayed and heaved as far as I could see in the gaslight; . . . The spectacle of those waiting thousands was enough to touch the heart and fire any man not made of wood and stone. It fired me so that I felt I had got the strength of ten men in me. My heart went out to every listener there, and that made my voice reach them too . . . I wanted them to know that I had been through what they were suffering now; that I was no professional agitator, but a working agricultural labourer, who was acquainted with their griefs from personal experience, and who was convinced that their one chance of social salvation lay in Union; . . . Yes, the dumb had found a voice at last; the despairing were filled with hope; the downtrodden slave had become a man again.'[29]

It was a highly emotional moment for all of them!

But sentiment and emotion were of limited value only. More prosaic matters must also be attended to, and when the executive committee of the new Union met on the Tuesday following the Good Friday demonstration, they appointed Arch organising secretary, at a salary of 21s. per week, plus travelling expenses,[30] while Edwin Russell, of Harbury, was appointed corresponding secretary for the next two months, also at a salary of 21s. per week, plus travelling expenses. Union offices were opened temporarily at the Guernsey Temperance Hotel — where, it will be remembered, Annie Arch was quite frequently employed as a dressmaker, and it may have been because of this connection that the Hotel was chosen as the first head office.

Joseph's most urgent task was now to try to settle the Wellesbourne strike. His efforts were made easier by the fact that already certain of the farmers and landowners were weakening in their opposition. Some had started to negotiate for a return to work and to grant wage increases to 14s., 15s. and 16s. a week, and in these cases the labourers accepted the offers and ended their strike. In other cases, too, threats of dismissal or eviction from tied cottages were withdrawn, and the London trade union newspaper, *The Beehive*, estimated that 'half of those on strike (had) got employment at the advanced price (of 16s.) . . .'

Among those who had agreed to withdraw notices of eviction and to grant an increase in wages was Sir Charles Mordaunt himself.[31] In addition, a number of the strikers had also migrated to better-paid employment in the urban north; the 'North Eastern Railway offered work for drivers and horsekeepers at one pound and twenty-three shillings a week,' for example, and there were many other similar offers both at home and overseas in New Zealand, Canada and, less genuinely, in Brazil.

By the 6th April, therefore, the number of men on strike in the Wellesbourne area had declined considerably. Altogether there were ninety-four still unemployed on that date — fifty-six of them at Wellesbourne, twenty-eight at Moreton Morrell and ten at Loxley.[32] When Arch and Russell visited them to distribute their 9s. dispute benefit, therefore, the union leaders decided that since there were ample opportunities for employment both in the North of England and overseas, the strike should be wound up. Twenty-five of the men agreed to go to a soap factory near Liverpool on the following Monday, while about twenty more were expected 'to follow some of their comrades to the dockyards of Gateshead'. The rest were advised to seek employment during the week, Arch remarking that the public could not be expected to keep them idle when work was offered at from 3s. to 5s. a day. Applications had been received for five hundred labourers from the new water works at Huddersfield, for instance, and 'any number were offered work at 7s. a day on the Government railway in New Zealand, the contractors engaging to tranship the men, though penniless.' Nevertheless, although a number of men did leave the Wellesbourne area in response to these offers or as a direct result of the dispute, the majority obviously did not. They were able to obtain employment under improved conditions in the vicinity of their homes. It is significant that by the end of May, 1872, the Wellesbourne branch was still the largest individual one in the county, with 210 members.[33]

Altogether the dispute had cost the Union about £214 7s. in strike relief and £112 16s. in migration expenses, but because of the great generosity of the public, there were still over £400 in hand, either in the form of cash, or in the form of a deposit at Lloyds Bank in Leamington.[34]

The success of the strike, despite the bitter initial opposition of many farmers and in the glare of considerable press publicity, gave a great impetus to the whole agricultural movement. Soon farm workers in many different counties were applying to the Warwickshire unionists for guidance and, above all, for the presence and advocacy of Arch himself. By this time his voice was hoarse with so much speaking, but in spite of his difficulties he continued to accept the invitations, and to travel all over the surrounding countryside. Yet, despite this formidable effort, he could not satisfy all the demands. For example, a bare three weeks after the establishment of the independent Milton Union, in Oxfordshire (it was later to form the basis of the Oxford district of the National Agricultural Labourers' Union), members were inviting him to come and address them. They repeated their invitation at intervals, until he finally spoke at a mass meeting at Oxford Town Hall on 23rd October, about five months after their original request.[35]

North Oxfordshire and Northamptonshire fared rather better. At the end of April, Arch, Russell and Edward Haynes of Ratley attended a meeting in Banbury Corn Exchange, for example, attended by over 2,000 labourers, and presided over by Mr Butcher, of Banbury Co-operative Society, who had earlier sent £1 7s. 2d. towards the Warwickshire strike fund. Significantly, although several of his fellow leaders spoke, it was Joseph the men had come to hear. His appearance was the 'signal for the greatest enthusiasm.'[36] And at Long Lawford, near Rugby, a week later, the devotion of the large open-air gathering was such that they were prepared to stand patiently in the pouring rain in order to hear him speak.[37]

Perhaps the labourers *needed* a man with these powers of charismatic leadership and so they attributed to Joseph qualities which he did not naturally possess, or perhaps the sturdy frame and strong voice could strike a genuine chord in the hearts of his audience. Whatever the truth may be, certain it is that he did exert a magnetic influence over the agricultural labourers during these feverish months. A description written at first hand by Joseph Ashby of Tysoe, who attended one of the early meetings (perhaps held in March, 1872[38]) gives a good idea of the flavour of such gatherings.

It had been announced that Arch was to attend a meeting in Tysoe. 'The excitement created by the announcement spread through the village, and, indeed, through the whole neighbourhood like a prairie fire, and there was not a little child even in the village school who did not seem to be affected by it.

'The old folk received the information with open-mouthed wonder, and regarded the innovation as we might now regard the invasion of our quiet streets by a detachment of a strange army whose intentions might be unknown to us.

'Our farmers seemed to regard the event as the beginning of a revolt which would lead to the complete ruin of their industry, . . .

'But my interest was chiefly centred upon the "young bloods" amongst the working classes. These assumed airs of triumph, talked in large groups of how old Grimes, and old Tommy at the top, and old Nickey at the gravels — these being abbreviations of names, along with others, by which some of our farmers were known . . . — would like to "put the waages up from a lebum to fifteen bob." They laughed

58

Stag Inn and Green, Wellesbourne, from a photograph taken in 1971. The old chestnut tree died in the summer of 1948 and its site is indicated by the large stone to the right of the picture. The present tree on the left was planted in March 1949 and was a gift from Councillor Herbert Farrington. A commemorative plaque at the base of the tree records the story.

"the agricultural labourer"

'Spy' cartoon of Joseph Arch from *Vanity Fair* of 26th June, 1886.

scornfully, too, at the sage councils (sic) of our old vicar as though the matter had passed already into their own hands . . .

'Although the meeting was announced to take place about seven o'clock in the evening, the streets of the village were gradually filling with visitors during the whole of the afternoon . . . . As the hour of seven approached, the strains of a brass band fell upon the ears of the gathering crowd, and every ear was strained to catch the distant music. . . .

'The band was now approaching us. The instruments twinkling in the soft glow of the evening sunshine; a swelling host to right and left of them, treading on the heels of each other, insensible of any sense of order or decorum till the street was filled to its utmost capacity, constituted a scene no man could soon forget.

'A waving of coloured cotton handkerchiefs hailed the band to the platform, and, as the last strains of the martial air, "See the Conquering Hero comes," fell from the instruments, JOSEPH ARCH, admittedly the unchallenged hero of that movement, was almost lifted on to the elevation.

'I am bound to admit that his manly form, and his quiet bearing, grotesquely clad as he seemed to me to be, for this meeting was held while he was still a labourer, won my young heart . . .

'. . . the excitement was inexpressibly intense when JOSEPH ARCH rose to address the meeting.

'Every voice was hushed as he rose from his seat and stepped forward to survey the crowd which was pressing to suffocation to catch his first words. . . .'[39]

It was heady stuff and to many of the excited audience it must have seemed like a dream come true; at last they had a representative from their own class who could express their inmost desires in a language they could understand.

But life for Joseph was not all excited meetings and adulation. Hostility had still to be faced from some of the farmers' organisations, despite the gradual ending of the Wellesbourne strike; and at a meeting of the Midland Farmers' Club at Birmingham on 4th April, for example, a resolution was carried declaring the Club's intention to resist 'the interference of designing political agitators, who seek, for their own selfish purposes, to sow dissensions between employers and employed in the agricultural districts of the Midland Counties.'[40] The members unanimously pledged themselves to oppose the Union 'by any and every means.'

There is no doubt, too, that a number of agriculturists were still following the earlier policies of eviction or dismissal in order to crush the Union — even if few went as far as Farmer Garrett of Tadmarton in North Oxfordshire, who literally flogged a middle-aged labourer

(Isaac Bodfish) in his employ because he had joined the Union![41]

Fortunately, however, wiser counsels prevailed in most cases. The Warwickshire Chamber of Agriculture for instance made several attempts to negotiate with Union representatives, and at a meeting of the local branch of the Chamber at Henley-in-Arden on 12th April, resolutions were passed condemning the perquisite system and 'recommending that all wages be paid in cash'.[42] Later, on 25th May, Joseph, Edward Haynes of Ratley, and Mr A. Arnold, a gentleman sympathiser and land law reformer from Henley-in-Arden, met representatives of the Chamber of Agriculture at Warwick, in order to discuss those Union proposals which Chamber members considered unfair and unacceptable. Altogether, the meeting lasted three hours and although no satisfactory compromise was reached, the atmosphere in which discussions were carried on was at least one of reasonableness and not of unthinking, bitter hostility.[43]

Then, of course, the attitude of the labourers themselves was another matter of some concern to Joseph and his fellow leaders. Many of them were taking advantage of the apparent improvement in their bargaining position and were coming out on strike independently in support of their demands for higher wages.[44] There was a danger that a too reckless use of the strike weapon would weaken the financial position of the Union, and would lead to its collapse. This obviously had to be guarded against, and Joseph sternly warned the men against thinking that the Union would keep them in idleness. At a meeting at Pailton, near Rugby, in the middle of May, he told a large gathering of labourers: 'You are not going to suck the blood of any working man, and if there is a loafer here tonight, a man who says, "I will get in the Union, and I shall get a good deal out of it," we don't want you in it at all. We want men who can work, men who will work in the Union.'[45]

This, then, was the situation which had to be faced. Joseph, as leader, had to discourage the men from becoming too demanding, since their organisation was still too frail to stand a prolonged and large-scale dispute, and yet he had to be ready to fight attempts at intimidation on the part of employers. Clearly the sooner the Union became stronger, the better it would be for all of its members. And it seemed to Joseph and his allies that the best way of achieving such strength was through wider united action — through the creation of a national organisation.

The possibilities of a national union had first been seriously explored by Arch and other committee members at a meeting held on 10th April in the Primitive Methodist Chapel at Wellesbourne. It had then been decided to hold a national conference in Leamington at the end of May and towards this aim to invite representatives from the other agricultural unions to participate. Each local union was to be urged to appoint two agricultural labourers as delegates to the Conference, while Mr George Dixon, M.P. was invited to preside over the gathering. It was hoped that a number of influential non-labourers would also attend in order to demonstrate their support.

Although Mr Dixon quickly accepted his invitation, not all of the Union leaders were prepared to follow suit and to agree to support the proposed amalgamation. In some cases, after consideration, the invitation was rejected — the Kent and Sussex Union, the Peterborough District Union, and the Lincolnshire Amalgamated Labour League are but three examples of agricultural unions which decided to decline the invitation and remain independent. Nevertheless, about sixty delegates *did* agree to attend. They came from approximately twenty counties in England and Wales — ranging from Radnorshire in the West to Suffolk and Norfolk in the east, and Yorkshire in the north.[46]

With the calling of this Conference everything was now ready for the next important step in the life of the Union — and of its leader, Joseph Arch.

[1] *Royal Leamington Chronicle* — 3rd February, 1872. The New Inn was situated near to the Wesleyan Chapel in Harbury — a fact perhaps of some signficance in view of the leading role played in the agitation by Methodist local preachers.

[2] *English Labourers' Chronicle* — 12th January, 1889. In the earlier accounts of this meeting two men only are mentioned, but in his autobiography, Arch mentions that three men came over to see him. He does not name them. — Joseph Arch, op.cit., p.68.

[3] Joseph Arch, op.cit., p.69.

[4] *Warwick Advertiser* — 10th February, 1872.

[5] Rev. F S Attenborough, op.cit., p.60.

[6] Gas lighting first came to Wellesbourne in September, 1864; rather ironically, in view of Joseph's experience, among the places chosen for the first trial was a lamp erected on the Green! — *Warwick Advertiser* — 10th September, 1864.

[6a] Joseph Arch, op.cit., p.73.

[7] *Warwick Advertiser* — 10th February, 1872.

[8] *Warwick Advertiser* — 17th February, 1872. In his autobiography, Arch wrongly dates this meeting for 21st February. — Joseph Arch, op.cit. p.74.

[9] *Royal Leamington Chronicle* — 24th February, 1872.

[10] Joseph Arch, op.cit. p.103 and *Birmingham Daily Post* — 9th March, 1872. Taylor was born in Luton, one of fourteen children — of whom only four were to survive childhood. He came to Leamington in 1869 to work first as a pattern-maker and then as a carpenter. — *English Labourer* — 17th June, 1876.

[11] Royal Leamington Chronicle — 9th March, 1872. The report noted that at Kineton Petty Sessions 'last week' John England (of Ratley) had been committed for three months' hard labour for compelling 'one Thomas Barnes, labourer, to leave the employment of Thomas Berridge, farmer. There was a strike in the village, but Barnes in spite of threats persisted in going to work; when defendant and others came and forcibly removed him from his master's premises'. Berridge was, significantly, the largest farmer in the village, cultivating at the time of the 1861 Census of Population 344 acres of land. At that date he employed, in all, fourteen men and six boys. — 1861 Census of Population, Ratley — P.R.O. R.G.9.916. There were five other farmers in the village at that time.

[12] Joseph Arch, op.cit. pp. 76–77.

[13] Ibid., p.94.

[14] Ibid., p.78.

[15] *English Labourers' Chronicle* — 23rd May, 1885.

[16] *Labourers' Union Chronicle* — 5th September, 1872.

[16a] Joseph Arch, op.cit. p.83.

[17] *Warwick Advertiser* — 30th March, 1872

[18] *Abingdon Herald* — 6th July, 1872

[19] F.Kleinwachter — Zur Geschichte der englischen Arbeiterbewegung im Jahre 1872 in *Jahrbuch für Nationalokonomie und Statistik*, 1875, p.385.

[20] J L Garvin — *Life of Joseph Chamberlain* (Vol. I) (London, 1932), p.148.

[21] *Birmingham Daily Post* — 5th April, 1872.

[22] Birmingham Trades Council Minute Book — Meeting on 14th May, 1872. — Birmingham City Reference Library.

[23] Report of the Federal Union of Agricultural and General Labourers, 1874, p.2 (in Howell Collection, Bishopsgate Institute) and *Royal Leamington Chronicle* 27th April, 1872.

[24] *Warwick Advertiser* — 6th April, 1872.

[25] See *Royal Leamington Chronicle* — 9th March, 1872, for details concerning the Union's approaches to Canon Girdlestone and George Potter. In July, 1872, Potter also came to speak on behalf of the agricultural trade unionists at meetings at Kenilworth and Leamington — *Aris's Birmingham Gazette* — 27th July, 1872.

[26] Joseph Arch, op.cit., p.85.

[27] *The Times* — 30th March, 1872.

[28] *The Times* — 29th March, 1872 and Thirty-third Annual General Report of the Emigration Commissioners, Parliamentary Papers, 1873, Vol. XVIII, p.8.

[29] Joseph Arch, op.cit., pp.89–92.

[30] *Royal Leamington Chronicle* — 6th April, 1872.

[31] *The Beehive* — 30th March, 1872 and *Warwick Advertiser* — 6th April, 1872.

[32] *Jackson's Oxford Journal* — 13th April, 1872.

[33] *Royal Leamington Chronicle* — 1st June, 1872.

[34] *Labourers' Union Chronicle* — 5th September, 1872.

[35] See meeting on 7th May, 1872 in Minute Book of the Milton Union in the Cole Collection at Nuffield College, Oxford.

[36] *Northampton Mercury* — 4th May, 1872.

[37] *Northampton Mercury* — 11th May, 1872.

[38] *Royal Leamington Chronicle* — 23rd March, 1872, describes a meeting held at Tysoe on 19th March very similar to the one Ashby mentions. Miss Ashby herself in *Joseph Ashby of Tysoe* suggests July as the date, however.

[39] J A Benson (pen-name of Joseph Ashby) — A 'Union Meeting' in *Land Magazine*, July, 1899 (Vol. III), pp.557–559. I am indebted to Mr E P Thompson for this reference.

[40] Reg Groves — *Sharpen the Sickle!* (London. 1949), p.53 and *Royal Leamington Chronicle* — 6th April, 1872.

[41] *Northampton Mercury* — 15th June, 1872 and *Midland Free Press* — 25th May, 1872.

[42] *The Times* — 13th April, 1872.

[43] *The Times* — 28th May, 1872.

[44] For example, *Royal Leamington Chronicle* — 25th May, 1872.

[45] *Midland Free Press* — 18th May. 1872. See also the Address in Appendix I(b) which was attached to the first rules of the National Agricultural Labourers' Union.

[46] *The Times* — 30th May, 1872 and Joseph Arch, op.cit., p.114.

CHAPTER FIVE

The coming of the National Union: 1872

I live:
For the cause that needs assistance,
For the wrongs that need resistance,
For the future in the distance,
For the good that I can do.

(Verse written at the back of Joseph Arch's
surviving account book/diary for 1876–77.)

IT WAS IN THE MIDST of considerable press publicity that the second
Leamington Conference opened on Wednesday, 29th May, 1872.
The labourers — the formerly despised and disregarded 'clod-
hoppers' and 'Johnny Raws' — had become 'news'; the living proof
that even the meekest and humblest members of society could show
spirit and independence, if pressed too far!

The venue chosen for their gathering was the newly-completed
Circus, a large wooden hippodrome in the centre of Leamington near
the Pump Room, which had been selected because it provided ample
accommodation for up to three thousand people.[1] And it was here that
Joseph and his fellow delegates assembled in some excitement on the
first morning of the Conference. George Dixon took the chair and on
the platform, supporting Arch and the other union leaders, were
several non-labourers who had agreed to speak as well. This rather
mixed group of sympathisers included Jesse Collings, W. G. Ward,
a somewhat unbalanced Herefordshire gentleman of passionate views,
who claimed to 'thirst for the blood of the farmers,' the Rev. A.
O'Neill, 'a Birmingham Baptist Minister who in 1842 had been imprisoned for his Chartist activities',[2] and J. Campbell, a J.P. from
Rugby. Letters of sympathy with the movement were also received
from a number of other friends, including the Hon. Auberon Herbert,
Thomas Hughes (the author of *Tom Brown's Schooldays*), and Canon
Girdlestone, whose own work for the labourers had done so much to

63

pinpoint the misery of their lives and to lead to the present revolt.

Joseph and the rest of the delegates listened closely as during the course of the first morning's work, a report was read concerning the condition of the parent Warwickshire Union, which now claimed a membership of 4,695 divided among sixty-four branches spread all over the county. Total receipts of £838 3s. 6¼d. were shown on the balance sheet, together with an expenditure of £400 9s. 6d., while the largest branches were listed as Wellesbourne, with 210 members, Cubbington, with 200, and Bidford, with 150, although there were several others which showed a membership of around 80 to 100. The report also indicated that a fair amount of migration of labour had taken place since the Union had first been established; altogether 200 had emigrated and 150 had moved to alternative employment within the United Kingdom.

Once this preliminary report had been considered, the sixty or so delegates soon settled down to discuss the nature and scope of the proposed national organisation. As a first step, Mr T. Strange, 'the leader of the Herefordshire Hinds', moved, 'that a National Union of Agricultural Labourers be formed, having district unions throughout the kingdom and its centre of management in Leamington.' His resolution was approved with 'ringing cheers' — 'passed by men whose honest faces shone with a new hope, whose stooping forms seemed to rise into erectness as they passed it . . .'[3]

During the often emotional discussions which then followed, there were frequent references made to the Bible, and a use of phrases 'redolent of the village pulpit.' This led one non-labourer sympathiser, the Rev. F. S. Attenborough, a Congregational Minister from Leamington, to discover that half of the delegates were local preachers (like Arch himself) — a fitting indication of the importance of Nonconformity in the creation of the agricultural trade union movement. Frequently, the speeches were punctuated with cries of 'Amen,' 'Praise Him,' and similar expressions, while one of the delegates prefaced his speech with the simple explanation: 'Genelmen, and b'luv'd Crissen friends, I'se a man, I is, hes goes about wi' a 'oss . . .'[4]

Many of the speakers seemed to feel that the movement had divine inspiration and would lead to more than a mere increase of wages. It would result in a 'brighter, happier and holier' world, in which 'man in trying to help himself shall be strengthened, and grim want and pauperism shall be rooted out.'[5] As one delegate passionately declared: 'Sir, this be a blessed day: this 'ere Union be the Moses to lead us poor men up out o' Egypt'.[6]

'The contrast in the appearance of the men, the striking difference between the pronunciation of the various speakers, and the homely honesty of all were very effective. The southern men seemed weaker and smaller than those from the shires and the north; the Norfolk and Suffolk men were the quaintest; the Kent, Dorset, and South Gloucester men the saddest; the Yorkshire men the most pertinacious; the Warwickshire men the most comfortable and buoyant. Now and again some simple ruralism, or odd allusion, or grotesque mistake, enlivened the earnest and almost sad assembly. . . .'[7]

For Joseph, of course, the meeting had a special significance. It was the culmination of weeks of hard work, and early on in the proceedings he had the great satisfaction of being elected President of the organisation he had done so much to create. His salary was fixed at £2 a week — nearly double what he had been earning as organising secretary for the Warwickshire Union.

Henry Taylor, who was already treasurer of the Leamington branch of the Amalgamated Society of Carpenters and Joiners, was elected general secretary, on the understanding that he gave up 'any other' union office he held — including the one with the Carpenters and Joiners. This provision indicates the labourers' continual fear that 'their' organisation would be taken over by urban trade unionists. As Joseph himself later wrote in his autobiography: 'We wanted neither outsiders nor professional Trades Union men; we knew our own business and we were determined from the outset to manage it in our own way.'[8]

For their third major official the labourers again looked outside their own ranks, however. J. E. Matthew Vincent, the sympathetic proprietor of the *Royal Leamington Chronicle* was invited to act as honorary treasurer, and it was as a result of his backing that the Union also decided to publish a newspaper — the *Labourers' Union Chronicle* — to act as its mouthpiece. Initially the newspaper was to be published monthly, the first issue appearing on 6th June, but in fact after four monthly editions had been produced, it became a weekly paper, from 21st September, 1872. It soon became quite popular and within two years could boast a circulation of over 50,000 (while from the autumn of 1873 it was even being sold by Messrs. W. H. Smith & Son on their railway station bookstalls). By this date it had emerged as a major source of information on the Union's activities and a powerful propaganda weapon in the Union cause.[9]

Therefore, through their selection of Taylor and Vincent to fill 'key' Union positions the labourers could hope to get the help of an experienced trade union official and also of a businessman well versed in the arts of publicity. Arch, as the central figure, was to provide inspiration and leadership.

In addition to the appointment of Union officers detailed rules for the new organisation were also worked out. The three main objectives were agreed upon as being: 1. to improve the general condition of the agricultural labourers in the United Kingdom; 2. to encourage the formation of branch and district unions; 3. to promote co-operation and communication between unions already in existence. As with the parent Warwickshire Union, members were required to pay an entrance fee of 6d. and a weekly contribution of 2d., although in 1873 this latter figure was amended to 2¼d., the additional farthing per member being retained by the branches for management expenses, and the rest despatched to the district headquarters. The district retained ½d. of this sum for its own administrative expenditure, and the remainder was forwarded to the central office of the Union in Leamington.

It was also agreed that an Annual Council of delegates from the various districts should be held, but that the day-to-day running should be carried on by a national executive committee, consisting of twelve agricultural labourers, plus a chairman. Of course, Joseph — as Union President — filled the latter position on most occasions, while among the first twelve men chosen for the committee were the original seven members of the Warwickshire Union executive committee — including men like Thomas Parker, who had attended Arch's very first meeting at Wellesbourne on 7th February.

In addition, a Consulting Committee of gentlemen 'favourable to the principles of the Union' was to be invited to attend the meetings of the national executive, but in an advisory capacity only, without any powers to vote. In this way it was hoped that the Union might get specialist assistance without any danger of overall control passing to non-labourers. Among the early members of this Committee were Canon Girdlestone, who continued to give the movement support until the autumn of 1873, despite his growing reservations concerning its increasing militancy, J. S. Wright of Birmingham, W. G. Ward of Perriston Towers, near Ross in Herefordshire, Edward Jenkins of the Middle Temple, Henry Duckett of Leamington Trades Council, Alfred Arnold of Hampton-in-Arden and the Rev. F. S. Attenborough of Leamington, who was later in the year to write the first biography of Arch.

Finally, it was decided that the funds of the Union should be invested in the names of four trustees, and the ones selected at this first meeting were Messrs. Arnold, Collings, Jenkins and Ward — none of whom had an agricultural labouring background, although Collings did originate from a fairly humble tradesman's family in Devonshire.

The important basic decisions necessary for the creation of the new National Agricultural Labourers' Union were thus taken on the first day of the Conference. For Joseph it was a most moving experience. When the delegates stood to sing the Union hymn, 'as with one mighty voice,' he told himself: 'Joseph Arch, you have not lived in vain, and of a surety the Lord God of Hosts is with us this day.'[10] As we have seen, this belief in divine intervention accorded well with the attitude of many of the other delegates present on that notable occasion.

The essential framework of the new Union having been decided upon, the evening of the 29th May was devoted to a public meeting, attended by nearly three thousand people, and during the course of which the establishment of the new National Union was discussed and warmly welcomed. Arch and several others made long speeches to the appreciative audience on the benefits which it hoped the Union would bestow, and upon the policy it was intended to follow.

The second day of the Conference was concerned with more general matters, considerable attention being given to special papers prepared, for example, by the Hon, and Rev. J. W. Leigh on 'Co-operative Farming,' Jesse Collings on 'Education' and Mr Butcher of Banbury on 'Co-operative Stores.' Since the Banbury Co-operative Society to which Mr Butcher belonged had branches in a number of Oxfordshire and Warwickshire villages, as well as in Leamington itself, this address was of practical interest to the Warwickshire labourers at least, and Joseph himself called it a 'capital paper'.[11] Nevertheless, Arch's general attitude towards these papers was one of caution, and the other delegates probably shared this feeling. As the N.A.L.U. leader later wrote: 'We wanted to get all the information we could from trustworthy sources, and from friends who were honestly interested in the movement; but at the same time we did not mean to be led away into starting all sorts of schemes before our own proper work was done, and was securely established. I was not going to have the cart of agricultural reforms stuck before the Union horse; . . . '[12]

During the evening of the second day the delegates met at the invitation of Mr Attenborough, to take tea in the School Rooms attached to his Congregational Church at Holly Walk, Leamington. After the meal was over further discussions took place and the meeting ended with the singing of the Doxology and the pronouncing of Benediction — a somewhat unusual finale for a trade union conference even in the strongly religious atmosphere of Victorian England!

Although the formation of the National Union was clearly an important milestone in Joseph's career as a Union leader, he could not afford to be complacent. Success was still too uncertain. By now permanent Union offices had been established at Balm Cottage, Forfield Place, Leamington, and Henry Taylor had, of course, been installed as general secretary, to carry out the administrative work for which Joseph had little interest or aptitude. Therefore, the new President's task seemed clear enough. As soon as the Leamington Conference had dispersed, he resumed his travels as union propagandist and agitator — into Oxfordshire, Hereford, Dorset and indeed

67

into most of the counties of central and southern England, where any incipient support for the Union might be detected. In the three months of August, September and October alone he addressed meetings in eleven different counties, ranging from Somerset and Dorset in the west to Norfolk in the east.

Even Thomas Hardy, the novelist, who heard Arch speak in Dorset in the early days, paid tribute to his powers of attraction. In an article entitled 'The Dorsetshire Labourer,' which was published several years later, during 1883, in *Longman's Magazine*, Hardy wrote: 'Nobody who saw and heard Mr. Arch in his early tours through Dorsetshire will ever forget him and the influence his presence exercised over the crowds he drew . . . . The picture he drew of a comfortable cottage life as it should be, was so cosy, so well within the grasp of his listeners' imagination, that an old labourer in the crowd held up a coin between his finger and thumb exclaiming, 'Here's zixpence towards that, please God!' 'Towards what?' said a bystander. 'Faith, I don't know that I can spak the name o't, but I know 'tis a good thing,' he replied.' Reactions such as this help to explain why Arch received so many invitations to speak!

Indeed, a detailed timetable of his travels during August gives some idea of the exhausting nature of his work — work which quite wore out many of his fellow activists, like Edwin Russell of Harbury, but which he, hardened by his years as travelling hedgecutter and labourer, seemed able to endure.

At the beginning of the month he was in Essex, staying with a Mr Charles Jay of Codham Hall, near Braintree; Jay was a Radical landowner and land law reformer. Immediately prior to this he had addressed meetings in Norfolk and Suffolk, and he was to speak at several meetings in the Braintree area, including one at South Ockendon. Here Mr Jay revealed that Joseph's schedule was so tight that it had been necessary to book his appearance a month in advance, for 'Mr. Arch had been sent for from almost every part of England . . .' At South Ockendon he was met by a band of music and an enthusiastic audience of about 1,500 people.

Following these various engagements in Norfolk, Suffolk and Essex, on 9th August he spoke at Byfield in Northamptonshire, preparatory to moving off to the West country. The 14th August found him addressing a meeting in Yeovil, and five days later he was at Sherborne in Dorset. Here he preached at the Primitive Methodist Chapel, as well as addressed an outdoor gathering. The most notable feature of the day's proceedings at Sherborne was, however, the fact that 'the brethren' paraded the streets singing hymns as a finale to their activities. At Yeovil, on the other hand, the meeting had ended in moonlight with the Montacute drum and fife band playing such stirring tunes as 'Britons never shall be Slaves'.[13]

The month closed with further assemblies in Somerset and in Warwickshire, but even then there was no respite. September saw fresh visits to East Anglia — and so it went on. The mere business of speaking was in itself extremely tiring — for Joseph always gave an address of about one and a half hours' duration — and during the period 13th–27th September inclusive he was, for example, expected to address a mass meeting on every day, save two.

And this was not all. As the movement grew in size and influence, the hostility of farmers and landowners, never far below the surface, was once more aroused. Farmers, squires and clergymen of the Church of England were noted by Arch as being particular opponents. The farmers were especially antagonistic towards him, as might be expected, and in the trade union leaders' own graphic language, at the sight of him they 'would start . . . off puffing and prancing and snorting, and crying, "Ha! ha!" like the war-horse in Job; they would gnash their teeth and butt. . . . like rampaging unicorns.'[14] Although the language is extravagant, it does indicate the strength of feeling which the mere mention of his name could call forth in some agricultural circles, as almost for the first time farmers faced industrial action on the part of members of their work force. In Gloucestershire, farmers were even reported to be ready to tar and roll him in feathers![15]

However, perhaps the most notorious dispute involving farmers and the National Union in its first months of existence did not directly concern Joseph himself, but rather a group of labourers from the Oxfordshire village of Wootton, near Woodstock. At the end of May, 1872, they had formed a Union branch and then about a month or so later, like their Wellesbourne predecessors, they had sent round a circular letter asking for an increase in wages. On receipt of this the local farmers had met together and had decisively resolved to discharge all men belonging to the Union. The Friday following this meeting (the first Friday in July) 120 labourers ceased work in Wootton — in some cases because they had themselves struck work and in others because they had been locked out. The long dispute had begun.

The local farmers organised themselves into a Defence Association, and as time dragged on and harvest drew near, they began to feel some anxiety. They did not wish to reach a compromise with the unionists, and so decided instead to appeal to the military authorities at Aldershot for the help of soldiers to get in the harvest. This was despite the provisions of Article 180 of the Queen's Regulations for the Army, which stated that soldiers were only allowed to assist in gathering in the harvest provided 'that the employment of the population is not interfered with.' Clearly by their intervention at Wootton, the employment of the civil population *was* being interfered with. Not surprisingly, loud protests were soon heard from both agricultural and urban trades unionists and complaints were made to the Secretary of State for War — Henry Taylor writing on behalf of the National Agricultural Labourers' Union (N.A.L.U.) and George Shipton, secretary to the London Trades Council, writing on behalf of urban unionists. Although the unionists' right of protest was later recognised and Article 180 was amended so as to prevent any repetition of the affair, the soldiers did in fact provide much-needed help for the Oxfordshire farmers. The exact number so employed is difficult to estimate, since reports often seem to be vague and unreliable, but it does at any rate appear that far fewer than the 200 originally requested were actually sent to give assistance — perhaps less than 100. In Wootton itself only about ten were engaged, and in the Bampton area, forty.

Although the employment of soldiers caused great local bitterness, after the harvest matters simmered down in Wootton. Nevertheless there is little doubt that the case did help to arouse public sympathy for the labourers' cause.[16] It certainly received wide coverage in the press, and Arch, of course, lost no time in drawing attention to it in his speeches and exploiting its propaganda effects.

However, if the farmers were some of Joseph's most determined opponents, a second hostile group existed among the squires, or landowners. They condemned him not only because of the agitation he was carrying on, but also because of the way in which they claimed he was upsetting the 'friendly relations' which had formerly existed between employer and labourer in pre-union days. An impartial examination of the labourer's position in the 1860's leads one to the view that the value of these 'friendly feelings' was grossly exaggerated anyway, and that most farm workers derived little benefit from them. Nevertheless, many squires would no doubt have agreed with Sir Herewald Wake, the lord of the manor and principal landowner at Courteenhall in Northamptonshire, when he wrote: 'Mr Joseph Arch and gentlemen "of his kidney" disturbed once and for all the life-long and friendly relations that had often existed between the farmer and his servants. . .'[17] Even twenty years later the mere hint of agricultural trade unionism could call forth similar opposition from such an enlightened landowner as Lord Wantage in Berkshire. According to his wife, in the early 1890's he warned his labourers 'against the specious promises held out by agitators and by associations such as that of the Agricultural Labourers' Union . . . The consequence of these observations was that in the Lockinge district this movement was dead in a week or two.'[18] (The 'Lockinge district' was the centre of Lord Wantage's estate.)

So strong was the feeling in the early 1870's however, that a friendly landowner like Sir Baldwyn Leighton of Loton Park, Shrewsbury, could anxiously express the hope that the Union movement might 'effect great permanent good, without inducing any feelings of hostility between employer and employed.'[19]

On occasion, too, the opposition of landowners was shown not only towards Joseph and the agricultural unionists, but also towards other members of the rural community who had befriended them. Thus Daniel Phipps, a small tenant farmer from Broadwell in Gloucestershire, who was a Union supporter, lost his holding because he had 'harboured (the) rebel Joseph Arch.' Phipps' offence was that he had given a night's hospitality to Joseph from time to time, and had thereby offended the squire. Broadwell was mainly in the ownership of a Mr Egerton Leigh and because of his hostility Phipps was unable to obtain any other land in the neighbourhood. He was eventually forced to move several miles away (to Moreton-in-Marsh) before he could again set up in business. Similarly, at Watlington in Oxfordshire, a butcher who allowed his close to be used for a union tea meeting, was shortly afterwards given notice to quit. He, too, had offended by his support for the Union. These and other like acts of petty persecution are indications of the animosity — and perhaps fear — which Joseph had aroused among certain of the more extreme members of the propertied class.[20]

With regard to the clergy, Arch's increasingly zealous advocacy of the cause of Church of England disestablishment was to lose the N.A.L.U. the support of most of those already few Churchmen who, like Canon Girdlestone, had come out in its favour in the early months of 1872. As the initially sympathetic vicar of Minster Lovell, Oxfordshire, noted before the Royal Commission on the Depressed State of Agriculture 1879–82: 'My opinion . . . was that Mr Arch was an honest man, and wished to benefit the agricultural labourer, and if he had adhered to that one object with a single eye, without mixing it up with class and abusing the Church, and making it a nail upon which to hang an attack upon the Church, and to speak against the gentry, nobility, and landed proprietary, the sympathy of England would have been aroused.'[21]

However, to do Joseph justice, there was some reason for his hostility, besides the normal suspicion and prejudice of an ardent Victorian Nonconformist towards the Established Church. He and his movement were often attacked by the clergy in their sermons, for example. In the very earliest days of the Warwickshire agitation, the curate of Bishop's Tachbrook had deduced from the words 'Lay not up for yourselves treasures on earth' that 'it was very wicked to agitate for more than 12s. a week as the income of a labourer's family.'[22] And at a meeting of the Peterborough Agricultural Society in July, the Bishop of Peterborough condemned the 'fussy, the officious, the selfish and the mischievous interference between labourers and employer, of those who had nothing to do with either.'[23] An even greater impact was made by a speech delivered at the Gloucestershire Agricultural Society's dinner on 2nd August by the Bishop of Gloucester, Dr. Ellicott. In this he declared with reference to the unionists that, 'There is an old saying, "Don't nail their ears to the pump and don't duck them in the horsepond".'[24] He went on to point out that they lived in times 'in which mischievous and evil efforts were being made to set class against class, and especially to set faithful English agricultural labourers against their equally faithful English employers.'[25] These remarks were interpreted by the Union leaders as a direct attack on themselves, and they responded not only with formal protests to the Bishop, but also by issuing an address under Joseph's name towards the end of September, in which they firmly denied that the Union had caused bad feelings. The Union, they declared, was not 'Republican or communistic; its claims were merely for just wages, proper house accommodation, and a garden.'[26]

After the various ruffled feathers had been smoothed again, the affair died down, but there is no doubt that it — and similar events — did help to strengthen Union hostility towards the Church of England. This led eventually to ever more provocative statements being made by Arch, in particular. The clergy's resentment was naturally reinforced by such speeches as the one he gave at a working men's meeting at Sheffield. In this he declared: 'If the Church were disestablished, and the clergy were to rest upon their merits and the affections of the people, instead of being propped up by the State, supported by laws which are class-made . . . they would win the respect of the agricultural labourer . . . But how frequently do we find that the clergy in our rural villages pass by our agricultural labourers as though they were some very low strata of society; and the squire and the wealthy tradesman they can recognise and shake hands with . . .'[27] Although this speech was made on 1st February, 1876, Arch was expressing similar views from quite early on. In one of his more dramatic statements, at an anniversary meeting held at Wellesbourne on 7th February, 1873, for example, he declared that the labourers 'might set up a free and independent church of their own.' And even at the Leamington Conference in May, 1872, it was noted by at least one observer that the cause of Church disestablishment was viewed sympathetically by the labourers.[28]

Many clergymen, for their part, felt equally strongly that the Union was responsible for a decline in Church attendance by labourers during the 1870's.[29]

Of course, despite this unfriendly approach some incumbents continued to express sympathy. Joseph himself notes the Vicar of Harbury as being in this category, and several other examples could be quoted, including the Vicar of Chalgrove in Oxfordshire (the Rev. R. F. Laurence), who even became a branch secretary.[30] Again, the Hon. and Rev. J. W. Leigh, vicar of Stoneleigh, spoke at a number of major Union meetings — including the inaugural meeting of the N.A.L.U. at Leamington in May.

Nevertheless, in spite of the various problems which still remained — and of which the growing hostility of agriculturalists and clergy was but one — Joseph and his friends could look back on the first months of the Union's existence with some satisfaction. Wages had been raised in many cases, perhaps by 20 to 30 per cent, and membership was growing fast. It was now approaching 40,000, of whom over 6,000 were found in Warwickshire alone.[31]

At the same time, much still remained to be done. Only a minority of the agricultural labour force were members of any rural union, and there were still a number of independent agricultural unions outside the N.A.L.U. fold. This lack of unity, coupled with the fierce sense of independence of several of the smaller bodies, seriously disturbed non-labourer sympathisers with the movement — particularly the London Trades Council, who had shown an interest in the labourers' affairs from early days. On 17th December, 1872, therefore, the Council called a conference at the Bell Inn, London, at which representatives of the various smaller unions and Henry Taylor of the N.A.L.U. met to discuss the unification of their organisations.[32] Unfortunately, nothing worthwhile was achieved as a result of the discussions, and despite repeated efforts by the London Trades Council to bring the various parties together in the months that followed, agreement could not be reached. Eventually the rift in the movement was hardened by the establishment of a rival Federal Union, covering most of the other independent organisations and having a membership of about 49,344 divided among eight districts. This took place in November, 1873, and, as Trades Council leaders had feared, it certainly did little to strengthen the movement as a whole. Indeed, when bitter inter-union rivalries arose later on, it had just the reverse effect.

However, this particular problem still lay in the future, and Joseph had good reason to feel satisfied with his achievements so far. Of course, he had not forgotten that at least part of the purpose of the Union was to secure the Parliamentary franchise for the agricultural labourer, and so when a Conference of the Electoral Reform Association was convened in London on 12th November, 1872, he readily accepted an invitation to attend. As early as April, G. O. Trevelyan, the doughty supporter of the extended franchise, had pressed for reform in Parliament, but Mr Gladstone, as Prime Minister, had declined to take any action because of the present 'state of Parliamentary business . . .' To the reformers this excuse was quite unacceptable — hence the need for such conferences as that proposed for November.

At this gathering Joseph Chamberlain presided, and other friends of the labourers' movement present included Edward Jenkins and Jesse Collings. About 120 persons in all attended, and Joseph's speech in favour of the 'assimilation of the county and borough franchise' was well received by the audience. The meeting ended with the unanimous adoption of a resolution in favour of franchise extension.[33] It is significant that virtually all of the supporters of the resolution were strong Liberals, and their zealous courting of Arch was, no doubt, at its lowest level, a desire to curry favour with the leader of the agricultural labourers, so that when the franchise was eventually conferred, the latter would be well disposed towards the Liberal Party. Certainly at least one active Liberal saw it in that light — A. J. Mundella, M.P. for Sheffield.[34]

As early as April, Mundella had viewed the labourers' movement as a chance to 'hit out' at both farmers and parsons —traditional Conservative voters — and to this end he had helped in the organisation of a 'monster meeting' to be held in support of Joseph Arch and the labourers at Willis's Rooms in London.[35] The conference had commenced on 30th April and had lasted for two days. Among those who attended, apart from Arch himself, were several other union leaders, like Thomas Halliday, President of the Amalgamated Association of Miners, and Daniel Guile, secretary of the Ironfounders' Society, but Liberal politicians were certainly present in considerable numbers. Mundella himself took the chair for part of the time on the second day.[36]

Furthermore, Mundella's enthusiasm did not diminish with the passage of time, either. Indeed, on 23rd July in the following year, when Trevelyan again tried to secure the passage of a franchise extension bill and George Dixon presented a petition signed by 80,000 labourers in support of it, Mundella's optimism knew no bounds. The downfall of the Tories in the country areas seemed imminent! Unfortunately, however, from his point of view, the jubilation proved somewhat premature, for despite support from leading Liberal Government speakers, the Bill was talked out and, in the event, another eleven years of struggle were to elapse before the final enfranchisement took place. Nevertheless, the partisan line taken by Mundella is very clear: 'The Government have played a trump card. We are going to enfranchise the rural population. The Tories . . . talked out the Bill in sheer despair. . . . I think this is the turning point in our career as a party . . .'[37] There is little doubt that other keen Liberals shared Mundella's sentiments, both in 1872 and 1873.

It is against this political background, then, that Liberal enthusiasm

Joseph Arch's cottage in Church Street, Barford. (Photograph taken in 1971.) The front porch of the cottage was, incidentally, constructed by Arch himself.

Joseph Arch as N.A.L.U. President in the 1880s
(*By courtesy of Radio Times Hulton Picture Library*)

for the November, 1872, franchise reform meeting should perhaps be seen. A similar view could be taken of the second large meeting held on behalf of the labourers in London at the end of 1872, namely that organised on 10th December at Exeter Hall. Yet, this would almost certainly be an over-cynical attitude, for there is no doubt that many of those present at Exeter Hall genuinely wished only to secure further support and financial aid for the labourers' cause, and disdained the mere scoring of narrow Party political points.

Originally it had been intended to invite the Roman Catholic Archbishop Manning to preside at Exeter Hall, but he had refused because he feared that in the somewhat anti-Catholic social climate of mid-Victorian England his presence in such a leading role would only harm the labourers' movement.[38] Nevertheless, he agreed to attend in a less conspicuous capacity and to speak in support of the Union. The Liberal M.P. Samuel Morley, (who was part-controller of the newspaper, the *Daily News*), then agreed to take the chair, and among others in attendance were Sir Charles Dilke, Sir Charles Trevelyan, A. J. Mundella and Sir John Bennett — all of whom were active Liberal Members of Parliament. Joseph Arch was there to represent the labourers.

The meeting attracted a large audience and after speeches had been made in favour of the Union — including one from Joseph, in which he declared that the 'labourer meant to be no longer starved and trampled upon' — the proceedings ended with an urgent appeal by Sir Charles Dilke for funds. Samuel Morley agreed to start off the list with a subscription of £500, and others followed suit, if rather less generously. Shortly after the meeting Joseph wrote to Sir Charles to thank him for the efforts made on behalf of the Union, and to hope that his 'sympathy for our deserving cause will not decline.'[39]

However, for both Archbishop Manning and Joseph Arch himself this meeting had some minor repercussions. The more 'respectable' members of the community deplored the Archbishop's connection with the movement, but he defiantly replied: 'To couple my name with that of Mr Arch gives me no displeasure. I believe him to be an honest and good man. I believe, too, that the cause he has in hand is well founded.'[40] Manning claimed the right to speak at the meeting on the grounds that for seventeen years, whilst he had been an incumbent of the Church of England, in Sussex, he had 'sat day by day in the home of the labouring men,' and had learnt their difficulties. Indeed, his interest in the agricultural situation was such that shortly after the Exeter Hall demonstration he wrote twice to Gladstone on the subject. His letters, dated 21st and 26th December, called either for the appointment of a Royal Commission to investigate the condition of the agricultural labourer, or else for the passage of legislation which would prohibit the employment of children under a certain agreed age, would cure rural overcrowding of cottages and would 'compel payment of wages in money.' In fact, his appeals do not seem to have met with any response from the Prime Minister,[41] but this did not prevent him from retaining interest in the National Union. In both 1878 and 1879, for example, he sent £10 towards the Union funds.[42]

For Joseph, the encounter with Archbishop Manning brought rather stranger results. It led Charles Newdegate, the notoriously anti-Catholic Conservative M.P. for North Warwickshire, to accuse him of being a Jesuit in disguise! The accusation was made at a meeting of the Rugby and Dunchurch Agricultural Association held in Rugby Town Hall soon after the Exeter Hall demonstration, and the M.P. appeared to feel that there was some unholy alliance between the 'two arches' — Joseph and Manning. He strongly denounced what he considered to be the secrecy of the Jesuits' normal methods of conducting their affairs and declared: 'I have been expecting for some time to find some of the ultra-Roman Catholic agents at the back of Mr Arch, . . . just as the Ultra-montanes were at the back of the unions when demanding unreasonable wages in Germany.[43]

To anyone who knew Joseph's background of passionate Nonconformity, such an accusation was quite ridiculous, and he had no great difficulty in refuting it. However, the fact that it was made, at a time when feeling against the Jesuits was strong in Protestant England, does indicate that for some opponents at least any stick was good enough to beat him with. Such tactics he rightly treated with the contempt they so richly deserved. They certainly did not prevent him from paying tribute to Archbishop Manning. As he later wrote: 'The testimony, at such a time and in such a place, of a man so respected, and who occupied such a commanding position in his Church, was of the greatest value . . . He . . . was a true friend through thick and thin.'[44]

Others soon joined Arch in condemning Newdegate's allegations. Mr J. C. Campbell, the Rugby J.P. and friend of the N.A.L.U., 'ridiculed as preposterous Mr Newdegate's insinuation that Mr Arch was a Jesuit in disguise,' while Samuel Morley, who had chaired the Exeter Hall meeting, was even more forthright. He scornfully remarked that: 'Mr Newdegate has eclipsed himself as a discoverer of mare's nests . . . From all that I have heard of the antecedents of Mr Arch I should be disposed to think he is somewhat less likely to be a Jesuit in disguise than Mr Newdegate himself!'[45] There the affair was allowed to rest.

[1] *Midland Free Press* — 1st June, 1872.

[2] Reg Groves, op.cit., p.56. O'Neill had shown his support for the labourers in April by writing to the Birmingham Trades Council on their behalf, appealing for financial help. Birmingham Trades Council Minute Book — Meeting on 6th April, 1872.

[3] 'Labourers in Council' — *The Congregationalist*, 1872, p.420. Although this article

is anonymous there is little doubt that it was written by the Rev. F S Attenborough, a Congregational minister from Leamington. Attenborough, himself the son of a Congregational minister, was born on 1st January, 1842, at Erdington. He came to Leamington as a Minister in 1868 and when the agricultural labourers' movement started he was one of the first to render assistance, speaking for it in a number of the nearby villages — *English Labourers' Chronicle* — 22nd November, 1879.

4 'Labourers in Council' — *The Congregationalist*, 1872, p.421.

5 J P D Dunbabin — 'The Revolt of the Field: The Agricultural Labourers' Movement in the 1870's' in *Past and Present*, November, 1963, p.76

6 'Labourers in Council', p.421.

7 Ibid.

8 Joseph Arch, op.cit., p.87

9 *Labourers' Union Chronicle* — 4th October, 1873, and 13th June, 1874.

10 Joseph Arch, op.cit., p.114.

11 Ibid., p.118. Mr Butcher hailed from Brackley in Northamptonshire and spent the early part of his business life at Buckingham, where he met G J Holyoake. He later moved to Banbury in about 1864–65 and became an enthusiastic supporter of the temperance movement. By 1865 he was in fact secretary of the local Temperance Society. He closely linked co-operation with temperance and was naturally anxious to secure the support of the labourers for both of these causes. He was intimately associated with Banbury Cooperative Society from its commencement in 1866, and remained with it until he resigned in 1873 in order to take up an appointment with the Co-operative Society in Leicester. I am indebted to Mr. B S Trinder and to Mr. J Hodgkin for this information.

12 Joseph Arch, op.cit., p.118.

13 *Labourers' Union Chronicle* — 5th September, 1872, This song was composed by a blind man named Reader from Stoke-sub-Hamdon, Somerset. — Information kindly provided by Mr E P Thompson.

14 Joseph Arch, op.cit., pp.232–233.

15 *Labourers' Union Chronicle* — 5th September, 1872.

16 P L R Horn — 'Farmers' Defence Associations in Oxfordshire — 1872–74' in *History Studies*, Vol. No. 1, 1968, pp.63–67.

17 See draft article written in 1894 by Sir Herewald Wake and entitled 'The Parting of the Ways' — Northamptonshire County Record Office, Wake Papers.

18 Lady Wantage — *Lord Wantage, V.C., K.C.B. — A Memoir* (1907), p.395.

19 Letter from Sir Baldwyn Leighton to A J Mundella, M.P., dated 29th April, 1872 — Mundella Collection, University of Sheffield.

20 Information concerning Mr Phipps has been kindly provided by his granddaughter in a letter to the author. His sympathy with the labourers' movement perhaps owed something to the fact that he himself had started his working life as a farm labourer — a position he occupied as late as the 1861 Census of Population. Census Return for Broadwell at P.R.O., R.G.9.1790. Daniel Phipps' daughter, Mrs. Sarah Bowerman, eventually became an Oxford City Alderman.

21 *Royal Commission on the Depressed State of Agriculture*, Minutes of Evidence, Parliamentary Papers, Vol. XIV (1882) — Evidence of the Rev. H C Ripley (Q.64,584).

22 *Warwick Advertiser* — 2nd March, 1872.

23 *Northampton Mercury* — 13th July, 1872.

24 F E Green — *History of the English Agricultural Labourer* 1870–1920 (London, 1920), p.37.

25 *The Times* — 6th August, 1872.

26 *The Times* — 24th September, 1872.

27 Joseph Arch on 'The Church and the Labourers' — A speech delivered at a Working Men's Meeting at Sheffield, 1st February, 1876. (Pamphlet issued by the Society for the Liberation of Religion from State Patronage and Control in the Howell Collection,

Bishopsgate Institute, London.)

[28] 'Labourers' in Council', p.424.

[29] Even in the county of Berkshire, where the Union was never very strong, in 1875 fourteen incumbents out of a total of 191 explicitly blamed the Union for a decline in Church attendance. For example, the Shrivenham incumbent declared: 'There has been a perceptible decrease in the attendance of the labouring classes since the formation of the Ag. Labourers' Union'. — See Bishop's Visitation Returns, Incumbents' Replies for the Berkshire Archdeaconry, Oxford Diocese — 1875; MS.Oxf.Dioc.pp.c.339 — Bodleian Library, Oxford. Similar comments were forthcoming from clergy in Oxfordshire, Leicestershire and Northamptonshire, to name but a few counties. At Little Oakley, in the Peterborough diocese, the incumbent noted: 'The evil influence exercised by 'The Agricultural Labourers' Union' over their members. The attacks upon the Church and Clergy in their paper the 'Union Chronicle' which is read by many in this Parish. I try and counteract the influence of this Paper by lending others such as the 'National Church', 'The Standard', &c." — Visitation Return dated May, 1875, at Northamptonshire County Record Office. I am indebted to the County Archivist for drawing my attention to this item.

[30] P. L. R. Horn — 'A Nineteenth Century Vicar of Chalgrove' (Part 2) in *Oxford Diocesan Magazine,* November, 1969   p.18.

[31] In January, 1873, the Union claimed a membership of 40,000 — See Report of 5th Trades Union Congress held in January, 1873.

[32] London Trades Council Minute Book — Meeting on 17th December, 1872.

[33] *The Times* — 13th November, 1872

[34] W. H. G. Armytage — *A. J. Mundella — The Liberal Background to the Labour Movement* (London,1951), pp.119 and 120.

[35] Ibid., p.120 and also a letter from Sir Baldwyn Leighton of Loton Park, Shrewsbury, dated 29th April, 1872, regretting he would be unable to attend — Mundella Collection.

[36] *The Times* — 1st and 2nd May, 1872. The London Central Aid Committee was set up as a result of this meeting.

[37] Letter from A. J. Mundella to R. Leader, dated 23rd July, 1873. (Leader was a proprietor of the *Sheffield Independent* and president of the Sheffield Liberal Association). Gladstone was not in the Chamber for the debate but he did send a message down to Forster, Vice-President of the Committee of Council on Education, stating that 'the extension of the franchise in counties was just and politic in itself, and that it could not long be avoided'. — A. Clayden, op.cit., p.189.

[38] V. A. MacClelland — *Cardinal Manning — His Public Life and Influence* (1865–92) (1962), p.132.

[39] Dilke Papers—British Museum, MS.43909 (No.315), written about 11th December

[40] V. A. MacClelland, op.cit., pp.132–133.   1872.

[41] Ibid., p.133.

[42] Joseph Arch, op.cit., pp.124–125.

[43] *The Times* — 28th December, 1872. Newdegate was well-known for his hatred of the Roman Catholic Church, which he displayed, for example, during the debate on the Bill for the establishment of a Roman Catholic University in Ireland, in 1867–68. Again, at a public meeting on 12th November, 1874, he 'expressed his joy that Mr. Gladstone had at last discovered the Popish religion to be slavery . . .' Repeatedly during the 1870's he sought to introduce Bills to demand permanent State inspection of Roman Catholic convents and monasteries, but without success. Newdegate was born at Harefield Place, Middlesex in 1816 and died in Warwickshire in April, 1887. He was M.P. for North Warwickshire from 1843 until his retirement in 1885. (For details of his anti-Catholic activities see E. R. Norman — *Anti-Catholicism in Victorian England* (Cambridge, 1968), pp.84, 96 and 202.

[44] Joseph Arch, op.cit., pp.124–125.

[45] *The Times* — 26th December, 1872 and *Midland Free Press* — 4th January, 1873.

CHAPTER SIX

Rise upward without ceasing: 1873

'We would have to be up and doing in 1873, and I said to myself
that the motto for the coming year must be, "Press forward,
push onward, rise upward without ceasing."'—Joseph Arch—
The Story of His Life Told by Himself (1898), p.134.

IF THE Exeter Hall meeting and its aftermath occupied much of
Joseph's attention during the last weeks of 1872, he soon discovered
fresh fields of activity opening up before him in the new year.
His first major engagement in 1873 was to speak for the Land Tenure
Reform Association at a meeting held in the Temperance Hall, Derby,
on 7th January. J. C. Cox, a Derbyshire magistrate, and Sir Charles
Dilke shared the platform with him, and, like him, they strongly
demanded a reform of the land laws. However, Joseph made his appeal
wider than that as well. He called for 'all artisans to stand at the back
of the agricultural labourers when demanding the franchise and help
them to gain their rights, and then as the wealth producing classes of
the community they could shake hands and work harmoniously for
the good of their country and the community at large.'[1] His remarks
were greeted with loud cheers. Clearly, therefore, despite his avowed
intention of steering clear of 'professional agitators' and urban
unionists, Joseph had recognised the need to secure — and maintain
—the goodwill of the town workers, if the agricultural trade union
movement were to succeed.

This became even more apparent a few days later. Arch had stopped
off at Derby on his way north to represent the National Agricultural
Labourers' Union at the Fifth Trades Union Congress to be held at
Leeds between 13th and 17th January. According to the Report of the
Congress, at this date the Union claimed a total membership of 40,000
and it gave a subscription of £5 towards the expenses of the Parliamentary Committee of the Congress.[2]

The urban unionists, for their part, soon made Arch very welcome, several of the delegates expressing keen gratification 'at the formation of Unions among agricultural labourers.'

Joseph himself spoke on two occasions during the Congress. The first was on 16th January, when he called once again for a reform of the land laws — particularly those relating to entail. These, he considered, interfered adversely with the free sale and distribution of land — and hence with the welfare of those who worked on it. This was a theme he had taken up at his Derby meeting and to which he was to return repeatedly and with increasing enthusiasm in the years that lay ahead. It was also, significantly, a theme somewhat apart from the earliest aims and intentions of the agricultural trade union movement. Already Arch was widening the scope of his operations and ambitions.

His second speech was made on the final day of the Congress, when he read a paper condemning the employment of women and children in agriculture. In this he demanded better education for the children, and firmly emphasized that: 'Wives must be at home, and the father must earn wages sufficient to maintain the family comfortably.'[3] This was, of course, no unexpected line of argument. From its very inception the Union had opposed the employment of female labour, both on the grounds of the competition it offered to the male workers and also because it was felt that the woman who was out in the fields all day was likely to neglect her home and family. It was formal policy to exclude women from union membership altogether and only on rare occasions did individual branches transgress by admitting them.[4] In this instance Joseph's sentiments with regard to the undesirability of female and child field labour were 'heartily' endorsed by the whole body of delegates to the Trades Union Congress.[5]

Nevertheless, while Joseph was in this way earning the approval of the Congress in Leeds, his supporters elsewhere were faring less happily. Amongst the most constant of their problems was the securing of accommodation for their meetings. Because of the hostility of many landowners it was frequently impossible for them to hire public rooms, or even rooms in an inn or public house. In some cases the use of Nonconformist chapels might be secured, but this depended very much on the attitude of the Trustees and, in any case, such buildings were frequently quite small and unable to house a large audience. Outdoor meetings thus remained extremely common, even during the inclement winter weather. However, in January, 1873, in the Berkshire village of Littleworth, even this last bastion of free speech seemed under attack.

The labourers were, of course, just as unable to obtain a field in which to hold their meetings as they were to hire a public hall.[6] Therefore, the village green or market place was often their only recourse. At Littleworth a group of local labourers held a meeting in this way early in the New Year, but owing to the objections of what Arch calls 'an ill-conditioned farmer,' the three leaders of the meeting were summoned shortly afterwards to appear before the Faringdon Bench 'for having caused obstruction on the Queen's highway.' Although the men correctly claimed that this spot had previously been used for meetings by the Primitive Methodists without any action being taken, their arguments were brushed aside and they were convicted.

Arch and the other Union leaders rapidly realised the danger of this for their movement. If it were allowed to continue unchecked, Union meetings would become almost impossible in many areas. Therefore, Joseph and his allies, including some non-labourers sympathetic to the movement, decided to hold an outdoor meeting at Faringdon Market Place towards the end of March, in order to test their continued right to hold open-air assemblies.

On the appointed day the old Market Place was about half-filled with labourers, as Joseph and his fellow speakers mounted a waggon which had been drawn up to serve as a platform. Scarcely had the meeting got under way, however, when the local superintendent of the police and a constable appeared on the scene, and asked that it be broken up as an obstruction was being caused. The Union leaders refused to budge, and were thereupon asked to give their names and addresses. These were taken down, and the meeting was then allowed to proceed without further interruption.

The unionists, for their part, had of course half expected this interference and were well prepared to deal with it. For example, the chair at the meeting had been taken by John Charles Cox, a landowner and Justice of the Peace from Belper in Derbyshire, who had spoken with Arch at the Land Tenure Reform meeting in Derby a few weeks earlier. Cox was described in the *Ripley Advertiser* of 31st August, 1872, as 'a remarkable man, a landowner and a magistrate, and a free lance for the farm labourers . . . a colliery proprietor, and a lecturer to colliers upon combination and trades unions; a churchman, the son of a parson . . . pleading for religious equality, and the separation of Church and State . . . How rare it is to find a man without class prejudice . . . a landowner who advocates land tenure reform . . .'[7] In 1873, Cox became President of the Reformers' Union, which was in favour of franchise reform, and in the months which followed he was to prove a sincere friend of the labourers. He was, by his experience, eminently fitted to provide help for Arch at Faringdon.

The other active participant at the Faringdon meeting, apart from Joseph himself, was W. Mackenzie, a London barrister, and it was these two prosperous Radicals, Cox and Mackenzie, who, along with Arch, were soon afterwards summoned to appear before the Faringdon Bench on 15th April, to answer charges of obstruction in connection with their March meeting.

Powerful help was now called in on the Union side. Fitzjames Stephen, a well-known London barrister, was engaged to defend the three men, while barrister Edward Jenkins, the 'constant friend' of the labourers was also retained, along with Mr Shaen of Shaen and Roscoe, a firm of London solicitors. In addition, a surveyor was employed to make out a plan of the Market Place, and to mark upon it the boundary line of the space covered by the crowd at the meeting.

For the local labourers, as well as for the Union, the case was of great significance, since on its outcome perhaps depended their right to hold future outdoor meetings. Consequently, on the morning of the trial the usual quiet of the sleepy old market town of Faringdon was rudely disturbed by the voices and marching feet of large groups of labourers who had decided to take a day off work and had anxiously come into town to learn the outcome of the prosecution.

Four magistrates were present to conduct the trial and one of them, the blind T. L. Goodlake of Littleworth, was described as 'one of the bitterest opponents of the Union that England could produce.'[8] However, despite his implacable attitude, it soon became apparent that no case of obstruction could be proved under the relevant section of the Highways Act. Fitzjames Stephen remorselessly exposed the weaknesses of the prosecution's case, and then went on to point out that there had in any event been a Parliamentary petition down for consideration at the meeting. He quoted clauses from the Bill of Rights 'setting forth the right of all subjects to petition the Crown and Parliament . . . ,'[9] and thus claimed that the mere fact that they had a petition to Parliament on the agenda protected the unionists from prosecution anyway.

In the circumstances, the magistrates had little choice in the matter. They retired for fifteen minutes, and then returned to dismiss the case, although they did warn the Union leaders against holding any more meetings in Berkshire.[10] This latter threat had, of course, no legal force behind it, and the Unionists had clearly re-established their right to hold outdoor assemblies. As Joseph noted, they 'had good reason to rejoice, as every public building in those parts was closed against (them).'[11]

The magistrates' verdict was greeted 'with some applause in Court' and on the defendants walking out into the street, they were quickly surrounded by a large, cheering crowd of labourers and their sympathisers. Joseph claimed that there were about four hundred men waiting and that they had armed themselves with sticks, ready to attack the police should the decision have gone the other way! The magistrates, for their part, decided that discretion was the better part of valour, and they left the Court by the back entrance.[12]

That same evening, in order to celebrate the Union victory, a further meeting was held at the village of Shrivenham, a few miles away, attended by Joseph and with J. C. Cox in the chair. More than 2,000 jubilant labourers assembled with them to share in their triumph and to reaffirm faith in the N.A.L.U. cause. [13]

Once again, therefore, the Union had managed to make its point, and to fight off attempted persecution. As with the Wootton strike of 1872, when the military were employed to bring in the harvest, the Faringdon case brought the Union much favourable publicity in both the national and local press. For example, the *Midland Free Press*, which was published in Leicester, declared: 'A foolish attempt has been made to stop the free and open discussion of the labourers' grievances. . . . The magistrates very wisely decided to dismiss the case.'[14]

Nevertheless, this triumph of free speech could not be bought cheaply. Legal fees of £88 15s. had to be faced, and the Union leaders decided to make a public appeal for contributions towards these, rather than to meet them directly out of Union funds. To this end they resolved that 'one or more places in London should be appointed for receiving subscriptions,' and that appeals to 'wealthy men' should be made.[15] At this stage in its career, the N.A.L.U. was very fortunate in the way that it could repeatedly and successfully ask for public contributions to help it out of its financial difficulties.

Joseph's own reputation gained very considerably as a result of the Faringdon prosecution. Indeed, his power over his fellow workers was such that a few months later, the *Newbury Weekly News* could declare, after he had addressed a meeting in the town on 18th July: 'Whether for good or evil, he has probably a greater influence over an outdoor assembly of labourers than any other man in England . . .'[16] Most newspapers and journals seem to have agreed with this judgment. Nevertheless, it is significant that despite the Faringdon case, this large demonstration in Newbury had had to be held in a 'meadow on the outskirts of the town' because the Mayor of Newbury had refused to permit the use of the Corn Exchange for the purpose.[17] If the Union could demand its rights, opponents were at least able to make sure that it got nothing more.

The *Newbury Weekly News* account is also of interest because of the description which it gives of Arch's appearance and of his mode of conducting a meeting at this stage in his career. He was dressed in 'a billy-cock hat, a short, round jacket with pockets at the side, and presented the appearance of an ordinary labourer in Sunday attire . . .' But he was no ordinary labourer. 'He spoke in the vernacular common to a Warwickshire peasant, but with a command that not a word was lost, nor an interruption occurred from the vast company, which was closely packed, and hung with bated breath on the lips of the speaker

83

for more than an hour, only relieving themselves by the applause following each sentence which was delivered with more than usual animation.'[18]

A further indication of the status which Joseph and his union had temporarily won was perhaps provided on 2nd May, when the N.A.L.U. President was called upon to give evidence before the Select Committee on the Game Laws then sitting. He was absent from home for two days in order to give the evidence, and received for this, £2 in expenses — £1 being to cover the journey to London and back and £1 for 'allowances during absence from home.'[19]

During the course of his lengthy examination before the Committee he lost no opportunity of expressing the labourers' dislike of the Game Laws — and, in particular, of the 1862 Poaching Prevention Act. He declared firmly that 'if a man killed a rabbit in the day-time,' he would not blame him for it.[20] He called, in fact, for a complete repeal of the 1862 Act and its replacement, if necessary, by stricter legislation with regard to trespass. He also emphasized that in his view game did not belong to any particular individual — hares and rabbits he regarded as wild animals and 'the fair property of anybody who (could) take (them).'[21] Under further cross-questioning he admitted that from time to time the *Anti-Game Law Circular*, the organ of the opponents of the game laws, was received in the N.A.L.U. office and that he had himself seen copies of it. (W. R. Cremer, a London Anti-Game Law activist was in fact a member of the Union's Consulting Committee, but Joseph did not mention this in his evidence to the Game Law Committee).

Finally, Joseph directed his remarks to exposing the iniquities of the game law legislation and the way in which it could be stretched to persecute the labouring population. Several cases were quoted, including one of a man 'who was made to pay £1 9s. 6d. because he was getting some liverwort for his afflicted wife. He went into the wood where it grew; . . . no doubt the man should have asked leave, . . . but (he) daresay he never thought about it; he only thought of the liverwort. He went just inside the gate and was picking the herb when up marches the keeper, apprehends him, and summons him for trespass in pursuit of game. On that charge the man was tried, and he had the option of paying or going to prison for twenty-one days . . .'[22] Although trivial in itself, this case exemplified all the evils which aroused the bitterness and resentment of most ordinary labourers against the game laws. Nevertheless, as Joseph recognised, his evidence could only throw light on the situation; it was unlikely to do 'much practical good,' from his point of view. Indeed, it is interesting to note that the 1862 Poaching Prevention Act remains on the statute book to the present day.

84

However, while the Faringdon case and preparation for his appearance before the Select Committee on the Game Laws occupied a good deal of Joseph's time during the spring of 1873, these were by no means his only preoccupations. There were, as usual, many meetings to address, including the first anniversary celebration at Wellesbourne on 7th February. And there was, too, the wider question of the need to regulate the supply of agricultural labour, including not only a consideration of the merits of the emigration of English labourers overseas but also the problem of the migratory Irish workers who came to England during the harvest season, and thereby under-mined the bargaining position of their English fellows at this busy period of the year.

The attention of the N.A.L.U. and its President had begun to turn in the direction of Ireland as early as 10th March, 1873. On that date it was resolved at an Executive Committee meeting that John Charles Cox, the Derbyshire magistrate and an enthusiastic supporter of the idea of Union intervention in Ireland, should 'communicate with several labour associations' in that country 'for the purpose of pre-venting' England from 'being overrun at certain seasons by large numbers of Irish labourers.'[23]

Just over a month later, on 21st April, the results of Cox's negotia-tions were reported to the Committee and it was then decided that since interest in the N.A.L.U. was being displayed by the Irish, two delegates should be sent to investigate the situation at first hand. One of those chosen was William Gardner, from Warwickshire, an ex-soldier who knew Ireland from his Army days, and the other was Peter O'Leary, an Irish exile living in London. The two men were to try to bring about the formation of an Irish Agricultural Labourers' Union, and on their departure they took with them an address signed by Joseph Arch, in which appeals were made to the Irish labourers to take 'the hand of friendship and brotherly love . . .' and to follow the example of their English brethren by forming a union.

Gardner and O'Leary arrived in Dublin on 2nd May, but once there they soon found themselves involved not so much in the question of establishing an Agricultural Labourers' Union as in political agita-tion and demands for 'Home Rule for Ireland'. Meanwhile, Joseph, in England, seems at this stage to have been blissfully unaware of the nature of the delegates' activities — as well as of the dangers posed by the disturbed political scene in Ireland and of the problems which could arise for the Union in sending delagates to that country.

Grounds for concern only began to appear when Gardner and O'Leary started to send back detailed reports of their work to Leam-ington. In addition, Gardner briefly returned to England for the 1873 Annual Council of the N.A.L.U. at Leamington at the end of May. He reported hopefully on the progress so far, and his words were 'listened to with evident interest, and on resuming his seat he was loudly cheered'. Although it was now agreed that care must be taken not to entangle the Union in the complexities of Irish politics (an almost impossible task, in view of the nature of the Irish political scene), it was nevertheless decided to carry on with the agitation. Gardner consequently returned to Ireland with this in mind.

Yet — perhaps not surprisingly, in view of the information now available — Joseph seems by this time to have become lukewarm about the whole project. But he certainly did not put forward any serious objections to it, and at a meeting of the N.A.L.U. Executive Committee on 30th June even agreed to accompany some of the other Union leaders on a visit to Ireland, in order the help establish an independent Irish Agricultural Labourers' Union.[24] It was eventually decided that 15th August would be a suitable date for the holding of this Irish conference.

In the meantime, the *Labourers' Union Chronicle*, as the organ of the N.A.L.U., was not only giving details of the activities of Gardner and O'Leary, but was also reproducing accounts of the 'Horrors of Irish Evictions' and other similar matters concerning life in that unhappy country.

Nevertheless, if Irish affairs were beginning to absorb some of Joseph's time, they by no means assumed a dominant role. Once more the fight against persecution by the opponents of the Union in England had to faced in an acute form in various parts of the country, and to this Joseph gave priority. Perhaps the most notorious case in this connection was that involving the village of Ascott-under-Wychwood in Oxfordshire. On 21st April, some Ascott labourers employed by Farmer Hambridge came out on strike, following the rejection of their claim for higher wages. Hambridge, who was the largest farmer in that small village, was determined not to be dictated to, and he tried to obtain non-union labour to replace the strikers. After some effort he managed to prevail upon two eighteen-year-old lads from a nearby parish to work for him. Then, shortly afterwards, on 12th May, the wives and daughters of the strikers decided to take a hand. They went to the field where the two young men were working to try to persuade them to stop. Seventeen women and girls were involved, and although some of them carried sticks it was generally agreed that their attitude was not very threatening. Indeed, they offered to buy the two youths a drink if they would cease work, but the offer was refused. Instead the two men left the field — only to return a little later under what *The Times* ironically called 'the powerful protection of one police constable'.

Soon after this the seventeen women were charged at Chipping

Norton Petty Sessions with a breach of the 1871 Criminal Law Amendment Act, which was a particularly harsh piece of legislation designed to restrict picketing. For their minor offence, sixteen of the women were sentenced to imprisonment — seven to ten days' hard labour, and nine to seven days' hard labour!

These savage sentences were greeted with expressions of outrage and disgust not only by N.A.L.U. supporters but by the general public as well. Criticism was levelled particularly at the two clerical magistrates who had imposed the sentences — especially in view of the fact that two of the women had young babies at the breast, who were also taken to prison with their mothers.[25]

Arch was as angered as anybody else at the treatment accorded the women and he and the other Union leaders decided to open a public fund to collect money for the unfortunate victims. In all, the sum of £80 was obtained for eventual presentation to the women.

As might be anticipated, the occasion of the women's release from prison was turned into a massive Union demonstration. The nine women who had been imprisoned for seven days were met outside the prison and taken home by train, but a more impressive display was arranged for the release of the remaining seven, who had been sentenced to ten days' hard labour. They were met outside Oxford gaol by several of the Union leaders, including the Oxford district secretary, Joseph Leggett, and were then driven home in style in a carriage drawn by four horses. Large and excited crowds assembled all along the route to cheer them on their journey home.

Arch, arriving a little later, received a similarly enthusiastic welcome. Indeed, just as he was leaving the centre of Oxford he and his companions were stopped by a group of labourers, 'one of whom sprang forward, and with his face beaming with joy, cried out: "How do you do, Muster Arch?" at the same time catching hold of Joseph's hand and wringing it as though it were in a vice. Immediately he let go another took hold of the President and said, "Be you Muster Arch? I did want to shake your hand, sur," and beyond all question he shook until dislocation seemed almost a certainty . . .'[26] Only after Joseph had spoken a few words to them would they let him continue on his way.

Eventually the party of women and Union officials arrived at Chipping Norton on the last stage of their journey and here they were greeted by fresh bands and banners, while a large crowd of about 2,500 excited labourers and their families surrounded them. Joseph, as the main attraction, had, of course, more speeches to make and more celebrations in which to share before the day's proceedings at last drew to a close.

Nor was this the end of Arch's connection with the Chipping

Norton case. About three weeks later, on 20th June, he made another trip to Oxfordshire — to Ascott-under-Wychwood. At a ceremony held outside Mr Hambridge's farm he presented each of the sixteen women with £5 and a silk dress in the Union colour — royal blue. The holding of the presentation outside Hambridge's property was an unmistakable sign of the unionists' defiance, but afterwards they moved elsewhere so that Arch could address a mass meeting and demonstration. According to an onlooker, his speech was heard with 'breathless attention', broken only from time to time by 'the earnest cheers of his delighted listeners.'[27]

Three days earlier than this, at an open-air meeting at Ham Hill near Yeovil (attended by over five thousand labourers and their wives), he had made clear his disgust at the action of the Chipping Norton magistrates and his disappointment that the Home Secretary, Mr Bruce, had not taken more action in the matter. 'I should like to know if one of these females had been a clergyman's wife whether Mr Bruce would have shelved it?' he declared, to the loud applause of his audience.[28]

Apart from the recurring problems of disputes, however — and, at the beginning of July, a spell of ill-health brought on by over-work — Joseph was also worried by another matter, namely that of emigration. In the early days of the movement he had been a firm opponent of emigration, despite the pressures exerted upon him by the representatives of colonial governments, keenly anxious to secure settlers.[29] It is significant, for example, that when an official of the New Zealand Agent-General's Office in London tried to interest him in emigration to that area, during the autumn of 1872, he rejected all offers, as 'he was at that time inimical to emigration movements amongst the agricultural class.'[30] The New Zealand government had consequently to look round for another Union emigration agent and eventually found him in Christopher Holloway, the chairman of the Oxford district of the N.A.L.U.[31]

Nevertheless, as time passed, Joseph's own attitude began to soften. Emigration agents were already active in the rural areas — as they had been since the time of the Wellesbourne strike in 1872 — and labourers were being persuaded to accept their offers of subsidized passages to a new land. In these circumstances it gradually seemed to him desirable that he should investigate at first hand conditions in at least one area of settlement, so that he could advise labourers on its merits from personal experience and knowledge.[32]

By the early summer of 1873 he had finally decided to accept the invitation of the Canadian Government to visit their country; in his choice of this particular Dominion he may, of course, have been influenced by Edward Jenkins, a Union trustee and friend, who, in 1874, was to become the London-based Agent General for Canada.

Be that as it may, the die was now cast. Canada it was to be. Two shipping companies offered Joseph free accommodation for the two-way journey, the Allan Line offering a free first-class passage out, and the White Star line offering similar facilities for the return.

On his tour of Canada Arch was to be accompanied by Arthur Clayden, a Berkshire gentleman who had been a friend of the labourers' movement from its early days;[33] Clayden was to publish reports of their journey in the English press — including, in particular, the *Daily News*.

Nevertheless, despite this offer of companionship and of first-class facilities for the duration of the tour, Joseph's decision had not been lightly taken. Although he had travelled widely in Britain, a long journey overseas was quite a different matter, and involved some considerable personal strain. Certain of the other Union leaders seem to have appreciated his feelings of disquiet, for there was a suggestion that a life assurance policy to the value of £2,000 should be taken out on his behalf and paid for from Union funds, so that his wife and family would be provided for should anything happen to him. In the end, this idea was rejected, as was a proposal that his salary should be raised from £2 a week to £3. Only after his return from Canada, on 15th December, did he in fact finally agree to accept the salary increase.[34]

Then, too, before he could actually depart for North America on 28th August, he had to face the ordeal of holding farewell meetings in England as well as fulfil his longstanding engagement to visit Ireland.

The last of Joseph's English village meetings was held at War-mington in Warwickshire, on Monday, 4th August, and although he was given an enthusiastic reception, the emotional character of the proceedings must have been rather unnerving. Many of the women wept as they shook hands with him, while John Haynes of Ratley, in a short but dramatic speech told the meeting that: 'The ship that was to take Mr Arch to America would never sink. It would be upheld by faith and prayers!'[35]

Soon afterwards, the *Labourers' Union Chronicle* contained letters from other Union members expressing similar sentiments, and there was at least one poem, 'hastily written' by 'a poor labouring man's wife . . . on the departure of our beloved President to America.' The last verse of this ran as follows:

'God bless our captain; safe him guard!
Through England echoes fly;
God speed our President's return!
We'll raise and swell the cry.'

In this atmosphere of undiluted sentiment, the trip to Ireland was, no doubt, a welcome and bracing diversion. On this journey Joseph was accompanied by Henry Taylor, the Union's general secretary, and by the erratic W. G. Ward of Ross in Herefordshire, who was a member of the Union's Consulting Committee.

The party arrived in Ireland on about 9th August, and they then travelled straight on to the small town of Kanturk in County Cork, which had become the Union headquarters in Ireland.

The ostensible purpose of the open-air demonstration on 15th August for which Joseph had come was, of course, the setting up of an Irish Labourers' Union. However, this aim was little in evidence as preparations for the meeting got under way. For example, around the platform erected for the speakers were flags bearing not Union slogans but such mottoes as 'No strength but the People', and 'God Save Ireland'.

Early on the morning of the 15th, crowds of people began to gather in Kanturk and it was estimated that in all an audience of between 3,000 and 4,000 people was eventually secured. But to the dismay of the N.A.L.U. representatives, these supporters were little concerned with genuine trade union agitation. Instead it was the question of Irish Home Rule which was clearly to the fore. The pro-Home Rule parish priest of Kanturk, Archdeacon O'Regan, took the chair, for example, while most significant of all was the choice of the President and Vice-President of the proposed Union. Isaac Butt, M.P. for Limerick and the founder of the Home Rule Party, was chosen for the former office, and P. J. Smyth, another Home Ruler and M.P. for West Meath for the latter! Smyth had earlier been a member of the Young Ireland movement and had escaped to America following the collapse of that movement in 1848. He had only returned to Ireland in 1856.

Although Arch spoke at the meeting, it is clear from the subdued tones of his address that he was unhappy in this company. His remarks about the way in which Irish workers undermined the bargaining position of their English fellows by migrating to England during the harvest season were, understandably, greeted with little enthusiasm. For Joseph himself the whole business was nothing less than an acute embarrassment. He, a loyal supporter of the Liberal Government, was apparently taking part in a demonstration against the very policies of that Government. Indeed, among the resolutions passed at the Kanturk meeting was one to the effect that, 'Ireland will never enjoy contentment or prosperity without the restoration of her right to legislate for her own affairs'. Isaac Butt, in his own speech, carefully underlined this view.[36]

Joseph's involvement in this 'seditious' gathering was quickly noted in *The Times* of 16th August, but it was the normally friendly Liberal *Daily News* and the *Economist* which were perhaps the most

Henry Taylor, first general secretary of the N.A.L.U.

Two women labourers in the later nineteenth century. The photograph was
discovered at Beausale in Warwickshire.

scathing of the English journals in their criticism. The *Economist* of 23rd August indeed warned Arch 'that by mixing himself up in political agitation of so dubious a character as that of the Home Rule association, he (was) exposing the cause to which he has devoted himself to very great danger . . . ' The *Daily News* contented itself by suggesting that Arch had been duped into giving his support to what was virtually a Home Rule meeting by the machinations of a cunning Mr Butt![37]

In the light of all this criticism, the N.A.L.U. began to back pedal quickly. On 30th August, the *Labourers' Union Chronicle* reported that the efforts to prevent the migration of Irish agricultural labourers to England for the harvest had failed; there was said to be a 'great surplus labour in the harvest labour market', and Irish labourers were reported to have come over 'in unusual quantities'. The Union's policy had thus failed in its main objective and it was agreed that the entire venture had been a mistake: 'To send delegates to Ireland was illegal, and apart from the imprudence of defying the law, it was imprudent to meddle in Ireland . . . ' In view of this it had been decided that: 'We cannot continue to narrate the history of the (Irish) movement any further so closely as we have done . . . '

Nevertheless, the disabilities and hardships under which the Irish peasants laboured were freely admitted, and sympathy with their position was expressed both by Joseph and the other Union leaders. Furthermore, if Joseph appeared rather half-hearted in his attitude towards Ireland on this first contact, such was not always to be the case. It is worth noting that thirteen years later, when Mr Gladstone and a large section of the Liberal Party embraced the policy of Home Rule for Ireland, Joseph was one of Gladstone's most devoted supporters. But all this lay a long way in the future, and in 1873 Arch's position was very much more equivocal.

On his return to England, immediately prior to his second and longer trip overseas, Joseph had to face considerable Union criticism for his part in the Irish conference, at a meeting held on 25th August at the Guernsey Temperance Hotel, Leamington. Mr Campbell, a Rugby J.P. and union sympathiser, who took the chair at the meeting, was one of those who declared that the effort to 'join the peasantry of Ireland in union with the agricultural labourers of England' was a mistake — and had been a policy which he had personally opposed from the beginning, although he knew it had had the approval of the Executive Committee and also 'of Mr Arch'.[38]

In this rather uncomfortable situation therefore Joseph was no doubt glad to shake the dust of England off his feet for a while and to set off, on 27th August, for Liverpool and ultimately for Canada. It is significant that although his Canadian trip received a great deal of attention in his autobiography, the Irish debâcle is mentioned only briefly and somewhat misleadingly as follows: 'I took a short run over to Ireland, and made myself acquainted at first hand with the condition of the people. From that day forth Home Rule was down strong on my programme . . .'[39]

Once on board ship, however, these unpleasant memories could be forgotten for a time. Arch and Clayden were to sail in the *Caspian* and it was at 2.30 p.m. on the 28th August that the ship moved off from Liverpool. For the first three days of the journey the sea was rather rough and Joseph found himself a victim of seasickness. During this time he apparently took his meals on deck, waited on by one of the cabin boys. Then, as he slowly found his sea-legs, he began to enjoy the trip very much. As he later wrote: 'I remember passing by the rocks of Newfoundland and New Brunswick on our left, and Labrador on our right; the scenery on both sides was splendid . . .' On 4th September he had the great thrill of seeing 'sundry monster icebergs' in the distance.[40]

Three days later, in bright sunshine, the *Caspian* steamed into the harbour at Quebec. Immediately on their arrival on Canadian soil, Arch and Clayden were met by a Mr Stafford of the Canadian Emigration Department and were taken to the St. Louis Hotel, where they were to spend their first night on foreign soil.

The next morning, thoroughly refreshed after his night's rest, Joseph was ready for what the day might offer. First of all a visit was paid to the editor of the *Quebec Mercury*, and then Joseph called on Mr Lesage, Deputy Minister of Agriculture and Public Works for the Province of Quebec, with whom he discussed the possibility of emigration schemes. Free grants of land were envisaged, 'with some provision for immediate starting in life of the man without capital . . . ' The ideas put forward in this direction seemed to Joseph to be satisfactory, and it was in good spirits that he went to inspect the Emigrants' Home, which had been erected by the Dominion Government to house emigrants on their arrival in Canada. He was extremely pleased with the standard of accommodation provided. The Home could cater for up to one thousand people: 'The women had a lofty wing set apart for their especial use, there were admirable lavatories, there was a capital laundry, and ample cooking accommodation. Upstairs the large rooms were fitted with sloping sleeping benches . . . '[41]

The following morning, 9th September, Joseph spent in sightseeing and in the afternoon he collected his railway tickets, passes, etc. ready for the next stage of his journey. Then, on Wednesday, the 10th, came an interview with Lord Dufferin, the Governor-General of Canada, who had himself only returned to Quebec five days earlier, after a prolonged summer tour of the country.[42] The interview lasted an hour, 'as the former farm labourer and the Queen's representative in

Canada' discussed on 'equal terms' the Union's hopes with regard to emigration to Canada.

On that same evening the Governor-General extended an invitation to Arch and Clayden to dine with him, and a carriage and pair, with attendant servants, was sent to collect them. Joseph later proudly recalled that as he entered the citadel 'the guard fired a salute . . . The dinner was a splendid one, and I relished it very much. There was a brilliant assemblage to meet me, and I had the opportunity of conversing with several public men . . . No one could have been more kind and courteous than Lord Dufferin was, and I fully appreciated the honour he did me, and through me the working men of old England.'[43] Among Joseph's fellow guests were the Mayor of Quebec and his wife, and the Speaker of the Senate of Quebec Province, together with a number of other leading citizens — including members of the judiciary.

Nor was this all. Lord Dufferin showed his further goodwill and interest by ordering a member of his staff, Colonel Denison, to escort Arch and Clayden around the country, while the Government itself paid all the expenses of the mission. In addition, the Governor-General provided the two travellers with a letter of introduction 'to his subordinates throughout the Dominion.'

It was on the Thursday, therefore, four days after their arrival in Quebec, that the two Englishmen at last started on their long tour of the Canadian hinterland. In all, the journey was to last for about seven weeks, and the initial stage of it was accomplished by way of the Grand Trunk Railway. The first stop was at a small town called Sherbrooke. Neither Arch nor Clayden was very favourably impressed with conditions here. The latter, in accounts, sent to the *Birmingham Daily Post* and the *Daily News*, spoke of the 'toilworn, narrow-minded farmers' of that part of Canada, and the 'miserable-looking, lank and hopeless labourers . . . in the service of these terrible task-masters.' He also reported that Arch told 'one of these worn-out landlords' that, 'if (he) thought that English labourers (were) coming out . . . to be (his) slaves he never made a greater mistake in his life.'[44] The unenthusiastic nature of this and some other reports was later to lead to friction between Clayden and the N.A.L.U. leaders in England, who had hoped for better things.

After visiting Montreal and the Provincial Agricultural Show there on 16th September, Arch and Clayden moved on to Ottawa, where their arrival was warmly welcomed by the local press. The *Ottawa Times* of 20th September, 1873, referring to Canada's need of agricultural immigrants, declared: 'We want, and grievously want, the very class that Mr Arch represents . . . It is the duty, then, of all the Provinces to be alive to the importance of securing by every legitimate means the settlement of bodies of agricultural laborers, to form in every locality a nucleus for still further additions to that which forms the strength of a country — a prosperous because an industrious yeomanry.' Three days later the same newspaper devoted a long article to a consideration of Joseph himself (whom it described as 'a fair type of an English workingman') and to the work that he had accomplished in England.

The Government was equally attentive. Arch and Clayden were accommodated at the luxurious Russell House Hotel and soon after their arrival, Joseph had a long interview with the Minister of Agriculture and several interviews with other members of the Agricultural Department. The Prime Minister, Sir J. A. Macdonald, gave the two men a very cordial reception, and impressed upon them the advantages of colonisation in Manitoba.

By now Joseph was becoming more favourably disposed towards Canada. As he later wrote: 'Here was a land of plenty! Why, it was a vast mine of agricultural wealth . . . There were farms of one and two thousand acres, well cleared, lying waiting for the farmer.'[45]

The next stop was in Toronto, which was reached on the 25th September, and where apartments were reserved for the two men in the expensive Queen's Hotel. Once again, friendly receptions were received on all sides. The *Toronto Daily Globe*, like its contemporary, the *Ottawa Times*, emphasized the need for a 'steady and continuous supply of imported labour.' It further observed that: 'So far as the delegates, Messrs. Arch and Claydon (sic) are concerned, they will, we are sure, be treated everywhere with the kindness due to their position in the movement they represent, and the importance of the mission they have undertaken . . . the greater the facilities afforded them for forming an intelligent and impartial estimate of the wants, resources and capabilities of Ontario, the more certainly will their visit prove beneficial to their constituents and to our own people.' (27th September, 1873).

The Premier of the Province of Ontario showed that he was fully alive to the significance of Arch's visit as a means of increasing his country's intake of agricultural labourers, and he extended a very warm welcome to the N.A.L.U. President. The outcome of the negotiations here was extremely satisfactory. The Government of Ontario and the Union agreed to co-operate closely to secure the emigration of labourers to that area. And as Arthur Clayden later wrote to the *Globe* on 15th October: 'I think . . . from the favourable impression produced upon Mr Arch's mind by what he has seen and heard during the past few weeks, it will be the farmer's own fault if an extensive emigration of English farm labourers does not take place . . . as the result of our mission. As far as the Government is concerned, there is little more desired . . . Few things have occasioned us more surprise than the careful thoughtfulness which everywhere characterizes the arrangements for emigrants on their arrival from England . . .'

Joseph then noted: 'That piece of business done, we had a bit of pleasure. We took a trip to Niagara Falls. It is a sight I can never forget; it was stupendous! It was sublime! As I gazed at that mighty mass of rushing, roaring, foaming water I could but exclaim, 'O Lord, thou layest the beams of Thy chambers in *mighty* waters!' '[46]

Arch and Clayden actually made their trip to Niagara on 27th September, leaving Toronto by steamer in the morning in order to cross over Lake Ontario. The weather was bright and sunny, and after about two hours their vessel entered the Niagara river. The next part of the journey was accomplished by train, and soon the breathtaking beauty of the Falls burst upon them — with the spray from the waters rising majestically up to meet the clouds in the sky. And as the water thundered down, in the spray itself a brilliant rainbow could be seen. As we have noted, for Joseph the visit was both exhilarating and unforgettable.

But this was only a brief holiday in the general rigours of the tour. Further official business had to be carried through and although Joseph realized that in certain regions of the Dominion the life of the farmers was as harsh as that of English labourers at home, he consoled himself with the fact that: 'The hardships of Canada were the voluntary hardships of free men toiling for themselves and their children'; in this respect at least even the most unfortunate of them were better off than their landless labourer brothers in England.

The exhausting Canadian tour finally ended on 24th October in Ottawa, when Arch visited the Parliament offices for a last interview with the Minister of Agriculture and the Secretary of the Agricultural Department. The Dominion Government offered him a regular position as an emigration agent, but this he rejected being, as he said, 'bound heart and soul and body to the Union cause.' Nevertheless, he did receive assurances from the Government that 'every assistance' would be given to encourage the emigration of agricultural labourers, and to this end 'books of warrants' were to be made available at the Union head office in Leamington for issue to members, to enable them to obtain special low-cost passages to the Dominion. It was also agreed that the signature of Arch himself, or another 'duly authorised' officer of the Union 'would be accepted in lieu of the usual signature required from a clergyman or magistrate, as a certificate of the fitness of applicants to receive Passenger Warrants for assisted passages'.[47] This latter provision was especially welcome since, on occasion, clergymen or magistrates would refuse to give their signature, and in this way were able to prevent men from emigrating.[48]

The special assisted passage rate of £2 5s. per person was obtained for agricultural unionist emigrants, while for those male emigrants willing to go to Ontario, the figure was reduced to £1 0s. 4d., since the Ontario Government offered a special bonus of £1 4s. 8d. to its proposed new inhabitants. Yet, 'even this sum was beyond the means of the great majority of labourers with families', and it was 'in a large number of cases, supplied from the funds of the Union'.[49]

Before Joseph left Canada he also had the great satisfaction of receiving two 'beautifully illuminated' addresses on parchment — pledging support from the 'representatives of the trade unions of the City of Hamilton,' in Ontario, and from the 'working men of Toronto.'[50]

The N.A.L.U. President thus had good reason to be pleased with his journey to Canada. He had seen for himself the advantages and disadvantages of the Dominion as a field of emigration for agricultural labourers, he had made useful contacts and had secured favourable conditions for those unionists who did decide that they wished to take the plunge and seek their fortunes overseas.

Now came the last instalment of the journey — a visit to the United States. It had been intended to spend several weeks in the U.S.A., but owing to the lateness of the season and the prolonged nature of Arch's Canadian trip, it was decided to cut short this part of the journey. Arch did in fact intend to return in the following spring to carry out an extensive tour of the United States,[51] but, as will be seen, events in England prevented him from keeping this promise.

Nevertheless, he did visit New York — although the constant press publicity, and annoyance at being exploited for the benefit of American trade unionism rather than for his own cause, made his brief visit to that city an unhappy one. However, he derived a measure of satisfaction from the fact that he was able to preach at one of the Primitive Methodist Chapels in Brooklyn on Sunday, 2nd November, before moving off to Boston on the final stage of his long journey.

On his arrival in that city he received the hospitality of Mr E. M. Chamberlain, head of the Labour Reform movement in Boston, while on the Wednesday following, a massive reception was laid on for him by various Boston trades unionists at Faneuil Hall in the city.

On this occasion Arch was escorted by Wendell Phillips, a well-known, rich Boston Liberal who had been nominated in 1870 by the Labour Reform Party for the Governorship of Massachusetts. Although he had been defeated, he continued to espouse Labour Reform policies, and was closely associated with the labour movement in his native city.[52]

There were about four thousand people present at the Faneuil Hall reception. Flags and bunting festooned the pillars, 'and mottoes met the eye in whatever direction it was turned'.[53] Wendell Phillips himself took the chair and after he had made a warmly welcoming speech to Arch, the latter was given a chance to reply. He spoke briefly on the history of the agricultural trade union movement in England and stressed the great odds against which he and his fellows had been obliged to contend. After several other speeches had been given, the meeting ended with loud cheers for Arch. Following this he was taken to a banquet organised, like the Faneuil Hall gathering, by the Boston trade unionists. Joseph appreciated their friendliness. As he later recalled: 'It was a very nice affair indeed, and I enjoyed my dinner. I am not above saying that I am every inch a John Bull in the latter respect; . . . I am a good trencherman as they say, . . .'[54]

Soon after this, on Friday, 7th November, Arch and Clayden were back in New York ready to go on board the *Republic*, the White Star line vessel on which they were to return to England. Their homeward voyage passed uneventfully, except for some rough seas, which were certainly not to Joseph's liking.

After the great attention paid to him in Canada and the United States it would be small wonder if Arch's vanity and self-love had not been stimulated to some degree. He was beginning to feel that he stood alone as the spokesman of the organised farm worker, and that the movement had been moulded in accordance with his ideas and must so remain. As this rather arrogant attitude developed it was to give offence to other Union workers in the years which lay ahead. But, as yet, that largely lay in the future and along with his natural feelings of self pride, there was a very real happiness when on November 18th he saw once more the coast of England.

Immediately he landed, Arch got in touch with the Union head-quarters and soon after his return, on 1st December, he and Arthur Clayden met the members of the Executive Committee at Leamington. This meeting was not an altogether happy one, in so far as criticisms were levelled at some of Clayden's reports from Canada, which were felt to be too discouraging, and the already troublesome W. G. Ward, by his intemperate speeches added to the difficulties of the situation. Nevertheless, it was eventually agreed that Clayden had acted in good faith and that Arch, in any case, was not responsible for what had been written in the dispatches. There the matter was allowed to rest.

That same evening the N.A.L.U. President addressed a crowded meeting at the Circus, Leamington. In his speech he gave a favourable account of his trip to Canada, and even volunteered to emigrate there himself 'with his wife and family if the Union would release him'. (Of course, he did not go, but it is perhaps worth noting that in about 1888 a member of his family — Edward, his third son, a cabinet maker —

did emigrate there, although he later moved on to Massachusetts in the U.S.A.)[55]

Shortly after the Leamington meeting, on 9th December, a more formal reception was given for him by Liberal friends and others in London. The venue was the somewhat surprising one of the Lambeth Baths and it was on an extremely foggy night that the celebration was held. However, despite the bad weather, *The Times* described the meeting as 'a large and enthusiastic one' which 'more than half filled the large bath' — although it did go on to state that the members of the audience were compelled to sit very close together because the fog rendered it difficult to see the platform and the speakers from the opposite end of the room![56] J. C. Cox of Belper took the chair, and in spite of the rather unpleasant surroundings, Joseph and Colonel Denison, who had returned with him from Canada, were both given a friendly reception, Denison speaking on the advantages of emigration to that Dominion.

As 1873 drew to a close, therefore, Arch and his colleagues had good reason to be pleased with their achievements. Membership of the Union had continued to rise steadily throughout the year, and even at the time of the annual conference at the end of May had reached a level of 71,835, divided among 982 branches and covering almost every county in central and southern England. The morale of the members was high, wages had been increased, and future progress seemed assured. Non-labourer friends were ready to hand, and even the emigration movement was, to some extent, under the control of N.A.L.U. leaders, since all of the Dominions were anxious to recruit union officers as emigration agents, wherever possible. It seemed a very solid foundation on which future expansion could be securely built.

[1] *Midland Free Press* — 11th January, 1873.

[2] Report of the Fifth Trades Union Congress — January, 1873.

[3] *The Times* — 20th January, 1873.

[4] *English Labourer* — 23rd October, 1875 noted that six women had joined the Old branch of the Market Harborough district, for example. At the 1874 Annual Council of the Union, Mr Airey, the Worcester district delegate, spoke 'strongly' in favour of women being admitted, but others argued that 'if they recognised women members of the Union, they would recognise women's labour. It was better, therefore, to discountenance the entrance of women altogether and this was the view ultimately adopted by the Council . . .' — *The Times* — 15th June, 1874.

[5] Report of the Fifth Trades Union Congress — January, 1873.

[6] *The Times* — 5th April, 1873.

[7] Quoted in R F Wearmouth — *Some Working-Class Movements in the Nineteenth Century* (Leicester 1948), p.293. Cox eventually took holy orders and was appointed to Christ Church, Lichfield. Ibid., p.296.

[8] A Clayden — *The Revolt of the Field* (1874), p.37. Goodlake's opposition was such that in 1874 he became President of a Farmers' Defence Association which was established for a short period in the Faringdon area. — See: P L R Horn — 'Farmers' Defence

Associations in Oxfordshire — 1872–74' in *History Studies,* Vol. I, No. 1, 1968, p.69.

[9] *The Times* — 17th April, 1873. In a biography of Fitzjames Stephen his brother, Leslie Stephen, noted that: 'Fitzjames . . .was at once a Puritan and a Utilitarian. . . . He called himself a Liberal . . .' — Leslie Stephen — *Life of Sir James Fitzjames Stephen* (London, 1895), pp.308–10.

[10] Joseph Arch, op.cit., p.138.

[11] Ibid., p.138.

[12] Ibid.

[13] *The Times* — 17th April, 1873.

[14] *Midland Free Press* — 19th April, 1873.

[15] *Labourers' Union Chronicle* — 7th June, 1873.

[16] Quoted in A Clayden, op.cit. p.75 and also in *Labourers' Union Chronicle* — 26th July, 1873. Clayden wrongly dates the meeting for 18th August.

[17] *The Times* — 19th July, 1873.

[18] *Labourers' Union Chronicle* — 26th July, 1873.

[19] Select Committee on the Game Laws, Parliamentary Papers, 1873, Vol. XIII.

[20] Ibid., Q.8,326.

[21] Ibid., Q.8,776 and also Joseph Arch, op.cit., p.159.

[22] Joseph Arch, op.cit., p.159.

[23] Cox's involvement in the matter was the subject of a Question in the House of Commons, when the Home Secretary was asked whether the Derbyshire magistrate's actions were 'consistent with the duties of a justice of the peace'. The Home Secretary replied that since Cox was acting on this occasion as a private person and not as a magistrate, and since he had done nothing illegal, his activities were quite in order. — *Hansard* (3rd Series), Vol.215, p.100.

[24] *Labourers' Union Chronicle* — 5th July, 1873.

[25] See R Groves, op.cit., pp.60–61, Joseph Arch, op.cit. pp.138–140, *The Times* — 23rd and 26th May, 1873, and *Labourers' Union Chronicle* — 7th June, 1873. According to the *Labourers' Union Chronicle* of 5th July, 1873, on the 31st May the governor of Oxford gaol received the Queen's Warrant to remit the remainder of the women's sentences and to release them forthwith, but 'as the whole sentence expired on that day . . .no practical effect could be given to the Warrant.'

[26] *Labourers' Union Chronicle* — 7th June, 1873.

[27] *Labourers' Union Chronicle* — 28th June, 1873. The last survivor of the women was Fanny Rathband (nee Honeybourn) who died, aged 81, in February, 1939, at Chipping Norton Public Assistance Institution. Fanny was the daughter of John Honeybourn, an Ascott carter

[28] *Labourers' Union Chronicle* — 28th June, 1873.

[29] One New Zealand newspaper, *The Otago Witness,* for example, encouraged its emigration agents as follows: 'The labourers at home have organised and emigration agents now-a-days, instead of obtaining one family at a time, can secure a ship load of suitable emigrants. As soon as this combination amongst the labourers is broken up, the agents will find themselves faced by the same difficulties that previously beset them . . .' — *Otago Witness* — 28th February, 1874.

[30] No. 26, Appendices to the Journals of the House of Representatives of New Zealand for 1874 — Emigration to New Zealand. Information kindly provided by the New Zealand High Commission.

[31] Ibid. Holloway was appointed in November, 1873. See also P L R Horn — 'Christopher Holloway — an Oxfordshire Trade Union Leader' in *Oxoniensia,* Vol. XXXIII, 1968, pp.130–131.

[32] Of course, there may have also been an anxiety to avoid a repetition of the unhappy experience of the emigrants who went to Brazil in 1872 and whose ill-health and distress on reaching their new home had become a matter for national concern and for Govern-

ment inquiry. — See, for example, Parliamentary Papers — *Report respecting the Condition of British Emigrants in Brazil,* 1874, Vol.LXXVI, pp.3–4. *Twenty-third annual General Report of the Emigration Commissioners,* Parliamentary Papers, 1873, Vol. XVIII, p.8.

[33] Arthur Clayden, op.cit., pp.31–32.

[34] *Labourers' Union Chronicle* — 5th and 19th September, 1874.

[35] *Labourers' Union Chronicle* — 9th August, 1873.

[36] It is significant that an Irish landowner and friend wrote to Butt after the Kanturk meeting: 'The way in which Home Rule and some other topics were treated as part of the proceedings was, on the whole satisfactory'. — Letter from W Vesey Fitzgerald to Butt, dated 26th August, 1873 — Butt Papers, MS.10,415 (4) National Library of Ireland. Clearly neither Butt nor his friends had any real interest in sponsoring an Agricultural Labourers' Union on the lines of the N.A.L.U.

[37] *Daily News* — 20th August, 1873.

[38] *Labourers' Union Chronicle* — 30th August, 1873.

[39] Joseph Arch, op.cit., p.174.

[40] Joseph Arch, op.cit., p.181 and A Clayden, op.cit., p.203.

[41] Joseph Arch, op.cit., p.182.

[42] G Stewart Jr. — *Canada under the Administration of the Earl of Dufferin* (1878) pp.274–275 notes that after their return to Quebec Lord and Lady Dufferin embarked upon six weeks of, 'Dinner parties, receptions, theatricals, dances and other social gatherings'. Joseph's dinner party fell under this general heading.

[43] Joseph Arch, op.cit., p.182. *Quebec Mercury* — 11th September, 1873.

[44] *Labourers' Union Chronicle* — 4th October, 1873.

[45] Joseph Arch, op.cit., p.187. See also *Ottawa Times* — 23rd October, 1873.

[46] Ibid,. p.188

[47] *Labourers' Chronicle* — 29th November, 1873.

[48] For example, at the village of Southstoke in Oxfordshire, the branch secretary complained that three young men who desired to emigrate had taken emigration papers to the clergyman, their late employer (a farmer), and the village doctor for signature, and all had refused to sign, despite the fact that the farmer had agreed that they were men of good character. Because of this opposition the men were thwarted in their efforts to emigrate — *Labourers' Union Chronicle* — 1st November, 1873.

[49] Report of the Minister of Agriculture of the Dominion of Canada for 1874, p.vii.

[50] *Labourers' Union Chronicle* — 29th November, 1873.

[51] *The Times* — 22nd November, 1873.

[52] Wendell Phillips was born on 29th November, 1811, and died 2nd February, 1884. During the Civil War he had strongly expressed his opposition to slavery and after the War he devoted himself to a variety of causes, including the labour movement. See *Dictionary of American Biography,* Vol.XIV, (1934).

[53] *Labourers' Union Chronicle* — 29th November, 1873.

[54] Joseph Arch, op.cit., p.197.

[55] Information kindly provided by Mrs. M A Fabyan, Edward's eldest daughter, who still lives in Massachusetts.

[56] *The Times* — 10th December, 1873.

PART THREE
1874-79

CHAPTER SEVEN

Reversals: 1874-75

IT OFTEN SEEMS, almost paradoxically, that triumph and disaster go hand in hand; that the time when any enterprise appears to be running smoothly and effectively is just the time to beware. So it certainly was to be for Joseph Arch and the N.A.L.U.

Joseph's Canadian tour had been triumphantly carried through; his position as the country's leading agricultural trade unionist was virtually unchallenged; and the N.A.L.U. itself seemed to be going from strength to strength. Then, on the horizon appeared a small cloud, 'no bigger than a man's hand', which was soon to extend and darken the entire union sky and to blight the previously successful careers of both it and its President.

The immediate cause of this change of fortune was a dispute involving some agricultural trade unionists in the small Suffolk village of Exning. As early as September, 1872, the Exning labourers had asked for a 2s. per week increase in their basic wages to bring them up to 14s., and had met with a firm rebuff from their employers. The latter had in fact joined with other farmers in the Newmarket area of Suffolk and Cambridgeshire to form the Newmarket Defence Association, whose express aims were to secure co-operative action in the case of any future dispute between their workers and themselves, and also to discourage 'agitation, and generally (ameliorate) the conditions of labour'. At about this same time other farmers in East Anglia similarly decided to form Defence Associations — some of them 'more aggressive than . . . the Newmarket Association'.[1]

The following spring (1873) further wage demands were put forward from Exning, and this time with a measure of success, since the Newmarket district farmers did agree to raise wages by 1s. per week, although they emphatically denied that they had in any way been influenced by trade union pressure. Not surprisingly, the men themselves thought otherwise, and a year later, on 28th February, 1874, they yet again demanded a rise of 'is. in their weekly wages.' When this was rejected they came out on strike.

The members of the Newmarket Farmers' Defence Association, for their part, showed an equal solidarity. They responded by locking out all Union men in their employ; and in this virtually unplanned, almost casual, fashion, the great Eastern Counties lock-out began.

It soon spread far beyond the confines of Exning and the New-market area. By 23rd March at least 2,500 Union members had been locked out in Suffolk, Cambridgeshire, Norfolk, Essex, Bedfordshire, Lincolnshire and Hampshire, and a Union lock-out fund had been established.[2]

As Joseph Arch and the other N.A.L.U. leaders quickly appreci-ated, this was the beginning of a massive counter-attack by the farmers, many of whom had joined local Defence Associations with the express purpose of destroying the Union movement. Joseph under-stood only too well that it was not against the demand for a wage increase that the lock-out had been called, but against the very principle of agricultural trade unionism. As he told a packed meeting of Leamington trade unionists on 21st March: 'The question . . . with the farm labourers was not a rise of a shilling a week but, Shall these labourers have a Union? These men had struck a blow for freedom and their freedom they would have; . . .'[3] He called upon urban unionists everywhere to give financial assistance to enable the Union to fight the lock-out and to pay the men affected their 9s. a week dispute benefit. At this Leamington meeting a general collection was made which yielded £5.

Indeed, Joseph realised only too well that, as with the Wellesbourne strike two years earlier, the Union's success, or failure, in the conflict depended very largely on whether the labourers could secure generous financial help from town workers and from the general public. Without adequate funds little could be achieved. To this end, therefore, he and Henry Taylor appealed personally for support at a meeting of the Birmingham Trades Council on 18th March; they were not disap-pointed, and the Council's efforts eventually produced the useful sum of over £200 for N.A.L.U. funds.[4] Appeals were made to other similar organisations elsewhere, but Arch appreciated that this was not enough. He decided to embark upon an intensive fund-raising campaign, touring the towns and cities of the Midlands and the North, and addressing as many mass meetings as possible. At the same time, he and the other members of the Executive Committee des-patched delegates to the East Anglian storm centre, to give support and encouragement to the men locked out. Arch in fact allowed his Union colleagues to cope in the Eastern counties almost entirely on their own, apparently paying only one fleeting visit to Newmarket at the end of May. To the N.A.L.U. President the need to raise funds was all important.

Soon after he had taken this decision, Arch travelled to Leicester, at the end of March, to address a meeting at the Temperance Hall there, and to support the formation of a local Relief Committee to organise future help for the farm labourers. He was accompanied by J. C. Cox of Belper, and shortly afterwards both Arch and Cox went on to Clay Cross in Derbyshire, where a mass meeting of eight hundred miners agreed 'to subscribe 6d. a head towards the locked-out labourers, . . . and to continue to subscribe the same amount week by week so long as the lock-out lasted.' In their first week of subscriptions the Clay Cross colliers in fact sent £25 7s. 6d. to the Leamington Lock-out Fund. Meanwhile, Joseph had travelled to Ripley in Derbyshire, and then farther North in his endeavour to arouse public interest and support.[5] His days were passed in an exhausting whirl of railway journeys and mass meetings.

The pressure was tremendous. Despite efforts to encourage the men locked out to migrate to alternative work in the United Kingdom or to emigrate overseas, it proved impossible to limit the scale of the conflict. More and more men were being locked out. Joseph dare not spare himself and in these circumstances it is not surprising that he sadly overtaxed his strength — to such an extent, in fact, that early in April he became ill and was reluctantly forced to take a short rest. As he later recalled: 'I started off and travelled through the North of England, and in a month and four days — I worked desperately hard day and night, till I was about done up — we collected just over £3,000'.[6] Despite the fact that he was 'about done up', however, he would allow himself only the briefest break, and within a week he was back on his treadmill once again. It is nevertheless significant that at this time the first allegations were being made that he was becoming 'somewhat fond of a glass of brandy and a cigar . . .' The allegations were strongly denied both by him and by the other N.A.L.U. leaders, but it would not be surprising if in this atmosphere of tension and strain he had begun to rely on alcoholic stimulants to help him to carry on with his heavy programme.[7]

Nor was this all. The N.A.L.U. was not the only Union involved in the Eastern Counties lock-out — even if it was the major one. Among others affected were the Peterborough District Union and, most significantly, the Lincolnshire Amalgamated Labour League, both of which formed part of the newly-established Federal Union. It was unfortunate that between the leaders of these different organisations petty feelings of jealousy existed, which could do nothing but harm to the movement as a whole. The delegates of the various unions, for example, frequently refused to co-operate together even at the scene of a dispute. Indeed, the leaders of the Federal Union complained that their members felt that 'the tyranny of the National Union agents was far more intolerable than the conduct of the farmers!'[8]

This bickering must inevitably have preyed on Arch's nerves, especially when the leaders of the smaller unions expressed resentment at the fact that 'in consequence of the National Union gaining public attention and the notice of the Press, for a long time all public funds were sent to Leamington'.[9] Charges of unfairness and desire for self-aggrandizement were, in addition, levelled at Joseph himself.

In view of the attacks being made upon him, in particular by William Banks of the Lincolnshire Labour League, Arch responded in kind. He refused to speak on the same platform as members of the Federal Union 'on account of the attitude of that body towards him and (his) cause, which has been an immense hindrance to the great work in hand'. This ban applied, for example, to a meeting to be held on behalf of the Eastern Counties labourers at Liverpool on 5th May.[10] A similar situation developed with regard to a meeting to be held at Wolverhampton later in the same month. Arch again refused either to speak on the same platform as a Federal Union delegate, or to meet Banks, whom he condemned as a non-labourer (even though he was, of course, the leader of the Lincolnshire Labour League). Banks was a journalist by occupation.

Neither side can be considered blameless in encouraging this inter-union rivalry. But whatever the merits (or otherwise) of the case, the most important result was that it seriously damaged the *entire* Union cause, at a time when it was fighting for its very existence, with perhaps 4,000 to 5,000 agricultural labourers locked out in the country at large.

Nevertheless, despite his brief skirmishes with Federal Union leaders, Joseph did not allow such difficulties to interfere too disastrously with his main task. Although forced to take another short rest early in May, he soon set off once more for the North of England on his work of propaganda and fund-raising. At Bradford on 19th May, for example, he declared that if the dispute continued in the way it was going he would urge emigration on a large scale. He warned, at the same time, that 'he was resolved that whether the lands of England were tilled or whether they were barren, (the labourers) should have their freedom and their rights or they should leave the country'. The day after, at Newcastle, following a similar speech, he called upon his audience to show their 'practical sympathy' by contributing to the lock-out fund.

Meanwhile, friends of the agricultural labourers, including Samuel Morley and George Dixon, were trying to bring an end to the struggle by initiating discussions between the farmers and unionists. (Morley had already shown his typical generosity with a contribution of £100 made at a mass meeting organised for the labourers at Exeter Hall, in London, on 23rd April.) In Suffolk, these efforts at conciliation broke down, largely because of the opposition of the farmers, but in Lincolnshire there was a greater measure of success. There the farmers agreed to end the lock-out after 23rd May, provided that the leaders of the Lincolnshire Labour League, the principal union involved, agreed to withdraw certain 'offensive' rules in return, These included a demand for a minimum wage of 18s. per week. When the League agreed to these conditions, the lock-out was brought to an end in Lincolnshire, without any increase in wages being secured but with a recognition of the Union by the farmers.

Somewhat unwisely, however, the N.A.L.U. leaders chose to condemn the reaching of this agreement by the leaders of the League. Arch contended that, 'After the thousands of pounds which had been expended in support of the lock out, and after the great sacrifices the poor men had so heroically borne in defence of their rights, and in their fight for emancipation he could not be a consenting party to any settlement which did not give a rise in wages to the labourers'.[11]

Other N.A.L.U. leaders were equally outspoken, and many were more belligerent, despite the restraining influence of Morley, who considered that 'such conduct was not likely to do good, but would alienate the sympathies of some of their best friends and supporters'.[12]

Joseph had spoken brave words. Slowly he was to realise that words, and even the massive financial help of the general public and of the trades union movement (the Amalgamated Society of Engineers alone sent £2,000) were not enough. In some cases the locked out men were able to migrate to better paid employment elsewhere, or else to emigrate, while in a number of instances, too, individual farmers agreed to re-employ labourers without demanding that they first surrender their Union membership. But for very many a return to work was only to be obtained on the farmers' terms — which often included an abandonment of the Union. Those not prepared to accept these terms remained locked out.

Various devices were set in hand to help to raise more funds. For example, at the invitation of the local Relief Committee, Joseph attended a mass demonstration in Manchester on 20th June. ' Between sixty and seventy trades and friendly societies were represented, accompanied by almost as many bands of music. A number of farm labourers took part in the procession, and showers of copper and silver coins were cast into two huge money boxes, mounted on lorries, which they escorted . . .'[13] The Bishop of Manchester, Dr. Fraser, also gave his support. (Of course, as an Assistant Commissioner for the Royal Commission on the Employment of Children, Young Persons and Women in Agriculture, Dr. Fraser had earlier expressed

Thomas Parker, shortly before his death in 1912. Parker chaired Arch's
first meeting at Wellesbourne on 7th February, 1872.

Wreath being laid by Mr R. Bottini, present general secretary of the National Union of Agricultural and Allied Workers', on Arch's grave, on the occasion of the Union's Barford Rally on 20th June, 1970.

his strong condemnation of the miserable conditions in which most labourers spent their lives.)

The large procession wound its way through the Manchester streets to Pomona Gardens, where as a climax to the whole rally Joseph was to address a crowded meeting. As he later recalled: 'Many wealthy merchants were present at this meeting, and at its close cheques to the value of £340 were placed in my hands for the relief of the distressed labourers of the Eastern counties.'[14]

But if this was one method of raising funds, a second — and rather more original one — was to be attempted by the Suffolk labourers themselves. On 30th June a 'pilgrimage' of about one hundred locked out men set out from Newmarket, under the leadership of Henry Taylor, on a fund raising tour through the Midlands and North of England. Their first stop was at Cambridge, and according to the correspondent of *The Times*: '. . . on entering the town, each of the labourers seemed to have an appointed duty. Some carried small baskets, in which they received pence and other contributions; others sold broadsheets of Union songs; some were told off to sing, and walked in ranks to such tunes as they could from time to time raise; others, again, marshalled the procession, or sold copies of the Union newspaper. And so this quaint array . . . of English peasants, in velveteens, smocks, or other working dress, with Union blue ribbons prominently displayed, proceeded to the inn at which a dinner had been prepared for them. To judge by their looks, they were in need of a substantial meal . . .'[15]

A few days later, while this unusual procession wound its way northwards, Joseph himself again took up the task of fund raising, this time addressing a series of meetings in London — including one at Battersea Park on 8th July which was attended by about ten thousand people. A collection made at the end of the demonstration realised £21 3s. 3d. On the following Sunday he preached to an audience of about four thousand in the Standard Theatre, Shoreditch, when about £10 were collected. The *Labourers' Union Chronicle* noted that as a result of his visit to London, 'The zeal of friends of the cause in the Metropolis' had been 'greatly' stimulated.[16] Unfortunately, as events were soon to show, zeal was not enough to secure victory for the Union.

Meanwhile, the 'pilgrim' labourers were now approaching Yorkshire. On the 14th July they arrived in Sheffield, and Joseph hurried north to meet them. Altogether they spent two days in that city and Joseph addressed two mass outdoor meetings on their behalf. At one in Paradise Square about seven or eight thousand persons assembled to hear him. In the atmosphere of excitement which his speeches engendered, Joseph abandoned his usual moderation and warned instead that he could no longer continue to counsel the labourers to behave meekly if they were 'insulted' as they had been in recent weeks. He linked his condemnation of the intransigence of the farmers with a denunciation of the system of game preservation, under which thousands of acres of land, instead of being cultivated in the interest of the many, were overrun with game for the sport of the few. Communism or no communism, his doctrine was that the produce of the earth should be for the inhabitants thereof, according to the writing of old — 'The earth hath He given to the children of men'.[17] His words were well received, and altogether the sum of £140 was collected in Sheffield by the 'pilgrims'.

When they left Sheffield to travel by train to their next stop at Rotherham, Joseph accompanied them, in order that he might speak in that town. Once again, he was successful and according to one correspondent at least, his oratory 'excited his audience to a pitch . . . not seen . . . at any other of the meetings.'[18] This done, he returned once more to Leamington, while the labourers continued on their 'pilgrimage', until it was finally wound up, at the beginning of August, in Halifax. Altogether the net sum of £770 accrued to the lock-out fund as a result of this enterprise.

Nevertheless, despite the continuing sympathy of his urban audiences, by late July, Joseph's confidence in the ultimate victory of the Union cause had been steadily eroded. In spite of his brave language of early June, when he had declared that 'he could not be a consenting party to any settlement which did not give a rise in wages to the labourers', he slowly realised that the struggle could not go on much longer. The drain on Union funds was tremendous. For example, in the period March to August, 1874, the N.A.L.U. Central Executive Committee had authorised the payment of a grant of £14,984 10s. 7d. to the district of Newmarket alone, including, of course, Exning, the original storm centre. Admittedly, this was the worst affected area, but in the Sawston district of Cambridgeshire, £1,931 had been expended, and in the Wisbech district, also in Cambridgeshire, £1,550. These sums excluded any money which may have been raised and expended by the districts on their own account. In all, the large sum of £24,432 10s. 7d. was granted to the various districts affected by the lock-out between the months of March and August.[19] Despite the generosity of the general public, such expenditure could not be maintained indefinitely.

Then, too, the men's last real bargaining counter was whether the farmers could commence harvesting without them, or whether they would be forced to make concessions even at that late stage. By the end of July it was becoming clear, however, that a compromise was not on the cards and that by the greater use of machinery and by relying upon loyal non-unionists and unskilled female, child or town workers, the farmers were determined to overcome even this problem. It seemed to Joseph that further Union opposition was useless.

The end came almost as an anti-climax. At a meeting of the Executive Committee of the N.A.L.U. on 27th July, Arch and his colleagues decided that they could no longer keep the men out 'while the harvest was waiting to be gathered in'. Those labourers who were still unemployed were advised to migrate, or else to rely on their own resources. A further meeting of the Committee on 3rd August confirmed this decision, and agreed that one further week's dispute pay only should be given to each member still locked out. From 10th August, therefore, all assistance was to cease officially; in practice, however, the withdrawal of help does not seem to have been quite as rigid as this plan suggests.[20]

The curtly worded statement issued by the Committee on the winding up of their support for the locked out labourers reflects little credit on Joseph or any of the others who drafted it, especially in view of their confident language of a few months earlier. The statement brusquely ended: 'The committee does not feel justified or in any way bound to give permanent relief to such men who, by reason of age or infirmity, are unable to migrate and who are victimised by the farmers in being discharged. This committee does not feel justified in taking upon itself the duties and responsibilities of the Poor Law Board.'[21]

It was later claimed that of the men originally locked out in the Suffolk area about 870 had returned to work without surrendering their union membership, 400 had migrated, 440 had emigrated, and 350 had managed to find work for themselves immediately the lock-out had ended. But by the second week of August there were still 350 out of work — and some of the 350 who had been re-employed had been forced to give up their Union membership. (With great unfairness, four years later Arch referred to these latter as 'traitors' who 'bowed their necks to the employer, sold their brethren'.[22] He did not say what else they could have done!)

Not surprisingly, this outcome of the lock-out was regarded by some N.A.L.U. members as a 'betrayal' of all their efforts. But as Joseph realised, despite his later emotional language, there was no other course of action open to them. They just had not the funds to continue the dispute indefinitely in face of the farmers' refusal to compromise. Nevertheless, for the first time confidence in both the Union and its President was seriously undermined.

Joseph's enemies were soon at work to take advantage of this.

Meanwhile, membership of the Union began to fall from the level of about 86,214 achieved at the time of the Annual Council, at the beginning of June, 1874. In the Newmarket district alone there was an *admitted* decline in membership by early October, 1874, of 294 as compared with the position of a year earlier, and in practice the decline was probably much greater.

Nevertheless, despite murmurings of discontent in the upper echelons of the N.A.L.U., among most of the rank and file of the agricultural trade union movement Joseph could still command much support. For example, at a tea meeting in the village of Eversholt in Bedfordshire, early in October, he was greeted by the local brass band, and '. . . the women especially were in high glee; one of the fair ones, stepping behind him, pulled his coat, and, apologising, said she had long wished to "touch the hem of his garment" . . .'[23] The whole gathering was indeed turned into a festive occasion, with dancing and 'kiss-in-the-ring' to supplement the speeches which usually characterised most Union meetings.

But despite Joseph's continued outward air of cheerfulness and self-confidence, there is little doubt that the disappointing conclusion of the Eastern Counties dispute, from the Union's point of view, plus his own tremendous efforts, had taken their toll of him. In the autumn of 1874, many of his fellow officials (including Henry Taylor) were busy organising the large-scale emigration of labourers from the Eastern Counties to Canada and Australasia, but he played no part in this. However, it is perhaps worth noting that the vigorous unionist emigration campaign appears to have borne fruit. In all, 6,890 adult male agricultural labourers, shepherds, gardeners, carters, etc. emigrated in 1874, according to the officials statistic. This was the highest annual figure for the agricultural category of emigrants during the whole period 1860–1880.[23a]

Yet, even without his participation in emigration work, the other strains he had endured were to prove too great for Joseph. Eventually, at the end of October, his health finally gave way and he was forced to rest. As the *Labourers' Union Chronicle* of 31st October warned: 'The invitations . . . still come crowding in thicker, perhaps, than ever . . . The necessity for rest is, however, not merely urgent — it is absolute . . .'

(To some minor extent, during this period of essential relaxation, Joseph's role was taken over by his daughter, Annie, who preached in a number of villages in the Banbury and South Warwickshire area to labourer congregations.[24])

Although Arch was able to return to work by the end of November, it is noticeable that he addressed no mass demonstrations or public meetings for some time to come. According to the *Midland Free Press* of 28th November, 1874, he was only 'slowly recovering from a severe illness', and doubtless for this reason, not until December did he attend any large-scale gathering which was likely to tax his strength. On the

16th of that month, however, he spoke at Oxford Town Hall, on the occasion of the Oxford district's annual meeting.

In his address he called, as he had so often in the past, for a reform of the land laws and an extension of the franchise. But perhaps more significant was the fact that he also emphasized that: 'The Union was secretly doing its work. Other papers besides the Oxford papers had said they were all gone to sleep, or had swallowed some dreadful morphia and were in a trance; but when they saw an increase of funds every month at the central executive it did not look much as though their movement was dying out . . .'[25] These were brave words, but despite them, it was becoming increasingly clear that much of the former enthusiasm and driving force had now gone out of the movement. The early feelings of exhilaration and sublime self-confidence had disappeared for ever.

Nevertheless, Joseph's task in the months ahead was to try to re-kindle some of the earlier fire and vigour. As 1875 dawned the difficulty of achieving this became ever more apparent. Although he personally was still able to attract mass attendances at his village meetings, he could not be everywhere, and too often lethargy and indifference were setting in. Then, too, within the movement his critics were at work.

As early as the middle of August, 1874, W. G. Ward, the erratic Herefordshire gentleman sympathiser with the N.A.L.U., had criticised Arch's leadership and had claimed that he was trying to reap financial benefit for himself out of the Union.[26] Although these criticisms were strongly refuted and Ward was expelled from the Consulting Committee of the Union, some damage had already been done. In 1875 others were to add their voices to his. There were demands for a widening of the scope of the N.A.L.U.'s activities, so that it could hire or purchase land to let as allotments to members, and for the establishment of a Union friendly society. Joseph opposed these schemes, which he felt could only dissipate the Union's strength and thereby weaken it in the long run.

Nevertheless, at the beginning of 1875, all did not yet seem lost. Arch and Taylor both attended the Seventh Trades Union Congress held in Liverpool, in January, and were given a friendly reception. In 1874 and again in 1876 Arch was to be elected to the Parliamentary Committee of the Congress, which was the political pressure group of that organisation; in 1875 Taylor was so elected. The two men also had the opportunity (in 1875) of thanking in person some of the leaders of the trades unions who had come forward so generously with their financial help in the previous year. At this stage, the N.A.L.U. claimed a membership of about 60,000 — or approximately 26,000 members fewer than its level of the previous June.

Yet even at its peak in June, 1874, the N.A.L.U. had failed to recruit a majority of its potential members (there were over 922,000 male agricultural workers (excluding bailiffs) at the time of the 1871 Census of Population).[27] After 1874, however, the decline became more apparent, and as Joseph was soon to realise, the task of salvaging what he could from the wreck of earlier success was going to be rendered more difficult by the increasing hardships facing British arable agriculture from 1875 onwards. Bad harvests at home and growing imports of wheat from Russia and the U.S.A., in particular, hit grain producers in the Eastern Counties especially heavily during the later 1870's. In this situation, farmers were likely to be more determined in their opposition to the N.A.L.U. — particularly as the Union itself appeared to be growing weaker. Some of the wage rises secured by the unionists in the favourable conditions of 1872–74 had to be sacrificed — and this was done with Joseph's reluctant approval. Several years later, in 1881, he told the Royal Commission on the Depressed State of Agriculture that: '. . . since 1875, when the depression set in, I have advised the labourers, thousands of them, when they were under notice of reduction to accept it. I said, 'You must take it; the situation of the farmers is not at all good.' . . .'[28]

Although Joseph's attitude was merely one of facing the economic facts of life, to many still poorly paid farm workers, it was a grave disappointment. They were soon asking themselves why they should contribute their 2¼d. per week to a Union which could give them so little protection on the vital matter of wage rates.

Nevertheless, in the early months of 1875 Arch was fighting valiantly against these feelings of defeatism and frustration. And through his own personality he could still arouse enthusiasm and confidence in the future. Unfortunately, however, once his bracing presence was removed, the enthusiasm too often dwindled away.

A typical example of a Union meeting of this almost revivalist character held by Joseph in 1875 was one organised at Hungerford in Berkshire on 16th April. The *Labourers' Union Chronicle* of 24th April provided a detailed account:

'In the course of the afternoon and evening numbers of countrymen, wearing blue ribbons, were to be seen entering the town from all parts, while detachments came in carts and carriers' vans. . . . The Wickham band, which wore a military uniform played through the streets . . . and the procession was headed by a blue flag, bearing a suitable inscription.' The meeting was held on the Downs and, as was often the case, a waggon was used as a platform. The meeting started at seven o'clock but as the night advanced the proceedings were continued by moonlight. About one thousand people had come to hear Joseph speak, and in his long address he exhorted them to stand by the

Union. His harping on this point was significant, and he concluded his speech with the following warning: 'You men are right if you are in the Union and if you are not you are wrong . . . you are crying out, 'Where's Joseph Arch? We want him in this village or that village, and we want him everywhere.' Now, Joseph Arch, nor forty Joseph Archs, cannot keep up your Union if you do not keep it up yourselves. . . . If you won't try and work up, and keep up your branch, and dribble out two or three now, and two or three again, and so on till a branch of 100 members dribbles down to ten, and say well, we must have Joseph Arch, I'll tell you what, Joseph Arch won't serve no (sic)such humbugs . . . If you will stick well together, and true to the Union, then the life God has given me shall be devoted to your interests and welfare . . .'[29]

His words were greeted with prolonged cheering and for a time probably he had in that place inspired renewed allegiance — had stemmed the outflow. In the long run, however, when the memory of this meeting had faded, the process of decline would no doubt again set in — as the remorseless drop in Union membership figures bears out.

However, in addition to this continuing loss of membership, a second serious problem confronting the N.A.L.U. was the renewed outburst of recrimination and division within the ranks of the organisation itself. In this dissension, Joseph himself was deeply involved. By the spring of 1875 relations were, in particular, becoming increasingly strained between Henry Taylor, the General Secretary of the Union, and Matthew Vincent, the Honorary Treasurer and proprietor of the *Labourers' Union Chronicle*. Some of the trouble seems to have arisen because of Taylor's interference during a labour dispute in Vincent's newspaper office amongst his compositors. But the situation was further aggravated by a personality clash between the two men.[30]

The first important danger signals of future strife appeared at the annual conference of the Warwickshire district, held in April, 1875, when Edward Haynes of Ratley, a founder member of the Union, expressed discontent at the heavy expenses being incurred by the Central Office. In particular, he criticised the employment of both a general secretary and an assistant secretary – for Taylor had acquired an assistant at the time of the Eastern Counties lock-out to enable him to cope with the flood of work this entailed. The assistant was Robert Collier, a Leamington draper.[31]

Arch himself, who was in the chair at this meeting, seems to have shared Haynes's views. He certainly emphasized that some reduction in expenditure was essential, and that he 'did not know what there was for two secretaries to do . . He thought Mr. Taylor would see that it was to his advantage to be in the office and know what was truly going on. If they were to have a general secetrary, let him be the general secretary, and not have the honour of being the general secretary, and someone else do the work...' This statement was loudly applauded by his audience, and a resolution to the effect that the district considered it 'advisable to dispense with the expense of one of the general secretaries' was carried unanimously.[32]

Naturally Taylor did not welcome this criticism and it soon led to a coolness between himself and Arch.

All of these various problems came to a head at the Union's Annual Council at Leamington, at the end of May. The first conflict arose when, in the course of discussion, some mistakes in the Union balance sheet were revealed – an alleged deficiency of £150 being brought to light. This was, however, said to have already been made good by Taylor and Collier, with the help of outside friends; but the disordered state of the accounts can be gauged from the fact that one speaker, Mr Lenthall, a delegate from Cheltenham, claimed that when J S Wright of Birmingham, as a member of the Consulting Committee, had inspected them he had declared 'that it would take a better man than him to say where that deficiency occurred. . .'[33] No attempt was made to deny this state of confusion.

Joseph himself also raised the question of the deficiency, but the main outcome of the debate on the balance sheet was a quarrel between Vincent and Taylor. The entire conference, in fact, became dominated by a spirit of petty animosity – and this included a prolonged argument between Arch and Taylor over the latter's duties as general secretary.

In this atmosphere of public bickering, therefore, the growing divisions within the Union ranks hardened. Vincent decided to break away from the main organisation and to form his own Union – the National Farm Labourers' Union – which would have as its prime purpose the acquisition of land for distribution among members as allotments or small holdings. For a time he hoped that because of the disagreement between Arch and Taylor, Arch would join him as well. This was not to be.

Joseph quickly appreciated the essential instability and impracticality of Vincent's proposals. It would be quite impossible for his organisation ever to be able to purchase, or even to rent, sufficient land to make the scheme worthwhile, out of income derived from the labourers' meagre subscriptions of 1d. or 2d. per week. In N.A.L.U. circles, therefore, the New Union was soon maliciously nicknamed 'the Bogus', because of the false promises made by its leaders and the false hopes held out.

A second reason for Joseph's unwillingness to co-operate with Vincent was, of course, his reluctance to abandon the old Union, which he had done so much to create. In these circumstances, therefore, the quarrel between Taylor and Arch was soon patched up — at least on the surface. (Deeper down, the breach may still have remained, and it is significant that at the end of May, 1876, Taylor decided to resign as general secretary in order to take up a position with the Immigration Department of the South Australian Government. He eventually became an Emigration Agent for that Government and after 1876 never again held Union office, although he did remain a member of the Consulting Committee until 1879).

Meanwhile, Vincent saw only the outward reconciliation and through the *Labourers' Union Chronicle*, he now turned to attack Arch, just as previously he had been attacking Taylor. In a leader headed *Joseph Arch*, the *Chronicle* declared that: 'Mr Arch . . . has . . . linked himself with a system of corruption which even he will fail to purify . . .'[34] Later outbursts were much less complimentary, especially when W. G. Ward gave his support to the new Union. Ward, in an article published in the *Labourers' Union Chronicle* of 24th July, condemned Joseph's 'extravagance.' 'Joseph Arch had at one time £25 for outfit in clothes, &c. for a journey! A year's income of a farm labourer . . . for an outfit for Joseph Arch for a journey.' (Presumably the journey referred to was Arch's Canadian trip). Again, in the edition of 7th August, a long article condemned the false statements and 'froth' of Joseph Arch. It ended: ' . . . we leave the indignation and scorn Joseph Arch has earned to honourable men, . . . We have written more in sorrow than in anger; but we should be moral icicles if our anger was not moved at the ingratitude and indelicacy and gross selfishness of Joseph Arch.'

Then, at a meeting in Ashorne, Warwickshire, early in August, the conflict went even further. As Arch was addressing a large audience in the centre of the village, Ward and Vincent both appeared and tried to interrupt him. (Perhaps their antagonism was understandable in so far as Joseph was said to be 'on his mettle, and fully proposed so far as in him lay, to show up the trumpery thing called the new Union . . .') They received short shrift from the labourers, however, and Ward was literally thrown out of the meeting.[35] Although possibly justified in the circumstances, this type of action was obviously unedifying, and could only give encouragement to the N.A.L.U.'s non-labourer opponents—especially the farmers.

By now indeed Vincent and his National Farm Labourers' Union were doing everything possible to undermine confidence in the N.A.L.U. As the former openly admitted in the *Labourers' Union Chronicle*, he was seeking to expose 'the abuses, and corruptions, the inefficiency and the mismanagement of the Central Office of the National Union . . .'[36]

And because of the split at the top, at local level, too, Union branches became divided in their allegiance, some supporting one faction and some another. In this atmosphere, therefore, membership began to fall even more rapidly. By the end of 1875 the N.A.L.U. could claim only 40,000 members, while, according to one impartial observer, the new Union numbered merely 'from three to four hundred.'[37] Clearly, then, the prime result of this distasteful in-fighting was an increase in the farm workers' general indifference towards the whole principle of trade unionism.

For Joseph the entire affair was extremely distressing. Attacks were launched on him from all sides. Not only was there the constant barrage of abuse from Vincent and Ward, but leaders of the older independent unions equally turned their attentions to him, recalling the bitterness which had existed in the days of the Eastern Counties lock-out. By the early part of 1875, the Federal Union itself had broken up, but its constituent parts had returned to their original independence. Among the strongest of these was the Lincolnshire Amalgamated Labour League, whose leader, William Banks, soon seized the opportunity to attack Arch. Writing in the *Labourers' Union Chronicle* of 21st August, he accused Joseph of lack of co-operation during the great lock-out, and rather hysterically declared that he believed Joseph's plan had been 'to prevent public money from reaching the League, and thus starving us into joining the N.A.L.U.'[38]

Benjamin Taylor, leader of another independent union, the Peterborough District Union, and a high bailiff of the County Court, followed a similar line in another letter in the same issue of the *Chronicle*, headed: 'How Joseph Arch was Spoiled.' In this he claimed that Arch had been spoiled by the adulation given to him. 'He was petted and patted to such a degree that it made him vain-glorious; in fact, his speeches soon became heavily laden with self, and he seems to have been led to the conclusion that without him the Labour Union Movement could not be sustained, and, in fact, that he was absolutely necessary for the success of many other important movements. This led to his not being able to bear an equal, much less endure a rival; eventually, none but those he approved of must take part in any meeting where he was to speak, no matter how valuable the services of the party might be considered. 'He would not allow any one to ride into popularity on his shoulders' was his frequent declaration: in fact the extreme petting he got from the middle and higher classes was too much it turned his head, and, perhaps, but few of Mr Arch's obscure origin could have endured the amount of flattery he met with and maintained his equilibrium . . .'[39]

There is undoubtedly *some* truth in Taylor's rather bitter summing up. Arch had clearly been influenced by the adulation shown to him, but, at the same time, this correspondence reveals only too well the deep jealousy felt by other trade unionists towards his dominant position.

Counter attack was essential, and since the columns of Vincent's *Labourers' Union Chronicle* were now barred to N.A.L.U. views, Joseph and the other members of the Executive Committee decided to try and enlist the help of some of their middle-class friends in establishing a fresh newspaper to represent their opinions. In this they were successful. The new venture was financed by J. C. Cox, his brother, Henry, Ashton Dilke, brother of the well-known Liberal politician, Sir Charles Dilke, and Howard Evans, a journalist and member of the Union's Consulting Committee. Evans indeed became the editor, and the newspaper was printed and published in London under his eye.[40]

The first edition of the *English Labourer*, as it was called, appeared on 26th June, 1875. It had two main aims. The first was to emphasize Joseph's position as the leader of the movement. The second, unfortunately, was to abuse Vincent and his new Union as roundly as the *Labourers' Union Chronicle* was abusing the N.A.L.U. It seemed that the movement was about to tear itself to pieces, but in fact this did not quite happen. Partly because of the evident impracticality of Vincent's land scheme and partly because the name of Joseph Arch still carried with it an appeal far and away greater than that of any of his rivals, the steady draining away of members never became a torrent. As we have seen, by the end of the year, N.A.L.U. membership was down to about 40,000 — as compared with over 86,000 achieved in June, 1874. The situation was serious, but not beyond hope.

Meanwhile, Joseph turned his attentions towards both revival and a refutation of the charges levelled against him. By this means he was able to swing some of the doubters behind him again. For example, at the small Northamptonshire village of Evenley, the branch members met and decided to pay up their contributions 'now that they have heard Mr. Arch.'[41]

He still possessed his old ability to persuade his fellows and his powers as an orator were unimpaired. In a passionate speech at Akeley, near Buckingham, on the 12th August, he appealed to the labourers to stand by the Union, in quite his old dramatic style. 'Will you go back to Egypt under Pharoah? If you leave me and the Union depend upon it you will sink again into the ditch, and there you may stop. Joseph Arch will not come to your rescue; but will let you cry in agony. I am here to ask you as sensible men that if I do not suit you as leader to send me about my business . . . But don't break up your Union . . . I should feel grieved to see it broken up. It is the work of my life. Stick together, men, and no power on earth shall break it down.' His words were greeted with loud cheers.[42]

He also used his abilities as a speaker to pinpoint the weaknesses in his opponents' case — as at a meeting near Evesham in mid-July when he declared: 'I ask the labourers, how much land are you going to buy with your two-pences per week? In the next place, where are you to find the land to buy? . . . Before the labourers can obtain land in this country they must have conveyancing placed upon a cheaper scale. Be careful how you are led by these land schemers, who in reality will be only another class of landlords, . . . What care these land schemers about your political rights if they can get your money? They tell you that all your officers are blood suckers, and that they have sucked your Union fund dry. We have however got your brains to appeal to, and I would rather disown my name than hold out a hope to you that I am convinced you cannot realise . . .'[43]

Nevertheless, despite this spirited response, from 1875 onwards both the N.A.L.U. and its President were on the defensive. They were never again able to recapture the first fine careless rapture of 1872 and 1873, when members had flocked to the movement and the future had appeared bright and full of promise.

And if Joseph's official activities as a Union leader were giving him concern at this point, the same must be said of his private life. On 17th July, his second son and namesake, who was employed as a porter/clerk at Warrington Railway Station, was committed for trial on a charge of theft, at Warrington Petty Sessions. At the instigation of an older man, named John Sheldon (a telegraph instrument repairer), with whom he was in lodgings, on 15th July Arch had stolen a box of ten gold watches (valued at £150) from the parcels office. These Sheldon had later sold, along with other stolen property in his possession. The crime was traced to young Arch and he was arrested — although he had apparently received no share of the proceeds.

As the *English Labourer* then recorded: 'Directly the event became known, Mr. Arch, senior, had numerous offers of assistance, but he preferred to trust to his friend Mr. J. C. Cox, of Belper. Mr. Cox accompanied Mr. Arch to Warrington . . . and . . . their bail was accepted, and Mr. Arch's son released. We are glad to learn that the youth obtained employment immediately on his release from one of the most respectable firms in Liverpool. . . . The railway company's books kept by Mr. Arch's son were found to be right to a fraction . . .'[44] Although the affair was eventually smoothed over, for Joseph it must have been an unpleasant shock. The *Warrington Advertiser* noted that he had a 'most affecting interview with his son' on the night he arrived in Warrington.[45]

The incident was certainly one which his enemies did not hesitate to use against him. Thus the hostile *Labourers' Union Chronicle,* while pretending to sympathise with "the shame of one Joseph Arch and the sorrow of another", did not shrink from drawing attention to "the association with crime of Joseph Arch's son".[46]

Indeed, as Arch knew only too well hostile eyes were watching his every move, ready to criticize and to condemn. Not 'only had he to fight the farmers and landowners of England, but former colleagues as well. There is, of course. no doubt that, as Benjamin Taylor pointed out, he was often arrogant and overbearing, but without his massive self-confidence it is unlikely that the Union would ever have attracted widespread support anyway. Unfortunately, as time passed his growing egotism became offensive to other genuine workers within the movement, and it served as a ready target for those who were jealous of his success, or who wished to undermine the agricultural trade union movement as a whole.

These were troubled years. As Joseph later wrote in his typically Biblical style: 'All through the seventies the Ark of Union was storm-tossed; now it would be rolling in deep and troubled waters; but through storm and shine, in fair weather and in foul, it still sailed on, and I still stuck to my post. It had to suffer attacks from foes without and traitors within. I had to bear what I may call the slings and arrows of outrageous slander, assassin stabs in the back of my reputation were dealt me, my character was defamed, and the purity of my motives was called in question by those who should have known me better. Self-seekers and place-hunters strove to knock me down, trample upon me, and cast me overboard— but the fate of the fallen angels was theirs, and it was they who fell and were cast down and thrown over, while I stood firm, and true friends stood by me and struck many a doughty blow in my defence. Cast down in spirit I often was, and sore at heart, but never — no not when the storm was at its highest, or the fight waxed hottest and fiercest — did I lose heart altogether, and fall a prey to ugly old Giant Despair.... In my opinion these traitors to the cause were no better than heathen savages and cannibals, for what were they doing when all is said and done, but trying to swallow each other? It was a cruel shame and a bitter disgrace, and I felt it to the marrow of my bones when outsiders twitted us and pointed the finger of scorn at us, and hooted,... '[47]

The years 1874 and 1875 were, then, vital turning points in Joseph's career and in that of the agricultural trade union movement as a whole. The limitations of extensive industrial action had been revealed. Now Joseph's attention turned — as perhaps his Liberal friends had hoped it would — increasingly towards the field of politics in general, and the Liberal Party in particular. Although as yet the labourers were, of course, still without the vote, it could only be a matter of time before it was given to them. Joseph, like the Liberal politicians, had his eye on the longer term, and meanwhile he was ready to take advantage of any new opportunities for action which might open up before him.

[1] F Clifford — *The Agricultural Lock-out of* 1874 (London, 1875), pp.2–5.

[2] *Labourers' Union Chronicle* — 28th March, 1874.

[3] Ibid. See also A Peacock — *The Revolt of the Fields in East Anglia* (pamphlet, 1968), pp.7–14.

[4] Birmingham Trades Council Minute Book — Meeting on 23rd September, 1874.

[5] *Labourers' Union Chronicle* — 4th April, 1874.

[6] Joseph Arch, op.cit., p.222.

[7] *Labourers' Union Chronicle* — 11th April, 1874.

[8] Report of the Federal Union of Agricultural and General Labourers, 1874, p.6. (Howell Collection, Bishopsgate Institute, London.)

[9] Ibid., p.6.

[10] Ibid., pp.9–15

[11] *Labourers' Union Chronicle* — 27th June, 1874.

[12] Ibid.

[13] *Midland Free Press* — 27th June, 1874.

[14] Joseph Arch, op.cit., p.222.

[15] F Clifford, op.cit., p.133.

[16] *Labourers' Union Chronicle* — 18th July, 1874.

[17] F Clifford, op.cit., pp.138–140. Clifford's account is, however, somewhat hostile to Arch.

[18] *English Labourers' Chronicle* — 17th August, 1878, quoting from the *Hour.*

[19] F Clifford, op.cit., p.21.

[20] *Midland Free Press* — 5th September, 1874.

[21] *Royal Leamington Chronicle* — 8th August, 1874. A similar statement was made by the Executive Committee of the Federal Union at about the same time in respect of the relatively few men belonging to their organisation who were still locked out.

[22] *English Labourerss' Chronicle* — 14th September, 1878.

[23] *Labourers' Union Chronicle* — 17th October, 1874.

[23a] See Emigration Returns in Parliamentary Papers, 1876, Vol. XLII. In the ten-year period 1872–81, a total of 42,744 adult male agricultural labourers, shepherds, gardeners, carters, etc. emigrated — as compared with a total of 17,523 for this category in the previous ten-year period 1862–71. In the later 1880's, on the other hand, the U.S.A. proved a major attraction for agricultural emigrants — without Union intervention; 1882–91 saw a total of 132,827 agricultural emigrants.

[24] See, for example, *Labourers' Union Chronicle* — 7th November, 1874.

[25] *Labourers' Union Chronicle* — 26th December, 1874.

[26] *Labourers' Union Chronicle* — 5th and 19th September, 1874, for example, and *Midland Free Press* — 29th August, 1874.

[27] 1871 Census of Population. Indifference was perhaps the greatest enemy to agricultural trade union success. For example, the secretary of the Banbury district of the N.A.L.U. noted in January, 1875, that only about one in five of the labourers within his area were Union members. — *Labourers' Union Chronicle* — 9th January, 1875. And in the relatively heavily unionized counties like Warwickshire, Oxfordshire and Norfolk, members of the Union never formed a majority of the agricultural labouring work force. In Warwickshire, in 1874, for example, about one-quarter of the male agricultural labouring work force were union members; in Oxfordshire it was about the same proportion.

[28] *Royal Commission on the Depressed State of Agriculture* — Interview on 4th August,

1881. (Q.58,562). Parliamentary Papers, 1882, Vol. XIV.

[29] *Labourers' Union Chronicle* — 24th April, 1875.

[30] *Royal Leamington Chronicle* — 15th May, 1875.

[31] F White & Co's Directory of Warwickshire (1874).

[32] *Labourers' Union Chronicle* — 17th April, 1875.

[33] *Labourers' Union Chronicle* — 29th May, 1875.

[34] *Labourers' Union Chronicle* — 3rd July 1875.

[35] *Labourers' Union Chronicle* — 14th August, 1875.

[36] *Labourers' Union Chronicle* — 3rd July, 1875.

[37] Mr F J Dore's Report to the Canadian Minister of Agriculture, 1875. Mr. Dore was a London-based emigration agent for the Canadian Government

[38] Quoted in R Russell, op.cit., pp.89–90.

[39] Quoted in R Russell, op.cit., p.91.

[40] For a description of the establishment of the newspaper see H Evan's autobiography — *Radical Fights of Forty Years* (London, n.d.), p.44.

[41] *English Labourer* — 27th November, 1875.

[42] *English Labourer* — 21st August, 1875.

[43] *English Labourer* — 24th July, 1875.

[44] *English Labourer* — 31st July, 1875 and *Leicester Chronicle and Leicester Mercury United* — 31st July, 1875.

[45] *Warrington Advertiser* — 24th July, 1875.

[46] *Labourers' Union Chronicle* — 7th August, 1875.

[47] Joseph Arch, op.cit., pp.252–253.

CHAPTER EIGHT

A widening of horizons: 1875-79

DESPITE THE DIFFICULTIES and disappointments faced in the
months following the unsatisfactory ending of the Eastern
Counties lock-out, most of Joseph's time in the second half of
the 1870's continued to be devoted to Union affairs, and to the
promotion of a cause which he regarded as the 'work of (his) life'.[1]
Nevertheless, alongside this were developing other interests, including not only the old preoccupations with franchise extension
and reform of the land and game laws, but newer issues as well. These
included tentative proposals for Joseph's election to Parliament
under the Liberal Party's banner and his work for the cause of international peace.

Given Joseph's enthusiastic support for the Liberal Party from
early days, and his persistent desire to secure the enfranchisement
of the agricultural labourer, it comes as no surprise to discover that
by the mid-1870's he was giving serious consideration to the idea of
entering Parliament himself as a Liberal M.P. Furthermore, not
only through his Union work but also through his activities in connection with the campaign for electoral reform, he was frequently
brought into close contact with a number of leading Liberal politicans.
In July, 1875, for example, he approached John Bright with regard
to the presentation to Parliament of a franchise petition, signed by
about sixty thousand Union supporters. At the time of their meeting
on 6th July, Bright described Arch, in his diary, as 'a sensible, and I
think, an honest man.'[2] (Bright actually presented the petition to
Parliament on the following day, during the course of a debate on a
franchise extension bill put forward by G. O. Trevelyan. The latter
was to reveal himself a tireless advocate of rural enfranchisement
throughout the 1870's; unfortunately for the labourers, however, all
of his franchise proposals were rejected by the Commons.)

Then, in May of the following year, Arch again acted in close
harmony with a number of leading Liberals in connection with the

organisation of a large-scale franchise demonstration at the Memorial Hall, Farringdon Street, London. Many agricultural workers from various parts of the country attended, but some Liberal M.Ps., including Mundella and Plimsoll, were also present. Numerous petitions and demonstrations were organised along similar lines in the succeeding years; and always they could count upon the support of the 'advanced' wing of the Liberal Party, whose members saw an extension of the vote to the rural householder as a way to 'dish' the traditional Tory rural vote of squire, farmer and parson.

In view of the support which Arch could count on from this section of the Liberal Party and of the personal contacts he was making, it is significant that by 1875 he had become a member of the very large General Council of the National Reform Union. This was a Radical 'ginger' group on the fringes of the Liberal Party, which demanded not only franchise extension, but also (among other things) religious equality, involving 'disestablishment and disendowment of the English and Scotch Established Churches', and a 'thorough Revision of the Land Laws'.[3] At this stage therefore, Joseph was obviously among the 'progressive' Liberals!

However, from 1877, his personal political career began to move along more clearly defined lines. It is, of course, true to say that from quite early on the possibility of his becoming an M.P. had been canvassed. In 1873, for example, there were strong rumours that he might stand as a Liberal candidate for the Woodstock division in Oxfordshire. (As a borough constituency all of its male householders had been enfranchised in 1867; these included many agricultural labourers who lived in villages included within the constituency boundaries.) Some local observers, at least, considered that if Joseph had stood, he would probably have been returned. (See W Wing: *Parliamentary History of the Borough of Woodstock duing the Present Century*. (Pamphlet, 1873). In the event, however, the negotiations came to nothing. But in 1877, prospects seemed to be more hopeful.

In the spring of that year Arch was invited by the working-class electors of the borough of Southwark, in London, to stand as a Working Men's candidate for their division. Their previous candidate, George Odger, a former Secretary of the London Trades Council and an active trade unionist, had died in March, 1877, and a successor had consequently to be selected. Joseph had in fact attended Odger's funeral, along with a number of other labour leaders, and it may have been then that the first contacts were made.[4] Although an urban constituency like Southwark seemed somewhat unsuitable for one with Arch's essentially rural background, he nevertheless treated the request seriously, and at the May, 1877, Council of the N.A.L.U. decided to seek the approval of his Union for the candidature.

To his undoubted chagrin, the response was less than enthusiastic. Although permission was given to him to go ahead if he wished, several of those present expressed reservations — including Mr A Arnold, a member of the Union's Consulting Committee. Furthermore, Arnold did not allow the matter to rest with mere opposition at the Council meeting. On 12th June, he wrote a letter to the *English Labourers' Chronicle* now the organ of the N.A.L.U., repeating his earlier objections:' . . . I . . . am still of opinion that if Mr. Arch was ever to be elected for Parliamentary honours the Union (would) have to pay the piper. My opposition, however, to Mr. Arch's candidature was not based upon this, . . . but rather upon the fact that Mr. Arch's present work is too important to allow of him being taken away to perform those duties upon which I think we are apt to lay too much stress, . . .

'I also maintained that a man should be elected upon the ground of fitness for the work; that Mr. Arch was better fitted for the platform than for a deliberative assembly; and that class representation was a thing against which the advanced Liberals . . . had all along been fighting and would continue to fight. . . .

'My position, therefore, was this — that when labourers get the franchise they will do better to look elsewhere for a Parliamentary representative, and keep Mr Arch upon their own platform to advocate their cause and strengthen their Union . . . '5

Arnold's feelings on the subject may have been quite genuine. But to the detached observer it also seems quite possible that his concern, and that of some of the Union's other middle-class Liberal supporters, was primarily due to a desire to keep the labourers in their political pocket. They had no wish to see Arch or his fellow Union leaders demonstrating their independence by going into politics on their own account.

Another equally vehement opponent of Arch's candidature was Henry Taylor, the former general secretary, who was now engaged in emigration work for the South Australian Government. He was still a member of the Union's Consulting Committee, and on these grounds attended its Annual Council meetings. In the *Labourers' Union Chronicle* of 30th June a letter written by him was published; in view of his old connection with the Union, its contents were possibly more hurtful to Joseph's pride than had been Arnold's comments. Taylor suggested that Joseph would be no good at debating in the House of Commons and that his talents were better exercised outside. The letter then continued: 'Neither is Mr Arch a Worker in politics; he could not endure the worry and strain of close political life . . . ' In view of his formidable efforts in both the trade union field and in the cause of electoral reform, Joseph's feelings on reading that he was not a 'worker in politics' can be imagined!

Whether these critical attacks led to Arch's eventual rejection of the Southwark offer is not known, but what is clear is that the whole proposition did fall through. In his autobiography he himself explains this as follows (although he confuses the date of the Woodstock negotiations and wrongly suggests that these also were in 1877): 'In 1877 I was asked to contest two seats, Southwark and Woodstock, but I refused them both. In the first place, I felt the time was not ripe; and in the second, I was sure that I could do better work outside; also, I thought if I was sent to Parliament then, somebody would be sure to spoil the work already done. The Cause came first with me . . . whatever malicious enemies might say to the contrary. The very idea of my entering Parliament roused the anger and jealousy of several Union officials; . . . they were jealous and they could not bear the thought of my going so far up the ladder and leaving them behind . . . '6

However, this explanation may not be wholly reliable, for in the same section of his book he also claims that he had 'never seriously considered the question of . . . entering the House of Commons until in 1874, Mr W E Forster, in his speech on the Franchise Bill said, 'I should very much like to see Mr Arch in the House of Commons now' '. Forster was of course, a leading member of the Liberal Party and a former Minister, but Arch's statement at this point hardly accords with the evidence available from elsewhere in respect of his interest in the Woodstock constituency in 1873.

About a year after the Southwark offer came another opportunity. On 4th April, 1878, the honorary secretary of the Greenwich Liberal Association wrote to Joseph, asking him whether he would agree to be on a short-list of Liberal candidates for that constituency. This time he refused the invitation straight away, on the grounds of the 'importance of the work in which (he was) engaged among the farm labourers and others in (the) rural districts.'7 Although Joseph was obviously still in the market for 'Parliamentary honours,' he was not prepared to snatch at any chance which came his way, and it was indeed only in 1880 that he did actually agree to contest a seat. As will be seen, he stood in the Liberal interest at Wilton in Wiltshire, at the General Election held in that year.

During these years of the later 1870's, Joseph was addressing meetings not only on behalf of the Union but also for numerous local branches of the Liberal Party. Thus in late January, 1877, for example, he spoke at a series of Party meetings in Lancashire on the subject of franchise extension and on 'Tory misdoings and Tory misgovernings.' About six weeks later he went to Leeds to speak to Kirkstall Liberal Association in much the same vein. It is, however, interesting to note that neither of these trips was financed from N.A.L.U. funds; in the case of the former, a claim for travelling costs of 15/5½d. and lodging expenses of 8/- was disallowed, while as regards the latter, a similar claim for expenses of £1 2s. 8d. was likewise rejected.[8] Nevertheless, Arch was by no means discouraged. Two years later his interest was still equally strong, so that in January, 1879, he spoke at 'the annual tea party and soirée' of the Butterworth Liberal Association, and shortly afterwards, during March and April, addressed Liberal meetings at Bilston, near Wolverhampton, and at Northampton, respectively. Clearly his links with the Liberals were continuing close despite the steady drain away of N.A.L.U. members, and the consequent erosion of Arch's own standing to which this gave rise.

For his part, Joseph was anxious to impress continually upon the Liberals the necessity for electoral reform. He appreciated that the Conservatives were unlikely to displease their farmer and landowner supporters in the country areas by extending the franchise to rural householders, and since they were in power from 1874 to 1880, there was only a faint hope of franchise reform within that period. But by persuading the Liberals of the desirability of electoral reform, and at the same time indicating his strong support for their party, Arch hoped to keep the subject uppermost in the minds of the Party leaders, in readiness for the time when they would be returned to power. As he later wrote: ' . . . all the while I kept the franchise ball rolling, and the franchise petitions going round and up to "The Honourable the House of Commons of Great Britain and Ireland in Parliament assembled".' And in his efforts in this direction he received the whole-hearted support of the labourers: 'A sure sign that the franchise agitation was a genuine and deep-rooted one was the fact that the men sang franchise songs at their meetings; sometimes they would start with a well-known Union one, but just as often in the later years they would sing some political verses as well.' In these demonstrations during the later 1870's, Arch made sure that N.A.L.U. support for the Liberal Party never wavered.[9]

But apart from the tactical value of ensuring that the labourers stood well in the eyes of that Party — and especially in the eyes of the 'advanced' members of it — there is no doubt that Joseph was, in any case, a convinced Radical at heart. In his autobiography he boasted that: 'Some of (his) Warwickshire forbears fought with Cromwell at Edgehill, and in other battles of the Civil War, against tyranny and oppression and for the liberty of the people.'[10] Whether this was true or not, there is no doubt that he did frequently hark back, in his speeches, to the events of the Civil War, and he encouraged other Union members to do the same. For example, the 1875 Annual Council of the N.A.L.U. opened with the singing of 'The Fight for

Freedom.' The opening lines of this ran as follows:

> 'An army fought in years long gone
> While Cromwell led the way;
> In freedom's cause they nobly stood
> While victory crowned the day.'

Similarly, several of the romances serialised in the Union news-paper were concerned to portray Cromwell and his followers as great liberators. One example on these lines was 'From Serfdom to Man-hood' by Howard Evans, which compassed the period from the Civil War to the establishment of the N.A.L.U. in the 1870's.[11] Another story, called 'No Quarter!,' by Captain Mayne Reid was described as a 'Romance in the Parliamentary Wars,' and it ran in the Union news-paper from 31st July, 1880, for the remainder of that year. The Pro-logue to it began: 'There is no page in England's history so bright, nor of which Englishmen have such reason to be proud, as that covering the period between 1640 and 1650 . . .'[12] It is an interesting indication of attitude that this period, which included Parliament's execution of the King, Charles I, should be so described in the Union's own journal.

Nevertheless, perhaps the clearest example of Joseph's interest in the Civil War period was his encouragement of annual demonstrations at the Northamptonshire village of Naseby each 14th June, to celebrate the defeat of the Royalists at the famous battle on 14th June, 1645. The first demonstration was held in 1875, on the occasion of the 230th anniversary. The active help of the local Naseby branch of the Union was secured, and announcements advertising the rally appeared beforehand in the *Labourers' Union Chronicle*. On the date of the first demonstration, Arch and the other N.A.L.U. speakers were collected in a carriage from Market Harborough railway station by Mr Martin, the sympathetic landlord of the Fitzgerald Arms, Naseby. When they arrived in the village at about noon they were 'met by a procession gay with banners and noisy with bands. Blue ribbons and rosettes were to be seen everywhere and in almost everyone's hat or bonnet . . .' With the bands marching before him, Joseph was escorted to the place of assembly, and all present prepared to enjoy themselves on what was for most a precious and rare holiday. During the course of the meeting, petitions were organised calling on Parliament to extend the franchise and to relieve 'the monstrous grievance of the present Game Laws.' 'Tables supplied with pen, ink and paper' were put out in readiness for the signatures to be added to the petitions, but such serious matters as these did not darken the gaiety of the general scene. For most men and women, dressed in their simple finery, it was a time for laughter, dancing and a brief but blessed freedom from the harshness of the daily struggle to earn their bread. Nevertheless, in his speech later in the day, Joseph underlined the importance of the petitions,[13] and the meeting ended with the singing of 'an original song relating to the battle of Naseby!'[14]

Joseph spent the night with Mr Martin at the Fitzgerald Arms, and the next day the landlord showed his friendship still further by driving Arch and some of the local leaders to the nearby village of Guilsborough, where they were to address more meetings. This spending of a night with Union friends was, of course, a common and cheap way of solving the accommodation problem when Joseph was on his tours. But he was not always so fortunate. Although he normally stayed in a village inn — thereby growing to know some of the landlords extremely well[15] — the charges made varied very considerably. Thus, at Blandford in Dorset, during February, 1877, he paid 4s. 10d. per night for lodgings, but at Market Harborough, Leicestershire, during the following April, the charge was only 2s. per night; again, in Newcastle-on-Tyne, where he stayed for several nights during September, 1876, the cost was 2s. 6d. per night. Arch's surviving account book for 1876–77 gives many other examples of these local differences.

The success of the first Naseby demonstration led to similar celebrations being staged in the following years. Arch made a practice of attending each of them. In 1876, for example, the subject of his address was, 'The Battle for Civil and Religious Liberty,' and he was introduced to the audience by Howard Evans, who was also present, as 'Our Cromwell!'[16] Most of the other demonstrations followed this pattern, and it was only after 1880, in the face of a general decline in N.A.L.U. membership, that the practice of holding the special June meetings in Naseby was finally discontinued.

Apart from his interest in the Union and in Radical politics, however, a further important outlet for Joseph's energies in this period was his work for the cause of international peace — and this despite the fact that his eldest son, John, was by now a sergeant in the Royal Welsh Fusiliers.[17] It seems likely that Joseph became involved in this campaign through his friendship for Howard Evans and William Randal Cremer, who were both enthusiastic workers for peace, as well as members of the Union's Consulting Committee. In 1871, following the Franco-Prussian War, Cremer had been the main driving force behind the establishment of the Workmen's Peace Association, a small, largely working-class organisation, which sought to promote international arbitration as an alternative to War.[18]

To further his aims, in 1875, Cremer proposed that the Workmen's Peace Association should hold a Conference in Paris, early in September, at which both English and French working-men would be present. Among those invited to join the British contingent was Joseph

Arch. He and two other N.A.L.U. leaders decided to accept the invitation, and Arch's expenses were paid for entirely by the Peace Association—despite its small 'uncertain annual income of perhaps £500 ... [19] (Arch later complained that some of his 'traducers tried to make the labourers believe that (he) had been spending their money (their 'twopences') for a pleasure trip to Paris.'[20])

The party of three ex-labourers — none of whom could speak a word of French — was escorted by Howard Evans. They all stayed in a small hotel such as 'a French workman on a journey would lodge in, in a working-class neighbourhood' in Paris. Although Joseph was deeply involved in the major deliberations of the Conference, there was time for enjoyment as well. He bought for himself a blue 'smock frock or coat, like the ones French workmen wear' as a souvenir of his visit, and there were the usual misunderstandings over language. On one occasion, an effort to obtain milk for coffee, led instead to 'a plate of pickled onions being served' — to the amusement of all concerned![21]

But despite these light-hearted adventures there was, of course, the serious side of the Conference as well, and Joseph's sincere concern about this is perhaps most clearly revealed by his role, a few months later, in the widespread public agitation over atrocities committed by the Turks in Bulgaria.

Christian Bulgaria was at this time reluctantly still part of the predominantly Moslem, but crumbling, Ottoman Empire; it remained so attached at a period when Pan-slav propaganda, mainly emanating from Russia, was encouraging the 'emerging national consciousness of the Serbs and Bulgarians.'[22]

It was in an atmosphere of mounting resentment and growing nationalism, therefore, that insurrections broke out among the Serbs in July and August, 1875. And, despite vigorous punitive measures taken by the Turks, they could not be stamped out, but flickered dangerously on, their influence spreading elsewhere within the Empire. Then, at the beginning of May, 1876, it was the turn of Bulgarian nationalists to try to follow suit. In fact, their effort proved extremely feeble, but the Turks, 'harassed and exasperated, determined to crush it with exemplary ruthlessness.' Their solution was mass slaughter.

Altogether perhaps 15,000 Bulgarian men, women and children were murdered, and over seventy villages, two hundred schools and ten monasteries destroyed. Reprisals against Christians on this scale were by no means unusual in the Ottoman Empire during the nineteenth century; indeed, in 1860, it has been estimated that 12,000 were massacred in a similar fashion, and towards the end of the century, in 1894, perhaps 120,000 Armenians suffered a similar fate.[23] What marked out the 1876 situation from both its predecessors and its successors, was the effect that it had on public opinion in England.

At this time the Conservative Government, under Disraeli, was following a pro-Turkish policy, designed to maintain the integrity of the Turkish Empire and to avoid giving Russia any excuse for interfering in Turkish affairs. Largely to this end, and to fend off intervention by the other major European powers, in May, 1876, the Prime Minister ordered a squadron, 'shortly afterwards reinforced to a powerful fleet,' to sail to Besika Bay near the Dardanelles. Here, it was welcomed by the Turks as a symbol of British willingness to 'prosecute another Crimean War.'[24]

The timing was unfortunate from the Government's point of view. So far news of the massacre had scarcely begun to filter through to Britain, the press containing only vague rumours up to the end of May. But soon the true facts of the appalling situation began to emerge. To the rigid mid-Victorian conscience it was quickly to appear that the Government's policy of bolstering up the Turks, and even, later on, of attempting to minimise their atrocities, was nothing less than the condoning of murder. If Disraeli had sent the fleet to coerce the Turks into implementing previously promised reforms to ameliorate the condition of the Christian inhabitants of the Empire, then the Bulgarian agitation would never have developed as it did. But it was only too clear that Disraeli intended to follow the traditional pro-Turkish line and that the fleet was sent to help and not hinder the Ottoman cause.

The first 'alarm' about the Bulgarian situation was probably aroused by an article in the *Spectator* of 3rd June, 1876, but reasonably full and reliable accounts became available to the public only with reports which appeared in the *Daily News* from 16th June. Other newspapers followed this lead, and shortly afterwards, on 26th June, W. E. Forster, for the Liberals, in a Parliamentry question asked Disraeli to comment on the atrocity stories. Somewhat unwisely, the Prime Minister gave a flippant reply, and this further offended public opinion.

Soon, more facts were emerging, and the growing general disquiet began to reach fever pitch when J. A. MaGahan, a brilliant young Irish-American newspaperman, was sent out to the scene of the massacres as the special correspondent of the *Daily News*. He arrived in the affected area on 25th July, and in the light of the facts as he discovered them, he set out consciously 'to project his own sense of passionate indignation'. MaGahan's first dispatch appeared in the *Daily News* of 7th August.[25]

For Arch and the agricultural labourers, however, the Bulgarian question had been a matter of deep concern well before this, and MaGahan's dispatches only served to reinforce their opinions. N.A.L. U. supporters were indeed the first members of *any* national organisation to express concern about the situation, at meetings held by Joseph in Suffolk during the first week in July. For the labourers, the so-called 'Eastern Question' was of especial significance because of the potential danger it seemed to offer of leading Britain into a War on behalf of the Turks against Russia, should the latter seek to intervene militarily in the affairs of the Ottoman Empire. And since the British Army was considerably recruited from among the sons of farm workers, they clearly had reason to oppose the outbreak of hostilities. Joseph, in particular, feared the onset of War — and his apprehensions were not entirely without foundation, as Shannon has shown in his study of the Bulgarian crisis of 1876.[26]

To Arch the issue was a simple one. As he told a meeting of about one thousand labourers and their sympathisers at Sudbury, in Suffolk, on 3rd July: 'It would be one of the most disastrous things for the present Government to do to plunge (their) country into war. He said this as a member of the Peace Society, and also as an Englishman and a farm labourer who supported himself, his wife and family during the injudicious Crimean War in which one hundred millions of British money was spent, and 40,000 of England's brave sons died on the field. . . . He urged upon all the necessity of combining, and in respect to the present war, insisting upon the Government pursuing a strict line of policy of non-intervention. What would be the result if we were plunged into deadly conflict? We knew not how expensive it would be, or how many lives would be sacrificed. Should we be in-volved at a cost, perhaps, of twenty millions, in a war for a miserable Empire whose despotism deserved to be crushed either by argument or by the sword? . . .' He then went on to emphasize that: 'When they were called upon to wield political power by their votes they would tell Mr Disraeli that before plunging into war they would have the oppor-tunity of saying whether the sword should be drawn or not, for they would never pay a war indemnity to back up the ambition of war-like and bloody men . . .' His speech was loudly cheered and a resolution was unanimously carried, urging 'Her Majesty's Government to pursue the strict policy of non-intervention.'[27]

Shortly afterwards, a similar meeting was held at Bury St. Ed-munds, when Joseph again pursued this line of argument. It is signifi-cant that at this stage his main protest was against the possible effects of war upon the *English* working man, and not against the atrocities in Bulgaria, as such. However, as the *Daily News* correspondents revealed the true horror of the situation, and as the protest movement got more strongly under way, so Arch's opposition to possible war, on the *moral* grounds of Turkish treatment of Bulgarians, became plainly apparent. The *English Labourer* of 26th August, 1876, for example, included several reports on the atrocities, which were reproduced from the columns of the *Daily News*. A few days later, at the beginning of September, on a visit to the North Oxfordshire village of Souldern (and soon after he had narrowly escaped serious injury in a railway accident[28]), Arch made his views abundantly clear. In a passionate speech he expressed the 'bitterest indignation' at the Bulgarian situation and declared with deep emotion: 'I have read every letter upon it in the *Daily News*, and I have sat in the railway carriages thus engaged until my blood has boiled within me; and I have laid my head on my pillow and thought of those fond mothers and children who have been so cruelly sacrificed. . . . I wish I were in Turkey, I would avenge innocent blood . . .'[29]

Shortly afterwards, on 6th September, at Northend in Warwickshire he returned to this theme. He condemned 'the conduct of the Government in connection with the Turkish atrocities, and (demanded) the immediate re-assembling of Parliament in order that the voice of the country might be heard through its representatives. . . . There is not a labourer in this country who has heard of the atrocities committed by the Turks on helpless women and babes, whose blood must not boil in his veins. Any one who does not sympathise with those victims of rapine and massacre is not a man, but a demon in human form. I have been charged with making our Union the subject of Quixotic enterprises . . . There are in England hundreds of men who call themselves Christians, and who move in what are called upper circles, who are wonderfully surprised at the steps which I and my fellow-workers have taken in this movement of the farm labourers. . . . While we are anxious to keep to the proper text, the social elevation of the rural population, and their political enfranchisement, we shall not allow any farmer, squire, parson, or anybody else to dictate to us what text we shall take, or how we shall preach our sermon. . . .'[30]

It is a tribute to Joseph's deep sympathies for the Bulgarian cause, and his ability to convey these feelings through his speeches, that he was able to make such an issue of an event in a far-away country, of which many of the farm labourers he was addressing can scarcely have heard. Yet, by his graphic language he could bring home to them the misery of people suffering far worse oppression than they had ever experienced themselves. Joseph was anxious to avoid War, because — as he told a meeting of the Peace Association in May — labourers were 'made by the Great Supreme to be of use to their country, and not to be food for powder and mere tools in the hands of wicked and bloody men.'[31] But he was also anxious, on moral grounds, that this country should not appear to give succour and support to a nation who had committed atrocities on the scale which events in Bulgaria revealed. These were his twin beliefs, and it was on these grounds that he was to agitate so persistently, in the months ahead, against Government policy. (The fact that it was a, to him, much disliked Tory administration may, of course, have made his enthusiasm for the cause all the greater!)

By the late summer of 1876, many other people were sharing Joseph's concern. The anti-Turk campaign was growing rapidly in size and strength, and mass meetings were being organised in many parts of the country. Then, on 6th September, the former (and future) Liberal Prime Minister, William Gladstone, who had been watching the course of events with increasing unease, decided to join unequivocally in the protest movement. He issued a pamphlet, condemning Government policy, entitled: 'The Bulgarian Horrors and the Question of the East.' Gladstone wrote the pamphlet in four days 'at white heat,' and when it was published by Murray on 6th September, it became an immediate best-seller. By the end of the month some 200,000 copies had been sold.[32] Gladstone's pamphlet, backed by the statesman's own considerable personal influence, gave a great impetus to the whole protest movement — but it is important to note that Arch had been fully committed to the cause well before that date. Nevertheless, he obviously welcomed the active participation in the campaign of the leader he so greatly admired.

In these circumstances, therefore, between 1st September and 27th December, 1876, memorials and petitions flooded into Lord Derby, the Foreign Secretary, protesting against the atrocities committed by the Turks and the pro-Turkish policy of the Government. Altogether in these months 455 petitions were received, and of these 407 (ninety per cent) were received between 1st September and 9th October! Three only were presented in the name of *national* bodies — and one of those three was from the National Agricultural Labourers' Union.[33] Shannon, in his study of the Bulgarian agitation, notes that, 'no other union except the Cleveland miners so distinguished itself' in the matter of participation in the agitation.[34]

Later on in the same year, Joseph's enthusiasm for the cause found another outlet, when he became one of the conveners of the Eastern Question Conference which was organised at St. James's Hall, London, on 8th December. He also attended the Conference, which was called to coincide with the opening of an abortive international meeting at Constantinople designed to settle the Eastern Question. Although much had been expected from the St. James's Hall deliberations, in fact, in the end the only real development was the establishment of an Eastern Question Association, which was pledged to continue the work 'of keeping the public informed of the true state of the Eastern Question.'[35] Joseph seems to have taken little active part in the Conference's discussions, although his sympathy for the cause certainly remained undimmed — as did that of the Union as a whole. The

N.A.L.U. funds had, indeed, financed Joseph's journey to the St. James's Hall Conference — at a total cost of 16s. 9½d.[36]

Meanwhile, on the international front, the collapse of the Conference at Constantinople was followed, on 24th April, 1877, by a declaration of war on Turkey by Russia, who saw herself as the guardian of the Slav peoples within the Ottoman Empire. Gladstone, for his part, soon made clear his support for Russia in discharging 'single-handed a duty which the European Concert had shirked,' namely the duty of securing reforms in the treatment of Christian subjects living under Turkish domination. He was strongly in favour of pressure being brought to bear on the Turkish Government to initiate reforms, and certainly opposed to any British entry into the war on the side of the Turks.

'The outbreak of the Russo-Turkish war divided public opinion on an issue of foreign policy more acutely than at any period since the French revolution . . .,' writes Sir Philip Magnus, in his biography of Gladstone.[37] And it goes almost without saying that Joseph, the early supporter of non-intervention and the condemner of Turkish actions, did not draw back now. Throughout the long period of dispute and uncertainty which surrounded the Eastern Question, until this sorry problem was temporarily resolved at the international Congress of Berlin in July, 1878, he consistently gave support to a policy of non-intervention. For example, in January, 1878, he and the other members of the Union Executive Committee announced themselves 'unanimously and decidedly opposed to England becoming involved in any war on behalf of Turkey.' At the same time it was announced that arrangements had been made for 'holding thirty-one labourers' meetings in Northamptonshire' during that month, at each of which resolutions were to be submitted 'in favour of strict neutrality.' Twenty-five petitions were, in fact, sent from the Northamptonshire district as a result of these meetings — some going to Lord Derby, who was himself beginning to feel dissatisfied with the Government's Eastern policy.[38]

At about this same time, too, Joseph issued an address to the members of the Union, pointing out the 'lamentable results' which would accrue 'if Lord Beaconsfield should unhappily drag this country into war.' (Disraeli had been created Earl of Beaconsfield in August, 1876). He also warned that, 'if Lord Beaconsfield does precipitate this country into war for such a cause, neither he nor his party will be able to recruit the army to any very great extent from the rural population.' He advised 'every branch of the Union to hold meetings and to adopt a resolution against possible war on behalf of Turkey.'[39] The threat that the Union would try to hamper recruiting campaigns among the agricultural labourers was no isolated one; it was repeated on more then one occasion by Joseph and the other Union leaders, and it is an indication of their serious opposition to Government policy. Whether it would have been effective is, of course, another matter.

However, if Arch remained steadfastly loyal to his early beliefs on this question, public opinion showed fewer signs of such fixity of purpose. By the early part of 1878 a change was becoming apparent. No longer was feeling against the Turks so passionate, and when, early in January, 1878, the Russians heavily defeated the Turks and marched almost to the walls of Constantinople, fears began to be expressed about future Russian intentions within the Ottoman Empire. A storm of anti-Russian sentiment 'swept England south of the Trent.' Gladstone had the windows smashed in his house in Harley Street, because of his known opinions, and Joseph, in his more humble sphere, did not escape unscathed either from the change in public attitudes. At a meeting at Evesham Town Hall, at the end of February, for example, he was refused a hearing by a hostile audience composed very largely of market gardeners and their labourers. When he stood up to speak he was greeted with 'hooting' and cries of 'Russian bear.' The meeting ended in uproar, and as Joseph left, three cheers were given for Lord Beaconsfield.[40]

To Arch, with his strong self-confidence and firm belief in the rectitude of his cause, such outbursts were a matter for contempt — the mere outpourings of ignorant fools. They certainly did not cause him to be deflected from his avowed aims. On 4th May, he presided at an anti-war meeting organised by the Working Men's Peace Association at the Memorial Hall, Farringdon Street, London, and 656 delegates from the N.A.L.U. attended to represent Union rank-and-file support. They came from twenty-nine different counties and their mood was one of enthusiastic endorsement of their leader's pacifist line of argument. Randal Cremer and Howard Evans of the Peace Association joined Arch on the platform, but the latter was the main speaker. In his address to the delegates he praised the 'true patriots like William Ewart Gladstone,' who had so far kept the country from War.[41] In recognition of this loyal support, Gladstone shortly afterwards wrote to Arch, expressing his appreciation of the labourers' support of his policy of opposition to what he termed 'a causeless war' in alliance with Turkey against Russia.

Fortunately for all concerned, this festering Eastern problem was settled — for a time at least — in July, 1878. Lord Beaconsfield himself attended the Congress of Berlin then held to deal with the matter, and by the 13th July a practical compromise agreement had been produced and was ready for signature. Under it some of the territory which had already passed under Russian control was returned to Turkey, but the agreement nevertheless represented an abandonment of the policy of maintaining intact Turkish territorial integrity, and Bulgaria was given a measure of independence. The Ottoman Empire could not therefore, return to its pre-1876 position, and by a seperate Anglo-Turkish convention Great Britain herself received the island of Cyprus.

On 16th July, Disraeli was able to return to England declaring that he had brought 'Peace with Honour.' He was received with great acclaim, and the bitterness of the former Bulgarian agitation was allowed to slip into the realm of forgotten things.

For Joseph, with his passionate anti-Tory views, however, any praise was impossible. At a meeting in the small Warwickshire village of Frankton, at the beginning of August, he not only criticised the outcome of the Berlin Congress, but sourly stated that yellow fever had just broken out in the newly-acquired island of Cyprus, and he 'had no hesitation in saying that before the island became the absolute property of England, 10,000 English lives would be sacrificed. . . .'[42]

Furthermore, as was perhaps typical of his growing vanity in these later years of the 1870's, he was inclined to take a great deal of credit to himself for the peaceful outcome of the Eastern agitation. Towards the end of June, 1878, at a meeting at Stratford-on-Avon, he even went so far as to claim that, 'the Union had saved this country from war . . .' This tendency to over-dramatise his own role was unfortunately becoming increasingly apparent.[43] It was strongly revealed, for example, during his opposition to the brief Zulu War of 1878/79, which was waged by Britain to destroy Zulu military power in South Africa. (In the course of the hostilities a Zulu army of 20,000 destroyed a British force of some 1,200 men on 22nd January, 1879, at Isandhlwana, but the war ended with the final crushing of the power of the Zulu chief, Cetewayo, on 4th July, 1879, at Ulundi.[44])

Joseph's opposition to the Zulu War rested partly upon the pacifist ideals which had formed the basis of his attitude towards the Russo/Turkish dispute, but there was, as well, his deeply rooted suspicion of the Conservative Government and his determination to find fault with it, wherever possible. In a speech at the beginning of July, 1879, at around the time of the successful battle of Ulundi, he declared, 'We do not want a War, and I don't see for a moment why the Zulu campaign should be carried on, or why it was ever commenced . . . I enter my simple protest against the war-waging policy of Her Majesty's Government. I am not going to be badgered from the cause I have in hand, or brought from it. No gold will buy me; no threats will drive me, no misrepresentation will frighten me . . .'[45] Although Joseph's anti-war feeling was undoubtedly sincere — he was to retain his interest in the Workmen's Peace Association, and its successor, the International Arbitration League, at least to the 1890's—

this type of statement was a clear over-valuation of his own importance. It is unlikely that anyone would have wanted to 'buy' his silence on this matter.

It seems indeed unfortunately true that Joseph's conceit and attitude of self-commendation tended to increase in direct proportion to the decline in membership of the Union. It is now time to look again at the fate of that organisation during the late 1870's.

[1] *English Labourer* — 21st August, 1875.

[2] *Diaries of John Bright* — ed. by R A J Walling (London, 1930) — 6th and 7th July, 1875.

[3] See Pamphlet issued by the National Reform Union during 1875; Reform Pamphlets, vol. 4, 1875–86, Howell Collection, Bishopsgate Institute, London.

[4] *English Labourer* — 17th March, 1877.

[5] *English Labourers' Chronicle* — 23rd June, 1877.

[6] Joseph Arch, op.cit., pp.271 and 272.

[7] *English Labourer* — 13th April, 1878.

[8] Joseph Arch's account book/diary for 1876–77 at Museum of English Rural Life, University of Reading; entries for weeks 23rd January and also 12th March, 1877 and *English Labourer* — 10th Februrary and 24th March, 1877.

[9] Joseph Arch, op.cit., p.272.

[10] Joseph Arch, op.cit., pp.3–4.

[11] Howard Evans — *From Serfdom to Manhood*. (This was later published as a pamphlet by Vincent at Leamington, in 1874.)

[12] *English Labourers' Chronicle* — 31st July, 1880.

[13] P L R Horn — 'Nineteenth Century Naseby Farm Workers' in *Northamptonshire Past and Present*, Vol. IV, No. 3, (1968/69), pp.168–171 and *English Labourer* — 26th June, 1875.

[14] *Midland Free Press* — 19th June, 1875.

[15] See Sir Richard Winfrey, M.P. — 'Some Reminiscences of Joseph Arch' in *The Land Worker* — 18th September, 1919. On a few occasions Joseph might stop with distant relatives. The son of Mr Charles Moore of Gough Road, Edgbaston, Birmingham, recalls that his father remembered as a child Arch stopping at that address when he was speaking at meetings in the Birmingham area. The Moores were distant relatives. — Information kindly given to the author by Mr Moore.

[16] *English Labourer* — 24th June, 1876.

[17] As a matter of interest John Arch only once served outside the British Isles during the whole of his Army career — in West Africa, from November, 1873, to March, 1874 — Papers of John Arch, Public Record Office, W.O.97/2207.

[18] Cremer was born at Fareham in Hampshire on 18th March, 1828. His father deserted the family while Cremer was still an infant and his mother kept a small dame school in order to support her family. Cremer was a Radical politician and a supporter of trade unionism; he was later knighted for his services to peace. In 1903, he was awarded the Nobel Peace Prize. For an account of his life see — *Sir Randal Cremer — His Life and Work* by Howard Evans (London, 1909).

[19] Howard Evans, op.cit., p.84.

[20] *English Labourers' Chronicle* — 7th Februrary, 1880.

[21] *English Labourers' Chronicle* — 18th September, 1875.

[22] R T Shannon — *Gladstone and the Bulgarian Agitation — 1876* (London, 1963), p.17

[23] R T Shannon, op.cit., p.22.

[24] Ibid., pp.17–21 for full details of the diplomatic background to this action by Disraeli.

[25] R T Shannon, op.cit., p.54.

[26] R T Shannon, op.cit., p.21. He notes that the Turks welcomed the British fleet as 'a symbol of British willingness to prosecute another Crimean War. This, as later events indicated, Disraeli would have been quite willing to do had he thought it necessary; but his aim was to avoid a 'drift' to war in the alleged Crimean manner by an unmistakable show of firmness.' During February and March, 1878, similarly, there again seemed a danger of Anglo-Russian War over the Eastern Question — *Disraeli* — Robert Blake (London, 1966), p.639.

[27] *English Labourer* — 15th July, 1876 and *Daily News* — 7th July, 1876.

[28] *Midland Free Press* — 2nd September, 1876. Arch's train had collided with another passenger train near Stafford. He had 'sustained a severe blow on the neck and head', but nothing worse.

[29] *English Labourer* — 9th September, 1876.

[30] *English Labourer* — 16th September, 1876.

[31] *English Labourer* — 3rd June, 1876.

[32] Sir P Mangus — *Gladstone* (London, 1954), p.242.

[33] R T Shannon, op.cit., p.148.

[34] Ibid., p.233.

[35] Ibid., p.261 and *English Labourer* — 16th December, 1876.

[36] Joseph Arch's account book/diary for 1876–77.

[37] Sir P Magnus, p.246.

[38] Lord Derby in fact resigned from the Conservative Government over the Eastern question at the end of March, 1878. Shortly afterwards, just before the election of 1880, he also resigned from the Conservative party and joined the Liberals — R Blake, op.cit., pp.640–641.

[39] *English Labourers' Chronicle* — 12th January, 1878.

[40] *English Labourers' Chronicle* — 2nd March, 1878.

[41] *English Labourers' Chronicle* — 11th May, 1878 and also Howard Evans, op.cit., pp.100–102.

[42] *English Labourers' Chronicle* — 17th August, 1878.

[43] *English Labourers' Chronicle* — 6th July, 1878.

[44] R Blake, op.cit., p.672.

[45] *English Labourers' Chronicle* — 19th July, 1879.

CHAPTER NINE

Union Affairs: 1875-79

'But if we were singing Union and franchise songs at our meetings we were singing tunes of a different sort as well, and they were not songs to be proud of. Why, some of our conferences and meetings might just have come out of the Tower of Babel, there was such a confusion of tongues; officials trying to cry one another down, and trying to push one another out, and struggling to get the upper hand, beset us on every side and gave the enemy cause to rejoice.' — Joseph Arch — *The Story of His Life Told by Himself* (1898), p. 274.

ALTHOUGH the rival National Farm Labourers' Union, which had been established by J. E. Matthew Vincent in 1875, proved no very formidable opponent to the N.A.L.U., its gradual disappearance certainly did not end the problems afflicting the old Union.[1] Nevertheless, *some* easing of the situation did occur when at the end of March, 1877, it was announced that the *Labourers' Chronicle* (the organ of the National Farm Labourers' Union) and the *Leamington Chronicle* were to be sold by Vincent — ostensibly because of his ill-health. However, there is no doubt that the former newspaper at least was losing money quite heavily. Joseph and the other members of the Executive Committee of the N.A.L.U. were immediately concerned to acquire the *Labourers' Chronicle*, and although negotiations were carried on in a rather circuitous manner, the deal eventually went through.[2]

At about the same time, the Union also decided to purchase their own paper, the *English Labourer*, from its sponsors — for the sum of £1,500 (a figure which the Union Treasurer, the Rev. F. S. Attenborough, later criticised as excessive). The decision to purchase the latter newspaper was taken entirely as a result of pressure from the N.A.L.U. leaders. As Howard Evans, one of the newspaper's founders, later recalled, he had 'urged in vain that the Union could never make it pay, but, as Arch insisted, there was no alternative but to let the Union buy us out. My forecast proved correct. The Union lost money over the paper, which helped to drag it down.'[3]

The formal amalgamation of these two newspapers became effective from 7th April, 1877, and a new paper, entitled the *English Labourers' Chronicle*, was issued in their stead. Nevertheless, this merger, although removing from the scene one persistent press critic of the N.A.L.U. and its policies, did not stem the continuing outflow of Union members, as Joseph saw with growing anxiety.

In these circumstances of declining support, he and the other leaders vigorously pursued a variety of schemes designed to turn the tide and to lure members back to their old allegiance. One of the methods adopted was the establishment of a national Sick Benefit Society, to supplement the numerous independent local friendly societies, which already provided widows' pensions, funeral payments, etc. for small groups of members.

As early as 1872, Joseph had declared, in a discussion on the proposed establishment of such a benefit society, that there was 'a strong feeling that Warwickshire . . . should initiate this Sick and Benevolent Society . . .'4 In fact, however, although the matter was raised at the 1873 Annual Council of the Union, and periodically thereafter, nothing effective was done on a national basis — even though some individual districts boldly established their own friendly societies (many of them extremely unstable, from a financial point of view).5

Despite Arch's early interest in the idea, therefore, it seems that by the mid-1870's he had become rather lukewarm, seeing the pitfalls into which many similar societies had already fallen. Nevertheless, he appears to have raised no formal objection to the decision to introduce an N.A.L.U. benefit scheme during 1877 — in spite of a statement made later in his autobiography that he 'had always been against it.' There is little doubt that the venture was embarked upon in an effort to attract new members to the Union — or to retain existing ones — and on these grounds alone Joseph was probably prepared to give it a trial. At the annual meeting of the Oxford district of the Union in March, 1877, indeed, he 'introduced the National Sick Benefit Society, and . . . stated that the Executive Committee was determined to form a society that would be worthy of the support of the labourer . . .'6

Unfortunately, this promise was not borne out by the facts. The benefit society was based on no firm actuarial principles and in the early days members were admitted on a haphazard basis, up to the age of sixty. No proper checks seem to have been made as to their health at the time of entry, and as Joseph had perhaps feared, many of the older, or more infirm, men seized their opportunity to join. It was, of course, this type of member who was most likely to prove a drain on the society's funds. As Arch later wrote: 'So it came about that for almost every ten shillings paid in, twenty shillings had to be paid out. Then the neglect of enforcing a proper entrance fee, the amount of which should have been regulated by the age of the applicant, deprived the fund of considerable sums. The basis of the fund was false hopes, and so it was bound to collapse; but, unfortunately, it helped greatly to kill the Union, too.'[7] Sick benefit expenditure rose from £496 11s. 5d in 1878 to £2,434 1s. 10d. by 1880 — and the trend was upwards thereafter.

In addition to the instability of the scheme, however, there was the failure of the Union administrators to keep the sickness funds separate from the trade ones, which were designed to provide for dispute pay, etc. Towards the end of the 1880's this weakness, too, was to lead to considerable dissension within the Union ranks. And if it had been hoped that the establishment of a friendly society would tie members more firmly to the Union, then these hopes were doomed to disappointment. Membership, which had fallen to 40,000 at the end of 1875 and had then briefly picked up to 55,000 at the end of 1876, continued to show a downward movement from that date onwards which it seemed impossible to reverse. By the end of 1879 N.A.L.U. membership had slumped to a mere 20,000 — or less than one-quarter of the 1874 peak.

In these circumstances, and in the face of Joseph's ever stronger efforts to mould the Union to *his* will alone, the murmurings of discontent grew. As the figures indicate, desertions from the ranks grew apace, and the women, who had once been his staunchest supporters, now became among his most determined critics. In some villages they discouraged their menfolk from joining — or rejoining — the Union, as for example in the North Oxfordshire villages of Chilson and Cropredy, where the district secretary castigated them bitterly as 'men rulers.'[8] Other wives, only too keenly aware that the Union was now too weak to influence wage rates, deterred their husbands from contributing precious pennies to the cause by asking, 'why (they) wanted to keep ol' Joey Arch a gennelman.'[9] This hardening of opinion certainly formed a very great contrast to their attitude only a few years earlier, when many wives had clubbed together to buy Joseph presents, as a mark of their gratitude. In March, 1877, the 'women of Greatworth' in Northamptonshire had bought him 'a writing desk and inkstand,' for example, and a few weeks later the wives of members in the nearby small town of Brackley had presented him with a 'handsome tea-pot and butter cooler.'[10] By the end of the decade their faith in his powers had been lost, and resentment at his failure to achieve more permanent improvements began to take the place of any friendlier feelings.

Arch himself was only too painfully aware of the growing complaints that he was looking after his own interests to the detriment of those of the members. As early as September, 1876, he had told a labourers' meeting at Souldern, in North Oxfordshire, that some of the men were 'drivelling it about, "Arch has run away with the money". . . . I can leave the Union tomorrow and make £600 a year. I don't want your paltry twopences. If it were not for the nobility of the cause, and the good men who are allied with it, I would not stand your humbug.'[11]

Again, nearly two years later, in August, 1878, at the small village of Frankton in Warwickshire, he pointed out that 'critics . . . had twitted the Union with the money that he (Mr. Arch) had spent for the Union. But during the last twelve months he had travelled through thirty counties and reckoning his salary and all in, the enormous amount received and spent by him reached £256 2s. 6d. This he contrasted with the expenses of royalty, and more especially with the trip of the Prince of Wales to India . . . He would not stoop to any class of people, and if the Union could not afford to pay him his salary, he would be happy to resign . . .' He also noted that Parliament had approved the granting of £10,000 per annum to one of the Queen's sons, Arthur, Duke of Connaught, 'and this the country was giving to a man who had never done a tithe for the people of England what he, Joseph Arch, had done . . .'[12]

This comparison of himself with royalty was, of course, a symptom of the growing self-importance which irritated so many of his friends. Then, about six months later, at a meeting at Wellesbourne, he defended his record yet again in a similar vein, and concluded defiantly: 'If you think my salary is too high, it is in your own hands, . . . nor is it a question with me how much I can get, but the question is, "Can I live and maintain my family, and travel through the country, and expose my constitution and health for the wage. . . . I tell you candidly that whether I am a despot or Napoleonic, I will neither stand humbug from officers nor men.".' His long speech was loudly cheered on that occasion, and the audience sang the old Union song, 'When Arch beneath the Wellesbourne Tree,' before he left. But other critics were less easily satisfied, and it is significant that at the Annual Council of the Union held at the end of May in that year (1879), his salary was reduced from £3 per week to £2 10s., in accordance with general economies made to cut down overall expenditure within the Union. (And even this sum must have seemed a fortune to many labourers who were struggling to bring up a family on perhaps 13s. or 14s. per week — out of which 1s. or 2s. had to be found for the rent of an often cramped and insanitary cottage.)

Nevertheless, Joseph, too, had reason to be dissatisfied. Although lack of Union records makes absolute statements on the financial position difficult, such evidence as has survived indicates that he *did* behave honestly in the matter of his expenses. His travelling and expense accounts for a good part of the years 1876 and 1877 have survived, and these indicate that the extensive travelling he did was responsible for most of the seemingly considerable outlay. In fact, during the twelve months from Monday, 15th May, 1876 to 12th May, 1877, his travelling and other expenses together amounted to £98 5s. 11½d., while his wages over the same period were £156 — at £3 per week. Of course, weekly expenditure varied a good deal according to the programme undertaken; for example, during the week beginning 19th March, 1877, it amounted to £1 2s. 8d. — made up of 9s. 6d. travelling expenses and 13s. 2d. for refreshments, lodgings, etc. During the week beginning 23rd April of the same year, on the other hand, the outlay was £2 12s. 10½d. — of which £1 17s. 5½d. was expended in travelling and 15s. 5d. on accommodation, etc. As regards the latter, it is also clear that he normally stayed in the cheapest boarding houses or inns, and if possible, stayed with friends, at no cost to the Union at all. Travelling expenses, too, were kept to a minimum — the help of supporters again being used wherever possible, and it is significant that, when in London, Arch seems to have travelled on the Metropolitan railway only — never in a hackney carriage.

On the evidence of this one surviving account book, therefore, it would seem that Arch was normally very careful with Union funds — hence his natural indignation when charged with peculation. His travelling expenses also indicate the arduous nature of his work. Thus during January, 1877, alone he visited Peterborough, Cambridgeshire, Rugby, London, Red Hill in Surrey, Wiltshire, Dorset, Hampshire and Manchester. In February the same progress is apparent, with visits to Essex, London, Dorset, Worcestershire and Suffolk, in addition to purely local trips to Birmingham and some of the Warwickshire villages. These months are by no means exceptional and they indicate the essentially busy life which Joseph was leading throughout the later 1870's. Indeed, it could be argued that he travelled too much— for several of his journeys seem to have involved covering rather similar ground and with only a brief interval between visits. This policy inevitably added to Union outgoings, even if it did have the undoubted advantage of stimulating local interest in the N.A.L.U. and its work.[13]

Whatever the merits of the case may be, however, there is no doubt that Arch's critics were becoming increasingly vociferous in their opposition to his way of conducting business. At last, at the end of October, 1878, the first real breach came, when the West Dereham district (in Norfolk) decided to break away from the parent organisation. The local leader here was a Methodist lay preacher named George Rix; although Rix was now employed as a shopkeeper, he had earlier been a farm worker and it was generally appreciated that he was a very 'zealous worker in the (Union) cause.'[14]

With his defection, others began to consider following suit.

One of the main points at issue was the fact that under the existing Rules of the N.A.L.U. the various district organisations had to remit three-quarters of their annual income to the Central Office in Leamington, and could retain only one-quarter, i.e. ½d. per member per week, for the management of their own local affairs. Many of the district officers became resentful of this, especially when they saw their money being spent on 'heavy' office expenses, and what they considered were excessive salaries for Arch and the general secretary, Robert Collier. Several of these local leaders, including Thomas Bayliss, secretary to the Oxford District of the Union, were anxious to secure greater district independence — in other words, they were pressing for a federal system of organisation, which would give them a greater say in the running of their affairs — and would give Joseph a much smaller one. The general dissatisfaction was, of course, further exacerbated by the financial difficulties which existed in all parts of the Union, and during the later months of 1878 a special sub-committee was appointed to consider ways of reducing expenditure. Joseph played a leading role in its deliberations.

Finally, at the end of December in that year, the divisions had reached such a point that Arch realised that the time had come for the whole matter to be brought out into the open. In a letter published in the *English Labourers' Chronicle* of 28th December, he announced that a Special Council was to meet in London on 21st January, 1879, to discuss the future of the Union.

Among the possible economies which had been suggested by the sub-committee, with Arch's approval, was the proposal that the large and expensive Annual Council of the Union should be ended, and that it should be replaced by a Council of fifteen elected members who would meet annually. The abolition of the annual district meetings, the placing of an upper limit of £8 on the total annual expenses to be incurred by the districts for the use of an office (including rent, taxes, lighting and fire), and the reduction in the number of delegates employed by the Union for propaganda purposes to three, were other suggestions put forward. Naturally, as some of them adversely affected the position of the district secretaries, it was they who gave the most determined opposition.

When the London Council meeting opened in January it was soon clear that it was to be a very stormy affair. Mr A. Arnold, one of the early members of the Consulting Committee and a critic of Arch's Parliamentary ambitions, bluntly declared that Joseph had lost the support of the labourers — a view with which Henry Taylor, the former general secretary and still a member of the Consulting Committee, concurred. Bayliss, the Oxford district secretary, and Clarke, secretary of the Bucks. and Northants. district, both demanded a loosening of the ties with Leamington, and the adoption of a federal constitution. Their motion to this end was lost by 19 votes to 35, but despite its rejection it is clear that feelings within the Union were running high — and by no means all of the delegates were in sympathy with Arch and his policies. Long and disjointed discussions followed and the meeting broke up in confusion.

At this point Joseph decided to secure his own position by a direct appeal to the rank and file membership. As he later declared: 'I was determined that if I was to go, I should be dismissed in an open above-board manner; but that was just what my enemies did not want. They tried to hustle me off the Union platform, they tried to push me out of the President's chair. All I can say is, they did not know Joseph Arch when they tried that game.'[16] They did not, indeed.

Without referring to any other members of the Executive Committee, Arch prepared a questionnaire and sent it out to all of the branches, asking them to signify their support for him. In a letter which accompanied the questionnaire he wrote: 'You are being befooled and betrayed, and I cannot longer be silent. . . . I protest against the employment of so many paid officers, legislating for themselves rather than for you, preventing free speech, and thrusting aside your votes . . .I protest against the attempt thus being made to break up the National Union, . . .and to establish a number of weak and pettifogging local societies in its place. . . . In the Council, Mr Arnold of Birmingham publicly stated that I no longer possessed your confidence. I protest against this assertion unless it is supported by evidence . . .

'Weary of strife, extravagance, and abuses, I today raise a flag on which I have written 'Peace, Retrenchment and Reform' . . . I leave the issue entirely in your hands. May God defend the right'! There is little doubt that Joseph saw himself as 'the right.'

The questionnaire itself consisted of five questions asking the members if they had confidence in Arch as leader, if they wished the Union to remain a centralized national organisation and if they were satisfied 'with the present shameful expenditure.' Recipients were instructed: 'Resist intimidation; answer these questions yourselves; answer them honestly. Answer them at once'.[17]

But if Joseph himself felt that desperate circumstances justified desperate measures, other sympathisers with the movement viewed this attack on his colleagues in rather a different light — as another example of his pig-headed determination to have his own way at whatever cost. In practice, of course, it is clear that he was right, and they were wrong; that in the long run, the establishment of a Federal Union, consisting of a large number of weak constituent societies must quickly have led to the collapse of the entire Union movement. Nevertheless, emotions ran very high. Alfred Arnold, Howard Evans, Jesse Collings and J. S. Wright — all early supporters of the Union and members of the Consulting Committee — formally severed their connection with the movement at this point. (Later Collings and Evans agreed to speak at Union meetings, however, and Evans, for a time in the early 1880's, wrote a column in the Union newspaper.) Collings and Wright, who had been acting as Union trustees, along with Joseph, were replaced in that office by George Ball, a Lincolnshire-born Union official and ex-labourer, and George Mitchell, a London marble merchant who had been a strong supporter of the N.A.L.U. in his native Somerset. A few months later, on 26th May, just before the normal Annual Council meeting was due to be held, Henry Taylor, too, sent in a letter of resignation from the Consulting Committee. In this he bitterly wrote: 'The N.A.L.U. is now impotent; and wracked as it is by internal discord promoted by the ambition, jealousy and tyranny of the President, assisted by a few of his creatures, it can no longer exist for any good purposes . . .'[18] This was Taylor's final break with the Union he had earlier done so much to create.[19]

Meanwhile, Joseph's policy of appealing direct to the members was paying off, from his point of view. Those who still stuck to the Union were strongly loyal to him, despite what his other critics might say. It was claimed that about 23,000 of them actually sent in replies, supporting him and the stand he had taken against his opponents. Although the exact number may be exaggerated — it will be remembered that by the end of the year a *total* membership figure of 20,000 was reported — nevertheless it is clear that for the vast majority of unionists, Joseph remained their rightful leader. In addition, seventy-seven letters were published in the *English Labourers' Chronicle* of 19th and 26th February from the secretaries of different named branches within the movement, repeating their loyal support. A typical example is one written to Arch by H. Jaggard, secretary of the Starton branch in Suffolk, and dated 7th February:

'Sir, I honour the manly and dignified course you have taken; I think it most ridiculous to think of establishing a number of local societies in the place of the N.A.L.U. I am glad of the course you have taken; you have the good wishes of all my members. It is all Mr Arch here'.[20] The seventy-six other branch letters which were published were written in a similar vein.

Of course, not all members *were* satisfied and in May, 1879 Bayliss and Clarke led a breakaway movement based on their own districts. As Joseph had guessed, however, it proved both unsuccessful and extremely short-lived.[21]

Yet, quite apart from the damage which attack and counter-attack had done to Arch's own status and to that of the whole union movement, the gradual re-establishment of unity within the surviving remnants of the N.A.L.U. was not achieved without loss. Loyal friends, like Collings and Howard Evans, were alienated, many of the most independent-minded and able members had been driven away, and although Joseph was in supreme control again, the Union had become very much 'Mr Arch's Poodle.'

Nevertheless, under these conditions, the much-needed reductions in administrative expenditure were forced through at the Annual Council of the Union held at the end of May, 1879.

In accordance with this economy drive, from 1879 onwards no further district meetings were held, and the Annual Council became a very small affair — easily dominated by Arch. Under pressure from him, too, new rules were approved, which made it essential for any branch to secure the permission of the Central Executive Committee in Leamington before going on strike, either to obtain a wage increase or to oppose a reduction in wages. As Arch declared in his speech on this subject to the Council,' . . . it was absolutely necessary in the interests of the men themselves and the Union to put a stop to a loose system of strikes. There was no fund in the world that could stand a perpetual drain, and it would be much better to poll the whole Union than to let things go on as they had done in the past.'

There is no doubt that his anxieties were justified; economies *were* necessary. According to returns submitted to the Registrar of Friendly Societies, during 1878 the annual income of the N.A.L.U. had amounted to £11,226 0s. 3d. — and the yearly expenditure to £11,536 19s. 10½d. Of this latter figure, £5,364 9s. 1½d. were spent on 'working and other expenses.' In 1877 the deficit had been even larger — over £2,000 — and the favourable balances built up in earlier and happier years were thus being inexorably eroded. After Arch's 1879 purge of the organisation, however, some improvement became apparent. Although income in that year had fallen to £9,331 16s. 2d., expenditure had fallen as well, to £8,936 14s. 11d., and 'working and other expenses' were a mere £3,021 12s. 10d. of this. (See Appendix 2 for further details of the N.A.L.U.'s financial position).

Joseph had, therefore, got his way. The sturdy bearded figure was once more the undisputed monarch — even if of a much restricted Union domain. Furthermore, his old self-confidence was apparently still largely unimpaired. As he told a village meeting of labourers at Hanslope in Buckinghamshire on 7th August, 1879: 'Gentlemen, I have given you the National Labourers' Union. It is destined to accomplish great things unless you listen to misrepresentations without ferreting them out. . . .But, gentlemen, so long as I stand at the head of your Union, to neither prince, nor officer, nor agricultural labourer will I bow my neck in subserviency and humiliation. While I do my duty, I will stand on my own vantage ground, and when that will not carry me I will retire from the front and die in obscurity.'[22] In the event, both death and obscurity were to prove a long way off, and even the Union, apparently so frail, was to survive for about seventeen more years.

As Arch later acknowledged, on the Union front in these years 'Peace, retrenchment, and reform,' became the order of the day, and 'in spite of foes from within and without,' he was well able to keep his position in 'the van of (the) Union army . . .'[23] It is perhaps indicative of the spirit of the men who remained members of the N.A.L.U. at this time that one of their favourite songs began:

> 'All hands to the rescue, our Union's in danger,
> By sham friends in our ranks, which we plainly can see;
> So swelled with ambition, their togs it won't fit 'em,
> They vainly would climb to the top of the tree'.

Significantly, the last two lines of the song ran:

> 'With Arch, for our leader we never can mend him,
> Let all that would spurn him from us ever flee'.

It was on this core of loyalty that he depended. The labourers knew that, despite all his faults, Joseph was one of 'them'; he was of their stock and could understand their small daily concerns — the difficulties they had in making ends meet; the petty restrictions often imposed on their activities by the well-to-do members of the village community; and the persistent concern with the seasons and with the state of the crops. He, too, had known what it was anxiously to till a small garden or allotment in order to raise carrots, beans, potatoes and other vegetables to supplement a meagre family diet, and he, like them, had known hunger and distress in the bad years. This was the intimate bond of fellowship he had with all agricultural labourers and which his middle-class and urban sympathisers could never hope either to possess or to supplant.

---

[1] The National Farm Labourers' Union and its associated Land Company were finally wound up on 19th July, 1881, although as early as September, 1880, it had been discovered that the Land Company could no longer carry on its business: 'Finding that the liabilities exceeded the assets, the managers have stopped the concern', as the notice read in the *Oxford Chronicle* of 18th September, 1880. Vincent himself had withdrawn his support as early as 1877, and had emigrated to Australia, while in September, 1879, it had been recognised that the trade union side of the organisation had 'become virtually obsolete'. — See Records of National Farm Labourers' Union Co-operative Land Ltd. — B.T./31/2240 — Public Record Office. (Vincent eventually returned to England

and died in London just before the First World War — *Leamington Chronicle* — 20th March, 1919.)

2 The *Labourers' Chronicle* was first sold to Messrs. Curtis and Beamish, a firm of Coventry printers, and it was they who sold it to the N.A.L.U. Presumably this indirect approach was adopted to save the face of the two warring Union parties and to prevent contact between them. The N.A.L.U. paid £850 to acquire the *Labourers' Chronicle*.

3 Howard Evans — *The Radical Fights of Forty Years* (London, n.d.), p.44.

4 *Royal Leamington Chronicle* — 28th December, 1872.

5 See P L R Horn — op.cit. (Leicester University thesis, 1968), pp.175–179.

6 *English Labourer* — 31st March, 1877.

7 Joseph Arch, op.cit., pp.381–2.

8 *English Labourers' Chronicle* — 20th March, 1880.

9 C. Holdenby — *Folk of the Furrow* (London, 1913), p.152.

10 *Northampton Mercury* — 24th March and 28th April, 1877.

11 *English Labourer* — 9th September, 1876.

12 *English Labourers' Chronicle* — 17th August, 1878.

13 See Joseph Arch's account book/diary for 1876–77 at Museum of English Rural Life University of Reading.

14 *The Memoirs of Josiah Sage* (London, 1951), p.59 and R Groves, op.cit., p.64.

15 *English Labourers' Chronicle* — 1st Februrary, 1879.

16 Joseph Arch, op.cit., p.286.

17 *English Labourers' Chronicle* — 1st Februrary, 1879.

18 *English Labourers' Chronicle* — 7th June, 1879.

19 Taylor continued to work as an emigration agent for the South Australian Government until about 1881, when his services were dispensed with. He at once emigrated to South Australia, and after trying his hand in an agricultural implements business at Clare, he sold out and became the proprietor of the Sturt Hotel, Adelaide. He eventually died in Adelaide in November, 1919, at the age of 74. His obituary noted that: 'He assisted to form the Anti-Poverty League in Adelaide many years ago . . . He was a loyal supporter of single tax principles right up to the time of his death.' The reference to 'single tax principles' related to the ideas put forward by the American, Henry George, in his book *Progress and Poverty;* this envisaged the levying of one tax only — a tax on land, designed to deprive landowners of the revenue from their holdings. — Information on Henry Taylor kindly provided by the Agent General and Trade Commissioner for South Australia and George E. Loyau — *The Representative Men of South Australia* (Adelaide, 1883), pp.242–244.

20 *English Labourers' Chronicle* — 26th Februrary, 1879.

21 P L R Horn, op.cit., pp.127–132.

22 *English Labourers' Chronicle* — 16th August, 1879.

23 Joseph Arch, op.cit., p.299.

PART FOUR
1880-1919

CHAPTER TEN

Joseph Arch; M.P.; 1880-85

'Arch spent his whole Life pleading the Worker's cause. It was he got the Franchise for the Worker . . .' — The view of an old Norfolk poacher written many years after the vote was given to rural householders in 1884. (See ed. Lilias Rider Haggard — *I Walked by Night* by 'The King of the Norfolk Poachers' (1935), p. 100.)

POLITICAL MATTERS had absorbed a fair proportion of Arch's time during the late 1870's, both in connection with his work for the Liberal Party and for the cause of international peace. However, with the commencement of a fresh decade they took on a new and even greater significance — not only for him but also for the labourers generally. By the end of 1885 two of Joseph's main political ambitions had been achieved. He himself had been elected to Parliament — the first farm worker ever to obtain that honour — and, after years of striving, the vote had at last been given to all male householders living in the rural areas (including farm labourers).

Joseph's renewed efforts to enter Parliament came right at the beginning of 1880. Early in January of that year he was invited by the secretary of the Salisbury district of the N.A.L.U., a Mr Smee, to address a meeting of unionist labourers at Wilton Temperance Hall, in Wiltshire. During the course of a long speech, he began to put out feelers concerning his own political career. He referred to the depressed state of agriculture, which he blamed partly on the present 'miserable land laws', and then went on to observe that, 'at the general election, now not far off, this constituency would be called upon to elect a man to represent it. Equal security for farmers in their holdings and the labourers in their cottages should be demanded. . . . He had been given to understand that at the last election in Wilton his name was a good deal talked about. They lived in an age of surprises, and had been accustomed to them for the last seven years, so that at the next election for Wilton they must not be surprised if he came to talk to them.'[1] In this almost casual fashion, therefore, he tossed his cap into the electoral ring.

The largely agricultural constituency of Wilton was at that time represented by the Hon. Sidney Herbert, younger brother of the Earl of Pembroke, within whose estate much of the constituency lay. Herbert had been put forward as an 'Independent' candidate at a bye-election held in 1877, following the resignation of the sitting Liberal member, Sir Edward Antrobus. However, the Wilton Liberal Party, feeling a 'good deal of uncertainty as to Mr. Herbert's politics'. and unhappy as to the sincerity of his 'Independent' label, had decided to contest the seat. A Mr. Norris of Bristol had been put forward as their candidate on that occasion, but he had been defeated, and the Hon. Sidney had become the new M.P.

Once in Parliament, Herbert had realised the Liberal's worst fears, voting with the Conservatives on virtually every issue — including such matters as the retention of flogging in the Army. This latter point was one upon which Arch felt particularly keenly, perhaps because his own eldest son was a soldier. In any event, in July, 1879, he had led a deputation to wait on Members of Parliament who had shown their dislike of this extreme form of military discipline, and had demonstrated his support for their point of view.[2] Many of his speeches also contained outright condemnation of the system and under his influence a number of petitions opposing the use of the 'cat' were sent to Parliament from various Union branches.[3] Since the Army, as we have seen, relied considerably on the rural areas for recruitment, the issue was one in which Joseph could expect to receive the support of many of his followers, and it soon became a plank in his political platform at Wilton — as elsewhere.

For those anxious to secure Arch's return to Parliament, therefore, the Wilton constituency seemed a reasonable choice. Despite the influence which the Earl of Pembroke could naturally be expected to exert on behalf of his younger brother, it was noted that only about 250 of the 1,401 electorate actually lived in Wilton itself, 'and the rest lived in nearby villages and hamlets'. A majority of these would, of course, be agricultural labourers, who as residents of a borough constituency, had been enfranchised by the 1867 Reform Act. The main aim of the N.A.L.U. and the local Liberals was to secure their support for Joseph's cause.

During February, 1880, there were frequent rumours abroad that Arch *was* to contest the Wilton seat at the next general election, but no hard facts emerged until the middle of March. The formal announcement which was then published followed several weeks of detailed negotiation between Arch and the local Liberals, who had eventually agreed to defray the expenses of the contest so that 'not one penny

...would come out of the pockets of the agricultural labourers'.[4] As might be expected, the local Committee which had decided to press Joseph's candidature was composed primarily of 'working men', although there were also 'a few of the Liberal tradesfolk'.[5]

Arch's election address to the 'Independent Electors of the Borough of Wilton' was written at Barford on the 17th March. In it he called for reform of the land and game laws, enfranchisement of the rural householder and opposition to the 'foreign policy of the present Government', which he considered had 'lowered the standard of English freedom and justice in the eyes of the world, and created hatred and mistrust abroad, distress and poverty at home'.[6] In the course of the campaign he proposed to raise other issues—including that of flogging in the Army. (He was as good as his word on the latter point, speaking against the use of the 'cat', which he called a 'monstrous instrument of torture', at his very first meeting in Wilton.)

Although his proposals were, in practice, quite sober in tone, the copies of the address which were issued had an external flamboyance which seemed to bely this, appearing 'in flaming scarlet, blue being the Tory colours (at Wilton) scarlet or orange the Liberal'.![7]

Prior to Arch's arrival in the constituency, his Liberal supporters had begun to canvass the electorate, trying to secure promises of votes for him, but when he himself appeared he put an end to this. According to the admittedly partial *English Labourers' Chronicle* this decision not to canvass 'was unique in the history of the constituency'.[8]

The General Election (extended, as was then the custom, over several days) commenced from the end of March. And Joseph's first meeting as official Liberal candidate was organised on the 22nd of that month in the Temperance Hall, Wilton. Needless to say by no means all of the electors supported him, and it was in the midst of some considerable violence that this first meeting took place. Fortunately for his audience, the precaution had been taken of boarding up the windows of the Hall on the inside, for during his speech the hostile crowd which had gathered outside not only kept up a continuous barrage of shouts and jeers but also hurled stones at the building. The tinkle of broken glass and the roar of the mob provided a constant background to the proceedings. Joseph was not greatly disturbed, however, despite the unpleasantness of the occasion: 'The roughs outside hooted and howled in a most disgraceful manner; but for all the howls and stones I finished my speech to the end as I set out to do.[9] Such treatment merely aroused all the pugnacious spirit which had been nurtured by his years as a union leader and propagandist.

Naturally he and his supporters blamed the incident on their Tory opponents, but the *Salisbury and Winchester Journal* adopting a more impartial line, suggested it was the 'work of a mischievous gang of boys . . .'10

On the succeeding days Joseph's electioneering passed off more peacefully — partly because a bodyguard of Liberal working men from Salisbury had been secured to help maintain the peace. It was later alleged that some of them were paid as much as £1 10s. or £2 a week to act as bill-stickers and general guardians of the peace in the Liberal interest. In addition, it was also claimed that many of them were 'bounteously regaled' in the local public houses and that out of Joseph's total election expenses of nearly £513, £160 'was set down for messengers and bill-stickers, and this expenditure was not accounted for by vouchers, but put down in a lump sum.'11 Although these allegations were made with the intention of discrediting Arch, after the election had been held, in fact there is sufficient evidence to suggest that a bodyguard *was* employed. The events at the Wilton meeting on 22nd March showed that it was fully justified, especially as most of his later meetings were to be held out-of-doors, and would, therefore, be especially vulnerable to attacks by hooligans.

Arch had started out on his campaign with great hope. Indeed, the loyal *English Labourers' Chronicle* had confidently declared on 27th March, that he had 'every chance of success, . . . As the labourers have the majority of votes in that constituency, there should be no doubt as to the issue . . .' Gradually this confidence was eroded as the underlying strength of the Hon. Sidney Herbert's position began to reveal itself. Despite the enthusiasm with which Joseph was greeted at his village meetings, a note of caution started to creep into the press reports. Repeated assurances were given that as a result of the passage of the Ballot Act of 1872, the poll was quite secret. Attention was, at the same time, drawn to the penalties which faced anyone who attempted to coerce labourers against giving their vote to Arch, should they wish to support him; this was a theme to which he himself returned in many of his speeches. Even at his very first meeting at Wilton on the 22nd he had 'impressed upon his hearers that it was morally impossible for anyone to tell how a man had voted unless he was simple enough to tell himself. He had been told that at the last election in that part farmers were seen at the polling stations pretending to take the labourers' names, and telling them they should know how they voted, but he hoped that would not be done this time, . . . He would say to all electors present, 'At the polling be too old for them.'12

These points were raised at other meetings organised in the villages around Wilton; and at Coombe Bissett, on the 24th March, a 'splendid meeting' was held by the light of the full moon. Although at several of the gatherings the farmers tried to interrupt Arch, thanks to his 'bodyguard,' the annoyance was kept to a minimum.

Yet, despite all endeavours, when polling actually took place on 2nd April, Joseph was defeated — by 818 votes to 397.

Naturally, even if the result was not altogether unexpected, it was a disappointment. Arch's friends immediately blamed the result on the fact that the electors had been 'intimidated by base threats,' or else 'misled by false statements, seduced by delusive promises,' and had therefore failed to vote for him. As the *English Labourers' Chronicle* put it: 'Mr. Arch made a gallant attempt and did well, but not so well as we could have wished. Landlordism, Tory tyranny, and rowdyism triumphed over purity of election . . .'[13] Some of the local Liberals even contemplated lodging an objection against the Hon. Sidney's re-election (on grounds which were not made clear), but eventually wiser counsels prevailed and they withdrew their opposition.[14]

As for Joseph himself, there was nothing for it but to lick his wounds, return to his normal everyday tasks, and hope to 'live to fight another day.' In addition, now that the Union had lost so many of its members, and the scope of its activities had been reduced, he was able to spend more time at home than had been the case for many years. He could again give attention to his garden, with its plentiful yields of fruit, flowers and vegetables, and to the upkeep of his cottage. His wife, Mary Ann, could expect to see a little more of him, and since she had suffered a paralytic seizure in 1878 and had difficulty in moving about, this would be a considerable boon. The quiet monotony of her days spent in light household chores would to some extent be relieved. Several of the children had by now left home — although the two youngest, Edward (aged 18), who was training to become a joiner and cabinet maker and Thomas (aged 15), who was learning to become a compositor, were still living with their parents. On 12th August, 1880, Mrs Arch's loneliness was, no doubt, increased when her second daughter, Annie, married a Methodist minister, the Rev. J. E. Leuty, who was stationed at Middlesbrough.[15] Leuty, who had been born at Burnt Yates in Yorkshire, was about four years his wife's junior. Their wedding took place quietly at the Spencer Street Chapel in Leamington, and for her dowry, Annie like her sister before her, received 'certain tables and chairs' of her father's own making.[16]

For Annie herself, now aged 29, the marriage marked the beginning of a new phase in her life. Although her health was often poor — so that about two years after the wedding, Mr Leuty had to leave Middlesbrough to seek a new appointment at High Wycombe, because of 'the ill-health of his wife' — she played as active a role as possible in the religious field.[17] She was a very enthusiastic local preacher and at the time of her early death in Chester, on 3rd November, 1904, it was noted that she had preached in 'as many as seven hundred pulpits,' and had been a devoted worker in the temperance cause, and in the Methodist missions. She was deeply interested in the Primitive-Methodist Orphanage, and when she realised that she was dying she expressed a wish that 'any token of respect for her might be sent to the orphanage rather than spent upon her coffin or grave.'[18] However, in 1880 those unhappy events lay well in the future, and for Joseph and Mary Ann Arch it merely meant that through marriage they were losing a 'dear daughter.' Nevertheless, her poor health in the early 1880's would clearly be a source of worry.

Meanwhile, on the political front, Arch could not afford to remain passive for long. Since it was fairly obvious that for some time at least no new constituency would be offered to him, he turned his attention once more to what he considered were the two major issues of land law reform and the securing of the vote for the agricultural labourers. Since a Liberal Government had been returned to power as a result of the 1880 general election, his hopes on this latter score at least were extremely high.

Joseph's concern for land law reform was, of course, a long-standing one, and at the same time one which had received a great stimulus as a result of the depression which was facing many sectors of arable agriculture by the late 1870's. From the beginning of his campaign for reform indeed he had — quite wrongly — placed most of the blame for the depressed state of agriculture on the land laws, failing to recognise the crucial role of cheap imports of foreign wheat in driving down the price of that commodity. This continued to be his attitude, especially when he became convinced that many agriculturists were deliberately under-cultivating their holdings, and he began to put forward demands that legislation should be passed to *compel* them to fulfil their duties in this direction. He even toyed with the idea of promoting a peasant proprietary — the 'three acres and a cow' type of farmer — who might be recruited from the ranks of the agricultural labourers, and who would inevitably have to maximise his production, in order to obtain a living. Arch quite ignored the obvious economic flaws of such an argument (especially in the face of a world decline in agricultural prices) and he made no suggestions as to the possible source of working capital for his peasant proprietors. His views on these proposals were made clear in a letter written to Mr Gladstone on 11th November, 1879, when he declared:

'Do you in your judgment think that some of the large farms of England which are not much more than half cultivated, reduced to smaller ones so that sufficient capital could be found to cultivate them properly would be an advantage to the country at large by producing more work for the labourer and more food for the people? Permit me to ask you whether in your judgment if the land itself were made free from the feudal fetters that bind it, that such emancipation would tend in future to prevent Agricultural Depression?' The Liberal leader's reply (if any) has not been preserved.[19]

Nevertheless, many agriculturists shared Joseph's disquiet at the economic position of their industry, and even in 1879 some of them had demanded protection from foreign competition. Although this had been refused by the Government, Disraeli had agreed to set up a Royal Commission to investigate conditions in the industry. Joseph, for his part, was firmly opposed to protection — which he rightly appreciated would mean higher food prices for workers — but his own principal solution to the problem of agricultural depression, namely land law reform, was not very helpful either.

When the decision to set up a Royal Commission was announced in 1879, the N.A.L.U. leaders had hoped that either Arch, or another Union official, would be represented on it, but to their disappointment this was not to be. Consequently, the members of the Executive Committee decided to collect material for themselves, and to this end a circular was sent round to all the N.A.L.U. branches, asking local secretaries to provide details of the state of agriculture in their own particular locality. On the basis of the information collected from this and from other sources, the Union then issued its own pamphlet, entitled *Evidence on the Causes of the Present Agricultural Depression* In its modest way it was designed to act as a rival to the Reports of the Royal Commission.

Meanwhile, if Joseph had not been appointed a member of the Commission, he was at any rate twice called upon to give evidence before it. Both interviews covered a wide variety of rural topics. The first of them was on 4th August, 1881, and the second on the 6th December, in the same year. In addition to answering questions about his own Union,[20] Arch also gave his interpretations of the causes and results of the agricultural depression. He declared fiercely that: 'The farmers are starving the land, throwing the men off the land even now. ... When I see scores of fields, through almost every county where I travel, with three times more rubbish growing on the land than there is corn, I certainly must come to the conclusion that the land is not farmed properly....'[21] He quite failed to see that farmers on the high cost, heavy clay soils, in particular, were unable to compete with cheap foreign grain, and their only hope was to diversify their crops, if they had the capital and initiative to do so. If they lacked either of these qualities, however, they were gradually forced to farm 'low,' in an effort to minimise their outgoings. Soon their fields bore the poorly tilled appearance which Joseph so deplored.

At his second interview on 6th December, he also returned to a favourite theme, criticising the role of the laws of entail and settlement. In particular, he objected to the fact that under the existing legislation, land so controlled could not be sold and he informed the Commissioners that he knew there were 'landed proprietors today, who would be very glad indeed if they could dispose of some portion of their estates, but the law forbids them. . . .'[22] His opinion was that 'whatever was said it always resolved itself in the last resource to this — better security, more freedom. The farmer's hands were tied by fear of a twelve months' notice, and the landlord's hands were too frequently tied by the law of entail.'[23]

Although, after the Royal Commission had completed its deliberations, an Agricultural Holdings Act was passed in 1883, designed to protect the interests of tenant farmers should they be required to leave their farms, this did not satisfy Arch. His demands were for more radical changes than this. Indeed, in October, 1881,[24] he even attended a meeting in London to discuss the question of the nationalisation of the land, although he later denied that he had any sympathy with that particular cause, declaring, 'I do not believe in State-aid and land nationalisation.'[25] (And at the 1888 Trades Union Congress, when speaking on this same theme, he made clear that 'what agricultural labourers wanted was immediate relief. Although nationalisation of land might be very well in its place, the present generation of agricultural labourers would pass away before such a reform could be accomplished. . . .[26])

Apart from the broad issues of land law reform, however, Arch was also interested in more limited objectives as well — such as an increase in the number of allotments available to the agricultural labourers. In the early 1880's, therefore, he played an active role in support of Jesse Collings (now a Liberal M.P. for Ipswich) in his efforts to secure the passage of an Allotment Extension Act. This was intended to make charity land available, as far as possible, to all workers who wished to obtain additional allotments. It required trustees of charity land not used for 'ecclesiastical, educational or apprenticeship purposes' to notify the agricultural labourers of their parish that the land was available to be let as allotments. Great hopes were held out when the Act was passed, but unfortunately its intentions were seriously weakened by the House of Lords, so that the Charity Commissioners in London, who had opposed the Bill, were given the position of final arbiters when agreement between the trustees of charity land and the labourers of a village could not be obtained. In practice, therefore, the Act proved fairly ineffective. Nevertheless, Joseph did all he could to prevent it from becoming a dead letter; he repeatedly encouraged the labourers to take advantage of it, urging 'that they must see to it and have the pluck to move themselves, for they had to force the hand of the Charity Commissioners. . . .'[27] To help to make villagers aware of the charities in their own particular neighbourhood, the *English Labourers' Chronicle* also ran a series of articles in the autumn of 1882 detailing the charities available in various counties in England and giving advice as to how the labourers should proceed to take advantage of the new legislation.[28] With a few exceptions, it was all in vain.

However, an even clearer indication of Arch's feelings on the land question was provided in September, 1885, when he became a vice-president of the newly-formed Free Land League, which had as its first aim, 'the abolition of the law of Primogeniture', and as its third, 'Prohibition of settlement of land upon unborn persons and of the general power of creating life estates in land'. (*The Times* — 29th August and 16th September, 1885). Although this organisation does not seem to have enjoyed very much success, Arch was by no means discouraged. He carried his land campaign not only into his next electoral contest — as will be seen — but also into the deliberations of the Trades Union Congress. Even at the Sixteenth Congress, held in September, 1883, he had demanded 'radical changes in our land system', and in the following year, the abolition of the 'laws of settlement and primogeniture'. He also criticised the fact that land was being allowed to deteriorate through inadequate tillage, and proposed compulsory cultivation, in order to deal with this problem. Indeed at the 1884 Congress he had suggested that any landed proprietors who would not cultivate their land to its 'greatest extent' should have 'heavy taxation' imposed upon them. This attitude continued as long as he spoke at the Congresses. In 1887, he declared vehemently 'that our land was in the hands of brigands and those who succeeded in releasing it would be doing a great work for generations yet unborn...' And in his very last speech to Congress in 1888, it is significant that land law reform was a major theme. (Although he attended both the 1890 and the 1891 Congresses he did not make a speech at either of them.[29])

Land law reform was thus one persistent bee in the Arch bonnet. Another was franchise reform, and throughout the early 1880's he neglected no opportunity of making known his views on this subject. Franchise demonstrations continued to be held — and now with some prospects of success. For since 1880 a Liberal Government had been in power, and although to the agricultural labourers it seemed intolerably tardy in giving them the vote, it was widely appreciated that sooner or later this must come. Nevertheless, Joseph left nothing to chance. When, on 11th June, 1883, Birmingham Liberals organised a celebration for John Bright, he saw to it that the labourers were conspicuously represented, about two hundred union members marching in the procession. They carried a large loaf and a red banner on which were inscribed the words, 'We demand the vote as our right.'

Joseph himself, together with Robert Collier, the general secretary, travelled in the procession in a coach with the two Liberal M.Ps., Jesse Collings and Sir John Bennett.[30]

Then, on 28th February, 1884, Gladstone at last introduced his much desired Representation of the People Bill. The only doubt was whether the Lords would reject it when it reached the Upper House. In the event they did so — but only for the purpose of recommending that a redistribution of seats should be carried out at the same time. When this was accomplished, the Bill became law.

Meanwhile, in the last feverish months before final approval was given, Arch exerted all his energies. Although Union membership had slumped badly — it was down to a mere 15,000 by the end of 1883 — he did not allow himself to become disheartened, nor to cease in his efforts to revive flagging enthusiasm. This is shown, for example, in a speech made on the Reform Bill in March, 1884, at Radford in Warwickshire, where, as he said, a few 'good men and true' had kept 'the fire of unionism burning'. On this occasion he declared that: 'In view of the new duties they would soon have to discharge, he wished to urge upon them the importance of cultivating their minds by reading and also the importance of combining together so that they might learn to act in concert so that they might be able to secure for themselves and their families the greatest measure of benefit. Let them lay down their plans in an honourable and just manner, for the general welfare of their class in the country, and when they did that they would be able to wield a power which none could withstand . . . Again, for a long time a cry had gone up from the tenant farmers of England for security for their capital. But they . . . never would have it until the agricultural labourers had the vote.'[31] This latter sentence is significant, for even in the late 1870's Arch had been trying to win the support of the tenant farmers for labourer enfranchisement by suggesting that they should be given an adequate Tenant Right Bill, and pointing out that if labourers had the vote, they would support such a measure. This was a subject to which he was to return on a number of occasions.

Many of the village meetings he attended at this time were sponsored by the Liberal Party rather than by his own organisation. Nevertheless, on Easter Monday, 14th April, it was decided that it was time for the N.A.L.U. to show its mettle, and to organise a large franchise demonstration at Leamington. Plans were laid accordingly.

The day dawned cold and damp but despite the fact that the demonstration was to be held out-of-doors, several thousand labourers were estimated to have assembled for it. As the *English Labourers' Chronicle* reported: 'About mid-day (they) came trudging in from the surrounding district in threes and fours, some of them from a distance which would scarcely be credible to a Conservative. We ourselves saw two . . . who had come . . . (a) total distance of 23 miles . . .' The procession was headed by the town band and behind followed men carrying a 'new silk banner' on which were inscribed the words, 'Franchise Bill 1884'. Other bands and banners followed, as the procession marched from the centre of Leamington to nearby Milverton, where about ten to fifteen thousand people were said to have gathered in the field where the meeting was to be held. There was a buzz of suppressed excitement over the whole assembly, as labourers pressed together expectantly, talking among themselves as they waited for Joseph to arrive. Some had their womenfolk at their side and many were clad in their 'Sunday best'. All gazed interestedly about them, anxious to miss nothing of what was going off.

For Joseph, 'this was a proud moment, and as he stood forth in the presence of the vast multitude, welcomed by a deafening burst of applause, and with the franchise almost within the labourers' grasp, he seemed to fully realize (sic) the consummation of one of his dearest hopes; to take courage for his further work. . . .' The *English Labourers' Chronicle* then went on to note that: 'The warmth and wealth of welcome he received, proved that even in Leamington, where political conventionalism and expediency have been sadly shocked by his sterling and advanced Liberalism, and where jealousy like a being born with teeth, has tried to fasten itself upon his fame, his hold upon the masses is unshaken . . .' As so often before, in his speech he called upon the labourers to use their votes wisely, and also — significantly — demanded greater security of tenure for farmers, too, declaring: 'They wanted the farmer as securely fixed in his farm as the lord in his castle . . .'[32]

In view of this renewed activity in the last months before the vote was granted, it is noticeable that the N.A.L.U.'s recruitment showed a temporary improvement as compared with the period which had preceded it and that which was to follow. Membership rose to about 18,000 in 1884, as compared with approximately 15,000 in 1883 and 10,700 in 1885.

Slowly the months passed by. Petitions in favour of the Reform Bill were repeatedly organised and in September the Trades Union Congress supported a motion in favour of franchise extension which Joseph put forward. But now success was in sight. In Parliament, an autumn session had been arranged so as to clear the franchise legislation out of the way, along with other measures. Finally, on 13th December, the *English Labourers' Chronicle* printed a congratulatory report from the general secretary, Collier, to the agricultural workers on the ultimate passage of the legislation. The labourers had finally been given the vote!

For Joseph it was a dream come true. After years of striving the farm labourer was accepted, politically at least, as a full and equal member of the community. In his autobiography he called 1884 'the great year of my life. We had a vote at last; we were now politically alive and existent; and there were those amongst us who intended to use that existence to the utmost of our power in pressing forward our best interests.'[33]

Certain outside observers, too, considered that this was the 'supreme achievement of the Union, its culminating point as it were, . . . When that was obtained the Union was no longer politically necessary, . . . With the franchise the agricultural labourer became a free man'.[34]

In his New Year Message to the labourers, published in the *English Labourers' Chronicle* of 3rd January, 1885, Joseph soon showed himself anxious to emphasize to the labourers the importance of their new position, and to ensure that they used it to the best advantage. 'I would say to the labourers everywhere, "organise yourselves, educate yourselves; don't leave the work for other people to do it for you; do it yourselves, and the Union will help you". If you expect Tory parsons and Tory squires or any of their agents to educate you, you will be deceived. You must read and think for yourselves.' Indeed, if anything, he was inclined to over-stress the value and significance of the vote, as when he told a meeting at Swaffham in Norfolk, 'Now the welfare of the country depends upon you, and I should like you to use your power for the good of the country . . .'[35] By statements of this type the hopes and expectations of the labourers must have been aroused to a pitch far in excess of what was justified by the facts. They were led to expect that they would become the arbiters of the country's future; when events proved otherwise, they grew disappointed and disillusioned.

There is no doubt, however, that despite these faults, in the months which followed the passage of the Representation of the People Bill, Arch and the N.A.L.U. did carry out a considerable amount of good work in the rural areas. They were able to educate the labourers in the simple mechanics of voting, and to inform them how they could get their names on the electoral roll. Joseph reassured them regarding the secrecy of the ballot, and emphasized that there was no way in which their employers could find out for whom they had voted; he equally discouraged them from promising any candidate their vote and suggested that on polling day, 'all the working men of the village meet together, and march to the polling booth, with one of your best men at the head . . .' This advice was, of course, designed to overcome any timidity or diffidence which the individual labourer might feel, especially if he saw his employer in the vicinity of the polling booth![36]

Under Arch's influence, too, mock ballots were held in many of the villages — 'with a view to educating the new voters, and of impressing upon them the secrecy of the ballot . . .' As Joseph admitted, he wanted to be sure that they were not accused of being mere 'ABC voters', but were fully able to choose between the merits of the different candidates. A typical example of these mock ballots was held at the Wiltshire village of Crondall in January 1885. Here, after instruction had been given, ballot papers were handed out to the twenty-six labourers present, and they were asked to decide between Gladstone and Sir Stafford Northcote, the leader of the Conservatives in the House of Commons. As might perhaps be expected (given the political views of the N.A.L.U. leaders) Gladstone secured twenty-five votes, one ballot paper was spoilt — and Sir Stafford received no votes at all! Another significant point, too, was the way in which the Union frequently tried to identify the local Liberal Party candidate as far as possible with the much-admired Gladstone.[37] This policy was clearly demonstrated in the Crondall example.

And in general, the labourers themselves took the franchise question as seriously as Joseph could have wished. Politics often formed the basis of discussion during their brief leisure moments and when they met together for their evening half-pints, in the warm comfort of a local public house. This was noted by that eminently sympathetic observer of rural life, Flora Thompson, in respect of her own quiet North Oxfordshire hamlet, Juniper Hill, during the 1880's. Regarding the regular evening gatherings in the hamlet's public house, she wrote: "Politics was a favourite topic, for, under the recently extended franchise, every householder was a voter, and they took their new responsibility seriously. A mild Liberalism prevailed, a Liberalism that would be regarded as hide-bound Toryism now, but was daring enough in those days. One man who had been to work in Northampton proclaimed himself a Radical; but he was cancelled out by the landlord, who called himself a 'true blue'. With the collaboration of this Left and Right, questions of the moment were thrashed out and settled to the satisfaction of the majority . . . Sometimes a speech by Gladstone, or some other leader would be read aloud from a newspaper and punctuated by the fervent 'Hear, Hear' of the company. Or Sam, the man with advanced opinions, would relate with reverent pride the story of his meeting and shaking hands with Joseph Arch, the farm workers' champion. 'Joseph Arch!' he would cry. 'Joseph Arch is the man for the farm labourer!' and knock on the table and wave aloft his pewter mug, very carefully, for every drop was precious."[38] In many other villages up and down the country a similar scene would be equally typical.

Nevertheless, in the excitement surrounding the enfranchisement of the labourers, Joseph did not neglect his own political career, either. Throughout the early 1880's he had, of course, been maintaining his loyal support for the Liberal Party. This came before most of his other interests, and it is significant that, for example, when Gladstone and the Liberal Government were involved in war in Egypt during the summer and early autumn of 1882, Arch made no reference to this in his speeches. His attitude towards Disraeli's similar 'adventures' in the 1870's had been very different; furthermore, although the Workmen's Peace Association had prepared an anti-War pamphlet entitled *The War in Egypt*, in which the Government's action was criticised, the *English Labourers' Chronicle*, the organ of the N.A.L.U., declared itself unable to accept the pamphlet's conclusions 'in many particulars . . .' On 19th September, 1882, when Arch attended a conference of the Peace Association in Manchester, he confined himself to a general condemnation of all wars: 'Swords and guns and bayonets were never made for the benefit of the people, but to support the aristocracy and despotism . . .'[39]

This steadfast loyalty to the Liberal Party bore some fruit. In August, 1882, he was 'unanimously adopted by the Hull Radical Club as their candidate at the next Parliamentary election', and about a year later was elected an Honorary Member of the National Liberal Club in London, clearly in recognition of his work for the Party in the rural areas.[40] Around this latter time too, he was also elected the first President of the Birmingham Radical Association.[41]

Arch remained the Radical candidate for Hull for a number of months — at least until the spring of 1884 — although perhaps with rather less than complete enthusiasm and satisfaction. On 5th September, 1883, for example, it was necessary for him to assure the secretary of the Hull Radical Club of his continued support and to point out that he had received 'no official invitation to stand for Birmingham'. He went on to declare: 'I still hold to the pledge I gave the Radicals at Hull, when last with you, nor do I intend to break faith with them if they are prepared to carry out the arrangements we have mutually agreed upon'.[42]

Despite these protestations, however, in the end the Hull venture *did* fall through — and in his autobiography Arch is silent as to the reasons for this. But if he himself were silent, certain hostile sections of the press were less reticent as regards their attitude towards him and his doings. One such unfriendly account appeared in the London *Figaro* of 28th April, 1883, and in it the writer maliciously noted: 'To be candid, Mr. Arch has not improved since he began to wear broadcloth and to dine with Members of Parliament. In adversity all his best qualities exhibited themselves; he does not shine in prosperity. Nature did not intend him to pose as an orator or a statesman . . . A few weeks ago Mr. Arch was entertained by the Junior Reform Club of Liverpool . . . It was not pardonable for him to libel the clergy wholesale . . . In 1880 Mr. Arch was a candidate for the representation of Wilton. He was defeated by a majority of two to one. He may meet with the same fate at Hull, but a seat will probably be found for him. The Radicals will go on hoping that he may be able to serve their interests. Perhaps he may. Mr. Joseph Arch has ceased to be clad in fustian — he has taken to talking it. But if, since he became an agitator, his pockets have been lined, who shall blame him? He may die a wealthy man, and, after death, be extolled as a pious patriot . . .' Here, of course, the old charges of corruption and self-seeking were emerging, as they had done so many times in the past and were to do many times in the future. As usual, no attempt was made to prove the charges; by mere repetition his enemies hoped they would gain a measure of acceptance, and would thereby serve to discredit him.

Furthermore, during 1884, alongside his franchise work, Arch showed his support for the basic Liberal doctrine of Free Trade by writing (perhaps with some professional help) a pamphlet for the Cobden Club entitled *Would Protection Remove the Present Distress and Benefit the Working Man?* (Cobden Club Leaflet, No. XVIII — See Appendix 3). In this he concluded quite firmly that it would not — as certain sections of the Conservative Party were claiming. The pamphlet was quite well received and he had the gratification of seeing it run into several editions.

Nevertheless, despite his political interests, after the collapse of the Hull offer he was still waiting to be adopted by a constituency as a Liberal candidate. Not until the spring of 1885 was this problem finally resolved. On 5th May in that year, he and Sir Brampton Gurdon (whom he had earlier called a 'swell Whig'), were asked to attend a meeting of the one-hundred-strong North-West Norfolk Liberal Constituency Selection Committee at Blackfriars Hall, Kings Lynn, so that the Liberal candidate for the division could be chosen. The members of the Labourers' Union in the area had been very active in putting Joseph's name forward, while Sir Brampton was the man whom many of the middle-class Liberals had marked out. Eventually, after some considerable discussion — during which one of the delegates declared that Sir Brampton would have 'broader views' than Arch — the voting took place; Arch received 64 votes and Sir Brampton, 36. Arch was, therefore, chosen as the candidate, although eight of those present refused to endorse his adoption.[43] He, himself, of course, seized this opportunity with both hands, since North-West Norfolk, a strongly rural division, was just the type of seat in which he stood the best chance of success.

No effort was now to be spared in publicising either Arch or the

Liberal cause. The columns of the *English Labourers' Chronicle* were utilised fully to this end, and at the N.A.L.U. Annual Council, held shortly after Arch's adoption in Norfolk, a ten-point political programme was approved, calling, among other things for abolition of the game laws, payment of Members of Parliament, and the settlement of election expenses out of the rates.[44] At the same time it was also agreed that if Arch *were* elected to Parliament, the question of his salary would be left in the hands of the Executive Committee. (Since he normally dominated this, the decision was a satisfactory one from his point of view.)

But perhaps the most significant development during this period was the way in which Joseph was prepared to bury his own hostility towards the farming community, in the interests of his Party (as he had done earlier, to some extent, when pressing for a new Tenant Right Bill). In July, 1885, he and some of the other N.A.L.U. leaders met the Executive Committee of the pro-Liberal Farmers' Alliance, in order to consider co-operation during the election period. The two groups, after much discussion, managed to agree on certain common demands for land law and game law reform, but there is little doubt that the temporary coalition was formed primarily for electioneering purposes and was a rather cynical application of the idea of farmer/labourer co-operation which Joseph had perhaps envisaged in his advocacy of an adequate Tenant Right Bill.

In practice, the liaison does not seem to have worked out very satisfactorily. The farmers became jealous of the attention paid to the newly enfranchised labourers by the Liberal politicians, and on the eve of the poll, the *Mark Lane Express* of 30th November, 1885, acting as the mouthpiece of the Farmers' Alliance, declared that the politicians had 'ignored, or nearly ignored, the interests of those agricultural electors who, on previous occasions, have been considered as the arbiters of the county contests . . .', i.e. the farmers. It is significant that after the election all mention of co-operation between the N.A.L.U. and the farmers' organisations seems to have disappeared, although the secretary of the Alliance did write to congratulate Arch on his success in North-West Norfolk. The link-up was never apparently revived, and it seems likely that Joseph himself was not particularly proud of it. Certainly it finds no mention in his autobiography; in this indeed he criticises the Farmers' Alliance as having 'too much humbug and shilly-shallying and blundering about (them) . . . I had no kind of patience with them. I told the farmers they must look to the landlords to redress their grievances . . .'[45]

After these months of preparation, the General Election at last drew near. The political scene had been complicated by the fact that in June, 1885, Lord Salisbury and the Conservatives had taken office as a minority adminstration after the Liberal Government had been unexpectedly defeated on the Budget. The defeat is perhaps explained by the fact that the Liberal Cabinet was already in disarray over the policy to be adopted towards Ireland, and it had been out-voted by a combination of Conservatives and Irish Nationalists.[46] Such a minority adminstration could, of course, only be an interim arrangement, until a General Election could be called in the winter, when the new electoral registers were ready. It was, therefore, in November, 1885, that the election was at last held.

Joseph had now been given his second chance to enter Parliament. His opponent in North-West Norfolk (which had been a Conservative-held seat under the old franchise) was Lord Henry Bentinck, a pleasant young man, whom another political opponent later called 'a Tory of the old school, who felt a sense of personal responsibility for the welfare of the working classes, . . .' and, 'as fine a gentleman as ever lived.'[47] Nevertheless, as Joseph understandably pointed out, 'with the best will in the world he could not possibly enter into (the labourers') feelings and understand (their) needs. The two millions of new voters wanted some one of their own class to speak for them. I was ready.'[48]

Arch's election address was published in the middle of November, and it was a very much more Radical affair that its Wilton predecessor. Among the sixteen proposals put forward were those for 'disestablishment of the State Church, the entire separation of Religion from State control, and the application of State Tithes to the equal benefit of all classes of the community'; free secular education; Free Trade for all articles of food; a complete reform of the land and game laws; the Sunday closing of public houses, except to bona-fide travellers; the substitution of international arbitration for war (a harking back to his Peace Society interests); the reform of the House of Lords, so as to deprive it of its powers to obstruct any measure that had received the approval of the 'People's House'; and 'the Abolition of Perpetual Pensions'. (See Appendix 4 for a complete copy of the Address.)

In putting forward these demands, Arch was, indeed, very largely following in the footsteps of Joseph Chamberlain and his so-called 'unauthorised programme'. This called for the implementation, on a national scale, of a number of Radical reforms by any new Liberal Government which might be elected. Many of Chamberlain's proposals, e.g. free elementary education; land reform, particularly to give the labourer 'a stake in the soil;' disestablishment of the Church of England; and manhood suffrage, with payment of M.Ps., were designed to appeal to the newly enfranchised farm workers and to swing them behind the Liberals in the vital county constituencies.[49]

Meanwhile, from November onwards, with the pressure now on,

the N.A.L.U's full propaganda machine was devoted to securing Joseph's return. As early as June a Union fund had been set up to receive contributions towards his election expenses, and frequent exhortations were made to the labourers to support it. (In practice, not many of them seem to have done so, and most of the money appears to have been obtained from friends in the Liberal Party, rather than from agricultural workers.[50]) Nevertheless, as a result of these efforts the respectable sum of £223 1s. 8d. was eventually acknowledged in the *English Labourers' Chronicle* of 23rd January, 1886; the remainder of the election expenditure (which amounted in all to about £991, including returning officer's charges) was met by wealthy Liberals.[51] (See Appendix 8 for information on election expenditure. Until the Representation of the People Act, 1918, candidates had to meet the returning officer's charges themselves — an added burden.)

Joseph, for his part, loyally continued to extol the virtues of the Liberal Party. In an 'Address to the New Voters', published in the *English Labourers Chronicle* early in November, he called upon them to return 'good sound Liberals to Parliament at the next General Election . . . Do not be led aside by smoking-concerts, Tory tea-parties, Tory skittling, Tory blankets, nor Tory soup. You have very largely the future destinies of the country in your hand; let me beg you to do your duty like sensible Englishmen by placing Mr. Gladstone in power once more, as Prime Minister of England.'[52] (This Address was later published as a separate pamphlet by the London and Counties Liberal Association.)

The *English Labourers' Chronicle* of course, repeatedly called upon the labourers of North-West Norfolk to 'do their duty'. '(They) should never forget that it is to Joseph Arch they owe the franchise . . . We hope the electors in North-West Norfolk will not forget this fact, but send Mr. Arch to Parliament as their representative.'[53]

The campaign was a hard-fought one. Joseph began his election-eering in earnest from about the third week of November, when he and his wife travelled down to Norfolk. For once, Mary Ann had thrown off her natural shyness and reserve and had decided to come with him to see what she could do to help, though her health was poor. (For several years she had been suffering 'from the effects of paralysis down the left side' and obviously had great difficulty in moving about.)

Local Liberals played their role with equal enthusiasm, and at a number of their meetings test ballots of Arch *v*. Bentinck were held, to give the labourers a chance to 'practise' for their great day! Thus, at both Fakenham Heath and at Sculthorpe, during the first days of December, test ballots were held, and at each Joseph was an easy winner. Poor Lord Henry could only muster a total of two votes![54] (Of course, this Liberal encouragement of mock ballots was no doubt partly due to the fact that a number of the electors in North-West Norfolk were illiterate; official reports indicate that as many as 550 out of the 8,282 people who voted in the division at the 1885 General Election were 'illiterates.' (Cd. 165). Ten years later, the widening of educational opportunities had changed this rather disturbing state of affairs, for at the 1895 General Election a mere 206 out of the total of 8,337 who voted did so as 'illiterates' — *Parliamentary Papers*, 1896, Vol. LXVII.)

Most of the meetings seem to have passed off peacefully, although Joseph later claimed that at one of them at least plans were laid to attack him physically. Fortunately, thanks to the help of some friendly navvies who were cutting a new railway line to South Lynn, the attack was beaten off.[55] Some of the farmers, too, 'were bitter against the labourers having the vote,' and tried 'to intimidate their men to get them to vote for the Tory candidate.'[56] A few threatened to discharge for the winter months any of their labourers who went to the poll on election day, while 'those who refrained from voting were to be kept on at 10s. a week.'[57] Indeed, one old Norfolk man from the Bungay area later recalled that, 'The Master would go to the man and say, 'Wich (sic) way are you goen to vote John?' If the answer did not please him he would tell the man w(h)ich way he must vote, and John did it or the Master made a spare man of him . . .'

In addition, the same witness also recalled the difficulties Arch often had to face in his electioneering, and the covert hostility of the authorities towards him: 'I have seen Arch get up and make a speech on the green at my home, and the police would come along and move him on, or try to. They could not prosocute (sic) him, much as they would have liked to, and would if they could.'[57a]

Nevertheless, events were to show that most of the rumours of undue influence were exaggerated. When the poll took place on the 8th December it was clear that the vast majority of the labourers had voted — 8,282 of the 10,444 strong electorate registering their votes. Many of them, indeed, "voted early, and walked to the poll, scorning the use of vehicles." Another pleasing feature, according to the *Norfolk News* was the fact that the election passed off quietly; "strong drafts of police" had been sent into Fakenham and Lynn, in anticipation of trouble, but in practice their services were not needed.

Although the poll was held on the 8th December, the result was not due to be announced until the 9th. Joseph's excitement and anxiety during that long night can be imagined. Had he been successful?

The next morning, he and Lord Henry were both present as the counting got under way at King's Lynn Town Hall, Arch having arrived at the Town Hall in a humble donkey cart! Supporters of both parties began to collect outside the building as the hours passed by, but it was not until about half-past one that the result was made known. Then the High Sheriff came to the window and announced that Joseph had won — by the comfortable margin of 640 votes. He had polled 4,461 to Lord Henry's 3,821.

After the enthusiastic cheers of his friends had died down, Joseph made a simple speech of thanks to all who had helped him, and then went straight to the Temperance Hotel, where Mrs Arch was waiting to hear the news. As they left King's Lynn later in the day, enthusiastic Liberals were waiting to congratulate their new M.P. all along the route. A group of them even unharnessed the horse from their carriage and dragged the latter, with Mr and Mrs Arch inside, all the way to the rail-way station. A large crowd came on to the platform to bid farewell and repeated cheers were given until the train finally left. And as it chugged along on its journey to Swaffham, where the Arches were to spend the night of the 9th, Joseph exhibited a large signboard on which were inscribed the words 'J. Arch, M.P.' This was to inform his supporters of the victory as the train passed through the Norfolk countryside. At Swaffham another enthusiastic crowd waited to greet him and his wife, and more celebrations were held.[58]

And if the Norfolk Liberals were elated, they were certainly not alone. The *English Labourers' Chronicle* did not attempt to conceal its delight — no doubt reflecting Arch's own feelings. As the paper happily recorded in its edition of 12th December: 'It will be a memor-able return in Parliamentary history, for he is the first agricultural labourer ever elected a member of Parliament in this country. In Roman History there is recorded the case of a man who was called from the plough, in a time of great peril, to Senatorial honour and labour, but from the time of Cincinnatus down to the election of Joseph Arch, there is a great historical break . . . The agricultural labourers have done their duty at the polls nobly . . .'[59]

As the first excitement began to abate Joseph returned to Barford and his cottage home, in time for Christmas. He arrived at Barford on the 11th December, but unfortunately during the last stages of his campaign he had caught a chill, and this, combined with natural exhaustion following the strain of electioneering, led to his being forced to rest in bed for several days. He was, of course, now in his sixtieth year — a time of life when many men are beginning to think of retirement. Yet, he was just embarking on a new career, with all the uncertainties that that entailed; in the circumstances a reaction to the pressures of the past weeks was scarcely surprising.

Thanks to Mary Ann's careful nursing, however, he soon recovered and was ready to receive the congratulatory letters which came flooding in from every part of the country. On 22nd December, some of the leading Liberals of King's Lynn sent him 'a large portrait of Mr. Gladstone, handsomely framed,' as a token of their satisfaction at 'the gallant fight he made in North-West Norfolk, congratulating him upon the victory he won, and expressing a hope that he (was) now fully restored to health . . .' These marks of appreciation were all the more welcome in view of the rather disappointing years Joseph had passed as N.A.L.U. leader during the early 1880's, when support for the Union had slumped so drastically.

The press, too, conscious of the news value of a 'crow-scaring to Westminster' story, sent correspondents down to interview him, or published features about him in their columns. And it was in these last few days before he took up his Parliamentary duties that a correspondent from *The World* visited him at home. The account thus provided is an interesting insight into the private life of this now very public figure.

Much of Joseph's personal life, of course, remained largely as it had been in the early 1870's, before fame had come to him. The cottage itself was but little altered and only slightly more luxuriously furnished. Now, as always, it was well maintained, Joseph having fairly recently 'restored the front of his dwelling and . . . adorned it with a porch of red deal and a letter box.' The front door opened directly into the small living room and a screen, 'covered with paper,' shut out the draught from the broad chimney corner, which nearly filled up one side of the room. The rough grey flags on the floor were covered 'with striped drugget-matting, and a long Warwickshire press of black polished oak (was) placed beneath the window with the cheerful red merino curtains. The press (was) usually sacred to a desk, work box and ancient tea caddy, but just (then) it (was) littered with congratulatory letters and numbers of the *Labourers' Chronicle*, which Mr. Arch's youngest son (helped) to print in Leamington . . . Twenty years ago Joseph Arch (had) made a little bookcase for himself, but his library (had) long since outgrown its capacity, and so Mrs. Arch (had) appropriated it for her best china tea-service, and her husband (had) lined the wall opposite the broad fireplace with substantial shelves.' Here were to be found, standing cheek by jowl, all his favourite works — Bright's and Cobden's speeches, Green's *History of the English People*, *Pulpit Aids*, Wesley's *Commentaries*, and Spurgeon's *Sermons*. On the top shelf Mrs. Arch had carefully preserved all her husband's hedging and ditching medals.

Below the book shelves stood a mahogany and horsehair sofa, and in one of the corners of the room was a second chest, in which Mrs Arch kept 'the bill-hooks, the horse-hide "mittens," . . . and the flannel coat' which Joseph had worn in his hedging days.

The reporter then went on to note: 'Mrs Arch is to be seen most afternoons seated in a comfortable armchair, within reach of the kettle, and busied with the necessary preparations for her husband's visit to London. She is . . . not a little proud of his triumph . . . in North-West Norfolk, and takes no pains to conceal her satisfaction. She is comely still, and, as becomes the wife of a member of Parliament, wears a serviceable stuff gown of the brightest mauve colour, an apron in which the red and the yellow flowers struggle for supremacy, and a matronly cap with ribbons to match. Joseph Arch sits opposite her in the upright seat which once belonged to his grandmother, . . . He wears a woollen jacket and trousers of gray tweed. As he reads and writes, he smokes a well-worn briar wood pipe, replenishing it now and then from a tobacco jar. . . . Before him lies a confused mass of heterogenous correspondence. Here is a pair of warm gloves knitted for him by the grateful wife of some unknown Wiltshire labourer; . . . there the lithographed letter of Mr. Gladstone inviting him to be "in his place" at the opening of Parliament, which he intends to bring with him to Westminster as a convenient means of identification; . . . he pauses, however, to confer with. Mrs Arch on the all-important question of London lodgings . . .

'He will not forget . . . to take you up a perilously perpendicular staircase to the little room overhead, where more portraits of Mr Gladstone and the pictures of John Bright and Peter Taylor[60] look down approvingly on many-coloured patchwork quilts, spotless linen, and home-made furniture. You . . . will be conducted through the little workshop behind the house to the garden, where Joseph Arch raises more fruit and vegetables than he can possibly use, and rears the finest pinks, roses, and pansies in the parish of Barford. Mr. Arch . . . regrets that the snow has just now buried his finest plants out of sight. He hopes you will come to see him again when his Parliamentary duties are ended, and he promises you tea and fruit in the wonderful arbour of ivy and evergreen privet, which he grubbed from the leafy Warwickshire hedgerows. . . .

'Mrs. Arch now appears at the gate to tell you that tea is served in the front parlour, where Mr. Gladstone's letter, the Wiltshire gloves, and the Press Association's queries have for a time been brushed from the hospitable table to the press beneath the window, and where you enjoy more talk of the probable future of the British peasantry, till the deepening twilight reminds you that it is time to hurry back to Warwick and the busy world beyond it . . .'[61]

This, then, was one man's impression of the quiet and homely background of the new M.P. for North-West Norfolk — a background very different from that of most of his fellow Members. Soon it was all to be left behind — for a time at least — as Joseph's new duties called him to London and to the unfamiliar routine of Parliamentary life.

173

[1] *Salisbury and Winchester Journal* — 17th January, 1880.

[2] *English Labourers' Chronicle* — 19th July, 1879.

[3] *English Labourers' Chronicle* — 26th July, 1879, Among the villages where motions against flogging in the Army were passed were Churchill and Middle Barton in Oxfordshire.

[4] *Salisbury and Winchester Journal* — 27th March, 1880.

[5] *English Labourers' Chronicle* — 27th March, 1880.

[6] *English Labourers' Chronicle* — 27th March, 1880. See Appendix 4 for full Address.

[7] *English Labourers' Chronicle* — 27th March, 1880.

[8] Quoted by A. W. Humphey — *A History of Labour Representation* (London, 1912), p.88.

[9] Joseph Arch, op.cit., p.324.

[10] *Salisbury and Winchester Journal* — 27th March, 1880.

[11] *Salisbury and Winchester Journal* — 26th June, 1880. (See also Appendix 8.)

[12] *Salisbury and Winchester Journal* — 27th March, 1880.

[13] *English Labourers' Chronicle* — 10th April, 1880.

[14] *Salisbury and Winchester Journal* — 1st and 15th May and 5th June, 1880.

[15] At the time of the marriage, Mr Leuty was a minister in the Wesleyan Reform Church, but in 1889, he became a Primitive Methodist minister. — Information kindly provided by the Methodist Archives and Research Centre and by the Rev. A. Halladay. General Secretary of the Wesleyan Reform Union, Sheffield.

[16] *English Labourers' Chronicle* — 23rd January, 1886. (Article on *Joseph Arch at Home*.)

[17] Information kindly provided by the Rev. A. Halladay.

[18] *Chester Chronicle* — 5th and 12th November, 1904, and information kindly provided by Mrs M. A. Fabyan. Mr Leuty himself survived until 1945, when he died at the age of 91. (However, despite Annie's marriage it should be noted that she did not break all links with her native Warwickshire. In 1886 she opened a draper's shop in Leamington, prior to her husband's appointment as a Primitive Methodist minister at Sheffield in 1889, and between 1891 and 1893, Mr Leuty was stationed at Leamington as a minister.)

[19] Gladstone Papers, British Museum — Additional MSS.44461 (135).

[20] See, for example, the interview on 4th August — Q.58,371–58,380 and on 6th December, 1881 — Q.60,345 and 60,354 — *Royal Commission on Agricultural Depression* 1882, Parliamentary Papers, Vol. XIV.

[21] Ibid. — 4th August — Q.58,433 and 58,439.

[22] Ibid. — 6th December, Q,59,999.

[23] Joseph Arch, op.cit., p.342. Of course, the Settled Land Act of 1882 gave life-tenants power to sell landed estates.

[24] *English Labourers' Chronicle* — 22nd October, 1881.

[25] Joseph Arch, op.cit., p.404.

[26] Report of the 1888 Trades Union Congress.

[27] Joseph Arch, op.cit., p.348.

[28] *English Labourers' Chronicle* — 23rd December, 1882, for example, when Arch again drew attention to the Allotments legislation in his Christmas Address to N.A.L.U. members.

[29] See Annual Reports of the Trades' Union Congress in the Howell Collection, Bishopsgate Institute, London.

[30] *English Labourers' Chronicle* — 16th June, 1883.

[31] *English Labourers' Chronicle* — 5th April, 1884.

[32] *English Labourers' Chronicle* — 19th April, 1884.

[33] Joseph Arch, op.cit., p.354.

[34] Preface by the Countess of Warwick to Joseph Arch, op.cit., pp.xii–xiv.

[35] *English Labourers' Chronicle* — 3rd January, 1885.

[36] Ibid.

[37] *English Labourers' Chronicle* — 31st January, 1885.

[38] F. Thompson — *Lark Rise to Candleford* (Oxford, 1963 edn.), pp.58–59.

[39] *English Labourers' Chronicle* — 30th September, 1882.

[40] *English Labourers' Chronicle* — 19th August, 1882 and General Committee Minute Book, National Liberal Club — 15th August, 1883.

[41] *English Labourers' Chronicle* — 18th August, 1883.

[42] *English Labourers' Chronicle* — 15th September, 1883. As late as February, 1884, he was still described as a candidate for Hull. — *Midland Free Press* — 9th February, 1884.

[43] *Norfolk News* — 9th May, 1885.

[44] *English Labourers' Chronicle* — 23rd May, 1885.

[45] Joseph Arch, op.cit., p.335.

[46] Sir P. Magnus, op.cit., pp.328–330.

[47] Lord Snell — *Men, Movements and Myself* (London, 1936), p.151. Lord Snell was a Labour Party supporter.

[48] Joseph Arch, op.cit., p.356.

[49] J. L. Garvin — *Life of Joseph Chamberlain*, Vol. II (London, 1933), no doubt displaying considerable partisanship, declared: 'In the shires, the deep country, the "unauthorised programme" and nothing else saved Liberalism from total disaster.', p.124.

[50] See, for example, *English Labourers' Chronicle* — 6th June and 1st August, 1885.

[51] Joseph Arch, op.cit., p.376.

[52] *English Labourers' Chronicle* — 14th November, 1885.

[53] *English Labourers' Chronicle* — 5th December, 1885.

[54] *Norfolk News* — 5th December, 1885.

[55] Joseph Arch, op.cit., pp.356–357.

[56] *Memoirs of Josiah Sage*, p.34.

[57] *Norfolk News* — 28th November, 1885.

[57a] The old Norfolk witness was a poacher, and his autobiography was edited by Lilias Rider Haggard in the 1930's. See ed. Lilias Rider Haggard — *I Walked by Night* by 'The King of the Norfolk Poachers' (1935), p.101.

[58] *Norfolk News* — 12th December, 1885.

[59] Cincinnatus (b.c.519 B.C.) was a favourite hero of the old Roman republic. In 460 B.C., he was chosen consul, and two years later dictator. When the messengers came to tell him of his new dignity they found him ploughing on his small farm. He rescued the consul Minucius, who had been defeated, and surrounded by the Aequi. Sixteen day later, after entering Rome in triumph, he relinquished his dictatorship and returned to his farm. In 439, at the age of eighty, he was once more made dictator to deal with a plebeian conspiracy. — *Chambers Biographical Dictionary*.

[60] Peter Taylor was a Radical M.P. for Leicester who was a strong opponent of the Game Laws.

[61] *English Labourers' Chronicle* — 23rd January, 1886, quoting from *The World*. The 'Wiltshire gloves' referred to had, incidentally, been sent by Thomas Marsh of Avebury in that county. In a letter dated 6th January, 1886, he declared: 'I have sent you a pair of home-knit gloves that the Mrs. has made and sent as a small present for the new year. Wishing you and Mrs. and family long life, health and a happy new year . . .' — *English Labourers' Chronicle* — 16th January, 1886.

CHAPTER ELEVEN

The Wheel of Fortune: 1886-91

JOSEPH'S SUCCESS in North-West Norfolk was indicative of the result in other rural constituencies, where Liberal gains were also recorded. Consequently, despite the defection of many Irish and urban voters at this election, the Liberal Party managed to secure a majority of 86 seats over its Conservative opponents. (The Liberals had 335 seats, twelve fewer than in 1880, and the Conservatives, 249.)[1]

However, the issue was complicated by the fact that in addition to the two major parties, a third — the Irish Nationalists — was also represented in Parliament — and with exactly 86 seats. It was they who were to hold the balance of power. Their support was needed for either of the other two parties to govern effectively and, since they were concerned only to obtain political reform for their homeland, the 'Home Rule for Ireland' campaign cast its shadow over the new Parliament from the very beginning.

Nevertheless, despite any apprehension that Liberal Party leaders may have felt over this situation, they did not allow themselves to forget Joseph's victory. Although he was neither the first trade unionist to be elected to Parliament under the Liberal banner, nor the only one in 1885, it was he who was singled out for special attention. The National Liberal Club even decided to organise a special banquet in his honour on 16th January — shortly after the new Parliament was due to meet for the first time. To this end, a special committee was appointed to arrange the celebrations and Mr James Drake Digby, secretary of the Free Land League (of which Joseph was, of course, a vice-president) was appointed its honorary secretary. Joseph Chamberlain agreed to preside, and 'all the members of Mr. Gladstone's late government, who had so much to do with the enfranchisement of the agricultural labourers' were to be invited to attend.[2]

Arch himself was naturally elated by this attention and by the numerous congratulatory messages which continued to pour in from far and near. (He even had to reject proposals to give him public receptions at Barford and Leamington!) Nevertheless, as he assured members of the Leamington Liberal Working Men's Club at the beginning of January, he did not intend to allow his head to be turned by so much flattery, nor had he any desire to 'ape' his fellow M.Ps. in the matter of dress. Instead, he intended to take his seat in the same rough brown tweed suit and billy-cock hat that he wore to his country meetings. Events were to show that he was as good as his word on this point at least; and it was, consequently, in this attire that a waxwork model of him appeared in Madame Tussaud's during the course of April, 1886! Similarly, it was in rough tweeds that the famous Victorian caricaturist 'Spy' depicted him in the issue of *Vanity Fair* for 26th June, 1886. (The cartoon appeared in 'Spy's' 'Statesmen' series, but whilst this may have flattered Joseph, he probably appreciated far less the accompanying article on him by 'Jehu Junior,' which spoke of him as 'a demagogue with enough self-sufficiency to believe that he is a power in the land, . . . But Mr. Arch has his good qualities. Against his conceit — which is natural to half-educated men who have succeeded — may be set off his sincerity, courage and independence. In Parliament, where he was deposited by the Democratic wave of last year, he had chiefly made himself known by a few crude speeches and a pepper-and-salt suit, . . . He . . . worships Mr. Gladstone.')[3]

However, all this still lay a little in the future as, shortly after the Leamington meeting, he and Mrs Arch travelled up to London in readiness for his formal entry into Parliament. One of his chief worries had been the securing of accommodation for an outlay that he could afford, and this had at last been resolved when he had rented a room in Pimlico 'for a few shillings per week.' There he and Mrs Arch were to live for the next few months — the first and only time in fact that Mary Ann set up housekeeping outside her native Warwickshire.

Of course, finance was a matter of some concern to the new M.P. His weekly income at this stage came solely from N.A.L.U. funds and amounted to about £5, of which £2 10s. was his 'normal' salary as N.A.L.U. President and £2 10s. a contribution towards his 'expenses.' Although £5 might appear quite a large sum to the agricultural labourers, it was very small beer indeed to most M.Ps.

The first great event in Joseph's new political career came on the 13th January, when he formally entered Parliament to take his oath of allegiance as an M.P. Joseph Chamberlain and Jesse Collings were his sponsors, and Arch, clad conspicuously in his brown tweed suit, contrasted strangely with the more formal attire of his fellow Members.[4] It was a proud moment for him, as he later remembered: '. . . if I was smiling, it was an inside smile at the thought that my entry marked the triumph of our enfranchisement. I took my place in the Council Chamber of the nation as the representative of the labourer and the Prince of Wales — the Sandringham estates are in the North-

West division — and I said to myself, "Joseph Arch, M.P., you see to it that neither the Prince nor the labourer has cause to be ashamed of you".'5

Then, three days later, on the 16th, came the glittering banquet organised in his honour by the National Liberal Club, in the Grand Hall at the Criterion Restaurant, Piccadilly. Joseph was, no doubt, both excited and nervous as he set off to meet the distinguished guests who had gathered to do him homage. He himself was, as usual, rather incongruously clad in his faithful tweed suit, but the other 480 or so guests were all in formal evening dress.

It was a brilliant scene. The Hall was lit with 'numberless jets of electric light' and in the centre, hanging from the ceiling, was a massive chandelier of glass covered with electric jets. (This room must have been one of the first in London to be illuminated by the new wonder of electricity). The curtains and hangings were of rich dark velvet, and hothouse plants were ranged around the walls. The opulence and splendour of it all contrasted strangely with the stark simplicity of the village meetings to which Joseph was normally accustomed.

Many leading Liberals were there, including the Marquis of Ripon and, of course, Joseph Chamberlain, who was to preside. At the dinner Arch sat next to Chamberlain at the centre of the high table, and after the meal had ended Chamberlain proposed the toasts — including one to, 'The newly-enfranchised Agricultural Labourers and their first direct representative in Parliament' — Joseph Arch. In his speech, Chamberlain went on to praise Arch and the work he had done to help the members of his class. It was all very pleasant and gratifying for the ego.6 Joseph responded to the compliments showered upon him in a suitably grateful vein.

Nevertheless, these events, enjoyable though they were, were merely a prelude to the time when he might begin his work as an M.P. in earnest. At last the day came for which he had all along been waiting — the State opening of Parliament. Joseph and the ten other trade unionist M.Ps. decided to go as a group to the House for this great occasion. They all met first in the office of Henry Broadhurst, the secretary of the Parliamentary Committee of the Trades Union Congress, who was also an M.P. Then they strolled together quietly 'from Charing Cross to Parliament.' Joseph's own feelings of excitement were carefully masked as he marched stolidly along with the rest.

The Queen's speech had been prepared by the minority Conservative Government, which had continued in office after the election, but whose future depended on the attitude taken by the Irish Nationalists. However, even as the speech was being prepared the brief and fragile Tory/Nationalist alliance was breaking up, as Gladstone's conversion to the principle of Irish Home Rule became public knowledge. Nevertheless, the State opening took place as planned on the 21st — with Joseph among those present. The day was a memorable one for him; first and foremost, it was his real introduction to the life of Parliament, and secondly (and more trivially) during the evening debate he had the embarrassing experience of losing his way. He ended up in the Peers' Gallery, which was nearly empty at the time, and there he seated himself. He only discovered his mistake when the gallery began to fill up, and the peers present started to look askance at him, conspicuously dressed as he was in his serviceable tweeds![7]

On the political front, it soon became clear that the Tory Government could not long survive, deserted as it was by its former Irish allies. On the 26th January the inevitable happened and its defeat was secured when Jesse Collings moved an Amendment to the Address, expressing regret that no provision had been made for the supplying of allotments and small holdings 'on equitable terms as to rent and security of tenure' to agricultural labourers, and others, in the rural districts.[8] (Because of this Collings later suggested that the Liberals had come 'into power on the backs of the labourers . . .'[9])

For Joseph, the Amendment had a special significance, for it gave him the opportunity to make his Maiden speech in the House. He turned it into a passionate plea for the provision of more allotment land: 'We do not ask for borrowed funds, or for the land to be given us, and we have no desire to steal it. What the Amendment asks, and what I ask honourable gentlemen on both sides of the House is, whether the time has not come when these thousands of industrious and willing workers should no longer be shut out from the soil, and should have an opportunity of obtaining a fair freehold, and producing food for themselves and their families? . . .' (See Appendix 5 for the full text of his speech.) The speech was well received by the House and it has since found its way into at least one collection of 'Famous Speeches'.

With the defeat of the Conservatives on the 26th, the Liberals returned to power once more. Unfortunately, from the very beginning the spectre of Ireland haunted all their deliberations. As early as Christmas 1884, Gladstone himself had become convinced that it would be necessary to give Ireland a separate Parliament. However, perhaps regrettably for the future of his Party, he had kept this conversion a secret, and it was only after the 1885 election had been held that his son, Herbert, made known his true views on the Home Rule question to the world at large.

Immediately the differences which already existed among the Liberal Party leadership over Irish policy widened; Joseph Chamberlain, in particular, made it clear that he could not approve of any policy which gave Ireland a Parliament of its own. In the weeks that followed,

despite feverish negotiations, these internal conflicts remained unre-
solved, and that was still the position when, on 8th April, Gladstone
introduced his first Home Rule Bill to Parliament. As originally drafted,
it envisaged that Irish members would cease to sit at Westminster and
that instead an Irish Parliament would be established with powers of
taxation, and authority over 'every other matter not specifically excluded by the Act.'[9a] Among the excluded questions were to be foreign
policy, customs and excise, religious establishments, defence, posts and
coinage. And because of their existence, Gladstone vehemently denied
that he was seeking to repeal the Act of Union or to bring about the separation of Ireland from the rest of the United Kingdom.[10] His arguments
nevertheless quite failed to win the support of a large segment of his
Party; in particular, the Whig element, led by Lord Hartington, and
a group of Radicals, headed by Chamberlain, were outspoken opponents.

For Arch, this in-fighting was something quite beyond his power
of influence. As always, his sympathies were with Gladstone — the
Grand Old Man — whom he so deeply revered, and whose arguments
over Ireland he was more than ready to accept. Meanwhile, he pressed
ahead with his own work as best he could. Altogether, during the five
months or so that this Parliament was to last, he spoke in the House
on six occasions (including his Maiden speech). He was also sponsor
of an abortive Land Cultivation Bill put forward by Charles Bradlaugh,
the Radical M.P. for Northampton, which sought 'to make compulsory
the proper cultivation of the land of the country.' (This was, as we
have seen, a favourite bee in the Arch bonnet, and in a speech on
the Bill made on 14th April, he called for the Government to help to
keep the labourers on the land. 'Even if the Government were to
spend a few thousands in putting labourers to work upon the soil it
would be a far less reprehensible expenditure than that which had
been incurred by former Governments in unjust wars.' He confidently predicted that: 'There were thousands of men who would only
be too glad to cultivate the land, in order to grow their own food, but
they were not permitted to do so.'[11]) In the end, Bradlaugh was
persuaded to withdraw his Bill, however, and there the matter ended.
Arch's rhetoric had been in vain.

The N.A.L.U. President could, indeed, claim few positive achievements during his brief Parliamentary career, while one of his speeches
may actually have done him political harm. This was made in a debate
involving a Bill put forward by the Conservative M.P. for Mid-
Lincolnshire, Mr. Chaplin, called the 'Cottagers' Allotment Gardens
Bill'. It was designed to facilitate the acquisition of allotments by
labourers — 'If one-sixth of the cottagers in any parish . . . (wanted)
allotments upon fair and reasonable terms and (could not) obtain

them and there (was) land in the parish available for the purpose, they (should) be entitled to make a representation to that effect to the County Authorities.' The latter, in their turn, would seek to arrange for allotments to be made available 'by voluntary means.'[12] Arch himself condemned the Bill in no uncertain terms: 'I think a more flimsy or more worthless Bill was never introduced into this House.' Yet despite this strong language, many of his criticisms seemed to be of a trivial and carping character only, and it is difficult to escape the view that his prime objection was to the fact that the Bill had been sponsored by a Conservative. Because of this, he seemed to deduce, it must inevitably be useless to the labourer.

However, whether his criticisms were justified or not, they provided his Conservative opponents with valuable propaganda material to persuade the labourers that he put his Party interests before them. In the event, the Bill was thrown out by the Commons, but to those agricultural labourers who were genuinely anxious to acquire allotments, from whatever source, his opposition must have appeared somewhat frivolous. He himself seemed to recognise later that the speech had done him harm in his constituency, but he continued to defend his attitude on the ground that the Bill had been 'an insult to . . . agricultural labourers.' Nevertheless, it is significant that even six years later he was still seeking to justify his conduct in this matter.[13]

Meanwhile, on the national front, events were moving into a very much more serious phase. Increasingly, Irish affairs were dominating the Liberal Party's policy-making, until, on 8th June, there came the Second Reading of Gladstone's Home Rule Bill. After a debate carried on in an atmosphere of great bitterness and hostility, the Party split and the Government was defeated. In all, 93 Liberals joined the Conservatives in voting against the Bill; these rebels included Joseph Chamberlain and Lord Hartington, who, with their supporters, were shortly to form a separate Liberal Unionist Party devoted to the maintenance of existing links with Ireland.[14] In the light of this defeat, the Government was clearly unable to carry on in office. Gladstone decided to ask the Queen for a dissolution, so that he might appeal to the country on the Home Rule issue. This she agreed to, and a new election campaign soon loomed ahead for Joseph — as for all other Members of Parliament.

The Liberal Party was now in a state of extreme confusion, and as is the case with most fratricidal conflicts, 'the election campaign which followed was fought with unprecedented bitterness,' as Liberal Unionists and Gladstonian Liberals opposed one another in a number of the constituencies.[15]

Joseph, as one of Gladstone's most loyal supporters, became a strong advocate of the Home Rule for Ireland policy. Even at the time of his 1873 visit to that unhappy country, he had felt pity for the miserable lives of the peasants. Again, in his 1880 Election Address at Wilton he had called for 'a temperate, liberal and wise continuation of measures for improving the condition of the Irish peasantry . . .' (See Appendix 4.) His conversion to the Irish cause was, therefore, not *entirely* the result of his admiration for Gladstone, but there is no doubt that this was a very influential factor in deciding his attitude. After 1886, his desire for the adoption of a just policy towards Ireland was clearly very much more intense than it had ever been before. (At the same time, his deep respect for the Prime Minister was equally clear — for he has called Gladstone 'one of the mighty men of the earth,' and later wrote of an extremely brief visit he paid to Gladstone's home, Hawarden Castle, in 1884, as 'a red letter day.')[16]

It is significant, too, that Joseph's two sponsors when he entered Parliament (Chamberlain and Collings) were now abandoned, because of what Arch called the 'unholy alliance' they and their fellows had made with the Conservatives over the Home Rule issue. He saw the Tories as "making cats' paws of the seceders to divide the Liberal and Radical Party, and thus climb into office and power."[17]

When electioneering began in earnest on 17th June, 1886, however, Arch was to discover that his Irish policy was unpopular with a number of his former friends. At his very first meeting, in Fakenham Corn Hall, there was said to be 'some hooting at the further end of the hall' while he was speaking, and he took great care to try to minimise the impact of Home Rule and to 'ridicule the idea that (it) would tend to Imperial disintegration.'[18] Furthermore, his difficulties were increased by the fact that, as indicated earlier, a number of the agricultural labourers were already annoyed at his opposition to Chaplin's Allotments Bill. Indeed, at the Fakenham meeting, when he pointed out that on 'two distinct occasions Mr. Chaplin had voted against working men having allotments,' a voice in the audience called out — 'So did you.'[19] As the meeting progressed, other shouts of disapproval were heard concerning Joseph's allotments policy. It was a not altogether auspicious beginning.

As in 1885, Arch was to be opposed by Lord Henry Bentinck, and the *English Labourers' Chronicle*, realising that the fight was to be a close one, sought to extract the last ounce of labourer affection for the N.A.L.U. President. It declared: 'To Mr. Arch the farm labourers owe the vote more than to any other man. . . . Before he commenced his great life work they were like "dumb driven cattle," today they are "heroes in the strife" . . . To reject Mr. Arch would be an act of ingratitude, of which we can never believe the labourers will be guilty. . . .'[20]

On the day preceding the poll, a telegram of support was received from Mr. Gladstone, stating that he sincerely hoped 'the electors of North-West Norfolk (would) show an undiminished confidence in the representative who (had) well justified it.' This Joseph proudly took round with him on the last stages of his campaign. As he later recalled, when he drove round on polling day and was recognised by a group of men working in a hayfield, for example, he stopped the carriage, asked them if they had been to vote, and when they said that they had, he jumped down, pushed through the hedge 'and handed round copies of Gladstone's telegram.' When the men had read them, they stuck them on their 'forks and waved them, giving (Joseph) a hearty cheer.'[21] In some cases the haymakers shouted to him that 'they began work at 3 a.m. in order to have plenty of time in which to walk to the poll.'[22] Similar enthusiasm was shown on polling day in many other villages. In Rudham, Joseph was speeded on his way by about three hundred men and boys 'singing a local election ballad to the accompaniment of a drum and with faces flushed with enthusisam;' at Massingham railway station 'half-a-dozen porters hailed him with "Hurrah! we're all going for yo"'!'[23]

Yet, despite all these efforts, victory was not to be his. When the result was announced on 10th July, it was discovered that he had been defeated — although by a mere twenty votes. As the partisan *English Labourers' Chronicle* did not fail to point out, he had, of course, been battling against very considerable odds. For one thing, unlike his opponent, he had been unable to obtain conveyances to carry his supporters to the polls, and, in addition, at the busy summer season of the year, many labourers were at work until too late to register their vote. Not all were prepared to get up at 3 a.m. in order to give themselves an early start to the day's tasks! Then, too, it was later claimed by the local Liberal newspaper, the *Norfolk News*, that 'many of the farmers in the division practised the grossest form of intimidation upon the men.' The newspaper went on to quote one example in support of this sweeping claim; at the village of Dersingham, it reported that 'a squadron of farmers surrounded the voting place . . . and as each labourer came up, not only directed him how to vote, but threatened him with serious consequences if he did not put an X against the name of Lord Bentinck. This sort of thing was kept up for two hours of the afternoon, until Joseph Arch himself arrived upon the scene and scattered the farmers in all directions.'[24] In addition, the *Pall Mall Gazette* of 15th July claimed that 'some suffrages (had) been bought by the bribe of a two-shilling meat tea, provided by Primrose dames and others at sixpence per head.' (The 'Primrose dames' were, of course, members of the Conservative Primrose League).

It is impossible to decide to what extent these charges were justified by the facts. It seems likely that, as in 1885, *some* pressures were exerted on the labourers by a few reactionary interests, but it is obvious from the number of votes cast for Joseph on both occasions, that most workers were quite immune to either threats or promises — where such were made.

As soon as Joseph heard the result he demanded a recount, but, in the event, this did not yield any better outcome, from his point of view. He had to accept the fact that Lord Henry had won. His supporters meanwhile bewailed the sixty or so spoiled ballot papers which had been discovered, thinking that these were probably intended as votes for him. In all, Arch obtained 4,034 votes (or 417 less than in 1885), while Lord Henry Bentinck obtained 4,054 (or 241 more than in 1885).

Yet, despite Arch's natural disappointment, he would not allow himself to appear despondent, but immediately rallied his supporters in a short speech, telling them: ' . . . be not dismayed, for before long I shall come back and claim the confidence of my fellow-labourers.'

The *English Labourers' Chronicle*, for its part, rather bitterly attributed the defeat to: 'Abstentions and certain "cheap trips" to the Norwich Show . . .' Nevertheless, even this partial source admitted that *some* defection had taken place over the Home Rule issue, and that the Gladstonian policy which had been 'loyally accepted as we believe by a vast majority of agricultural labourers, was undoubtedly refused by some, and the great split in the Liberal Party, which followed the introduction of Mr. Gladstone's famous measure, was naturally felt in the agricultural districts . . .'[25]

Joseph himself attributed his defeat mainly to a lack of carriages to transport his supporters to the polling stations and to 'great territorial influence' — but whatever the true reasons were, the fact remained that he had now been pushed out of the Parliamentary seat he had valued so dearly. He must return to the sidelines of political life and to his failing Union. Nevertheless, he was determined to regard the defeat as a temporary setback only and to seize the first opportunity of fighting back. He had the doubtful consolation, too, of knowing that many other Gladstonian Liberals had suffered the same fate as himself, for only 191 had been returned to Parliament — as opposed to 316 Conservatives, 78 Liberal Unionists and 85 Irish Nationalists.

Arch's defeat did not go unnoticed, either, outside labourer circles. Many letters from friends and admirers came to his Barford home, regretting the result; several were later published in the columns of the *English Labourers' Chronicle* during late July.

Characteristically, Arch spent little time in repining his lot. By the beginning of August he had once more taken up his work as Union agitator, his first meeting being at Darsham in Suffolk. Yet, despite his obvious determination not to be downcast, there was an understandable trace of bitterness in his speech on this occasion. He declared that: 'In all his political experience he had never known an election where so much misrepresentation and lying were carried on by the Conservative party as the last one. Their conduct then was a disgrace to civilization . . .'[26] The use of such extreme language was undoubtedly an indication of the deep hurt he felt within himself at what he saw as his rejection by the Norfolk electors.

Unfortunately, too, he could gain little consolation from consideration of the position of the Union. By now, membership had fallen to around 10,000, and it is significant that at many of his meetings genuine support seems to have been lacking — except, perhaps, in East Anglia. At Northleach in Gloucestershire, for example, where he spoke at the end of September, he found it necessary to say, after a vote of thanks had been given to him, that the 'best vote they could give him would be to all join the Union . . .' But his listeners do not seem to have heeded the plea, and membership in Gloucestershire remained at a low level.

As before, opportunities were also given to Joseph to speak on behalf of the Liberal Party, and the early weeks of 1887 found him engaged upon a fairly lengthy speaking tour on their behalf in the North of England — especially Lancashire. During the course of January and the beginning of February it was reported that he had addressed nearly twenty public meetings, in about as many days, mostly within the Lancaster constituency. These meetings were, of course, not concerned with the Union at all, but with condemnation of the Conservative Party and with demands for land reform or for Home Rule for Ireland.

At the beginning of the tour he had apparently been offered a fee of £20 for his lectures, but this he had refused to accept. Instead he had asked that it should be sent to the Union's General Secretary, to be added to the N.A.L.U.'s general funds.[27] It is impossible to know if this was his normal practice in the matter of fees or whether he did, on occasion, receive some payment for his lectures.

Then, quite unexpectedly, early in 1887 he was given hope of an escape from the often dreary round of speechmaking and exhortation. This arose from the fact that during January of that year Lord Henry Bentinck, the sitting member for North-West Norfolk, had written a letter of thanks to one of his supporters, named Wasey, who lived in the village of South Creake. With the letter he had sent a postal order for £3, 'as some small compensation for all the trouble and worry you have had in connection with the election and afterwards.' As a postscript, Lord Henry had added, 'You had better not tell anyone that I sent you anything.'[28] Unfortunately for him, the letter fell into the hands of another Mr. Wasey, also of South Creake, who was an enthusiastic friend of Arch and of the Liberal Party. Allegations of corruption on the part of Lord Henry were soon being made, as it was claimed that under the Corrupt Practices at Elections Act of 1883, the time for payment of election expenses had expired in the early part of the previous August, and furthermore, that all payments should have been made by the election agent anyway and not by the candidate.

To Joseph the opportunity seemed too good to be true. A petition against Bentinck was quickly lodged on his behalf in the Queen's Bench Division of the High Court. It was to be heard on 5th April, and just before this date, Joseph, speaking at Swaffham in Norfolk, excitedly promised his audience that if the outcome of the petition were in his favour, 'before many hours were over he would be down in North-West Norfolk as a candidate for its representation . . .'29

Sadly, from his point of view, the result was *not* favourable. At the trial Lord Henry was able to satisfy the Court that the payment had been made not in respect of the election proper but rather in respect of Mr. Wasey's efforts in 'working up the (electoral) register for South Creake,' in the Conservative interest. It was therefore denied that 'the present of three pounds was made in respect of any expense prohibited by the Corrupt Practices Act.' The request for secrecy had been made because Bentinck was anxious to avoid creating jealousy among the other party workers who had not been similarly rewarded; he claimed that he had written the letter carelessly and it was this fact which had given the impression of corruption.

As soon as Lord Henry went into the witness box and made this explanation, therefore, Arch's counsel decided to withdraw the petition. As was usual in such circumstances, Arch had to pay the costs incurred both by his opponent and by himself. Since he personally did not have sufficient spare cash to meet this expenditure, the *English Labourers' Chronicle* of 9th April appealed for help, hoping that his 'many' friends would not allow him to suffer. It seems likely that supporters in the Liberal Party did oblige, although no information on the final financial arrangements was published at any later date, and the whole business is omitted from Arch's autobiography.

Here, then, was another dashing of his hopes. In a speech made at Sutton Bridge, Lincolnshire, shortly afterwards, Arch's feelings of frustration are only too apparent. There is more than a trace of 'sour grapes' in his claim that: 'Personally he should like to keep outside the walls of Parliament, for the life of members of that House, who wanted to see business done, was wearing and worrying. But in great public questions he did not consider his personal feelings, and, considering he held very great influence amongst the working classes from one end of England to the other . . . it would be a dereliction of duty in his part not to respond to the request of the labourers of North-West Norfolk to speak their voice in Parliament. Given health and strength, he quite expected again to occupy a seat in the House of Commons.'[31]

And if entry to Parliament remained his underlying ambition, he obviously thought that the best way in which this could be achieved was by continued support for Gladstonian policies — in particular, support for Irish Home Rule. At the twentieth Trades Union Congress, held in September, 1887, for example, he passionately appealed to the delegates on this point, saying that, 'He thought they would fail in their duty unless they were allowed to express their opinion about the tyranny of the present Government in Ireland . . .' Later in the same Congress he declared that: 'At the next election the first question should be that affecting Ireland: . . .'[32] A year or so later, at a Liberal Association meeting at Shipley, he expressed the wish that he might again enter Parliament so that he could 'record his vote in favour of justice to the Irish people, . . .'[33] And in a letter published in the *English Labourers' Chronicle* of 12th January, 1889, he was even more vehement in his criticism of the record of the then Conservative Government over Ireland. He declared that the Liberals must be 'determined that our Irish brethren shall be delivered at once and for ever out of the hands of the uncircumcised Tory Philistines.' Such emotional language, with its biblical overtones, obviously did little to endear him to members of the Tory Party!

The advocacy of Home Rule was, then, a major theme of many of Joseph's speeches during his often frustrating years on the fringes of public life in the late 1880's. But his lack of genuine progress in the political field was by no means his only problem at this stage in his career. Once more, allegations of financial corruption were being levelled against him by former friends and supporters. This time the offenders were George Ball and George Mitchell, who had both been fellow N.A.L.U. trustees with Joseph from about 1880 up to the Annual Conference of the Union in 1886.

There is no doubt that the real basis for the charges was provided by the slackness of book-keeping methods adopted by the Union officers and the evasive attitude many of them (including Joseph) adopted to try to conceal the true position of N.A.L.U. finances from friend and foe alike.

Despite the controversies and economies of the late 1870's, a considerable part of the Union's income continued to be swallowed up by 'working and other expenses' (See Appendix 2), while as early as the 1884 Conference it had been revealed to delegates that £900 of the Sick Benefit Society's funds had been used for trade purposes — to provide unemployment relief, strike benefit, etc. However, in response to anxious queries about the overall state of the funds, the then general secretary, Robert Collier, merely remarked soothingly that, 'the auditor had all the accounts submitted to him for his inspection,' and he had implied that all would be well.

The following year it was announced that £400 of the £900 had in fact been repaid to the sick funds by the trade section, and Mitchell and Ball both expressed satisfaction at this. However, when shortly afterwards the former was asked to sign a cheque for £500 'for sick purposes,' he refused to do so 'unless a proper statement was given' as to its exact composition. This was promised and Mitchell signed the cheque — but in fact the statement failed to materialise, despite repeated demands by Mitchell. The rift between Mitchell and Arch then rapidly widened, until at the conference in May, 1886, Mitchell and Ball were both asked to resign as trustees, while two minor union officials (both former labourers) were elected to act, with Arch, as replacements. This step, no doubt intended to rid the Union of unwelcome critics, was condemned by outsiders as well as by Mitchell. Its purpose seemed to be to bring the finances too closely under the personal control of Joseph himself, with the two new trustees acting merely as ciphers. It is a sign of the suspicions that his actions were beginning to arouse even among friends that in 1887, an urban union leader, George Howell, could comment on the controversy and on Arch's temporary assumption of the position of Union treasurer: ' . . . thus Arch is Trustee, President, ex.committee and general manager. God help the poor laborers (sic).'[34]

Mitchell, for his part, was not the man to allow himself to be pushed aside in this cavalier fashion. Not only did he refuse to authorise the passage of the Union's funds from his trusteeship to that of the two new appointees, but he issued a pamphlet, in the summer of 1887, which was designed to give the maximum publicity to the affair. At the same time, he wrote to the press vehemently condemning Arch's leadership and the policy of the N.A.L.U.

There is little doubt that great confusion did exist in the Union accounts and to this extent, therefore, Mitchell's anxiety was justified— although it would have been more to his credit if he had displayed greater interest earlier on, whilst he was still a trustee. Nevertheless, once called upon to surrender the funds to another duly appointed body of trustees, he had no legal right to withhold his consent. Consequently, after several abortive attempts had been made to persuade him to agree to a transfer, the new trustees decided to bring an action against him in the Chancery Division of the High Court, in November, 1887.

When the case came up, judgment was given for the new trustees, and Mitchell's objections to handing over the funds to them were overruled. The Judge declared that in the light of the facts at his disposal he could not 'assume that the present Trustees (were) about to commit a breach of trust . . .'[35]

Naturally this result gave considerable satisfaction in Union circles (even if it did mean that the sick benefit fund had had to be raided to the tune of £149 to cover the legal expenses, etc.)[36] This was felt to be a small price to pay to obtain justice, and ten thousand copies of the report of the case were immediately ordered to be printed by the N.A.L.U. Executive Committee, for distribution among members. Nevertheless, this decision could not eradicate all the effects of the unfavourable publicity which the case had already provoked and which had done serious harm to the already weak Union movement. By the end of 1887, N.A.L.U. membership had slumped to 5,300 — or about half of the previous year's total.

For Joseph, the case was especially unpleasant, as, despite the judgment given, Mitchell continued to write damaging letters to the press on Arch's 'infamous' conduct in regard to the Union funds. Not surprisingly, the whole affair was quickly seized upon by Joseph's enemies outside the Union, too. The Conservative *Leamington Spa Courier* of 28th May, 1887, for example, noted that 'intense indignation was expressed against Mr. Arch for his neglect of the Union and the sacrifice of its interests to his own as a Member of Parliament . . .' Another Conservative newspaper, the *Leicester Advertiser*, was even stronger in its criticism. In the issue of 20th August, 1887, it declared: 'We all know how bumptiously Mr. JOSEPH ARCH has posed as the champion of the Agricultural Labourers, but it was never difficult to see that, like all other glib-tongued demagogues, Mr. ARCH was first and foremost concerned for himself, and that so long as he was well paid for it, he was always ready for any sort of social or political agitation, . . . What good he has ever done for any of the farm labourers, excepting himself, has not yet been discovered, but it is well-known that he has done infinite mischief by his efforts to stir up strife amongst the farm labourers, and set class against class . . . This time there is an apparently very bitter squabble going on as to the distribution of the sick benefit funds . . . It seems Mr. ARCH regards that as a piece of information which is to be kept a profound secret from all but himself . . . Mr. MITCHELL alleges that the money which has been subscribed by the labourers to the sick fund of the Union has, contrary to the rules, been squandered in other ways; . . . and that notwithstanding that he is one of the trustees, and as such holds a responsible position, the particulars as to the distribution of certain funds are denied to him . . . In refusing his consent to this open and impartial investigation, Mr. MITCHELL confirms what many have long thought — namely that Mr. ARCH "is no friend of the labourers".' In a further report on the matter on 17th September, the newspaper noted triumphantly that, 'Mr. Arch is now a long way from having the confidence placed in him which he had once somehow acquired amongst his class.'

And as the months passed by, the controversy still rumbled on. It was now no longer confined to the ranks of the Union movement or even to the columns of the newspapers, but had reached the floor of the House of Commons. On 24th July, 1888, Major Rasch, the Conservtive M.P. for South-East Essex, asked the First Lord of the Treasury, 'Whether the Government (would) cause an investigation of the Agricultural Labourers' Union, in order to prevent further misappropriation . . .?' The First Lord, Mr W. H. Smith, replied, however, that as the 'Agricultural Labourers' Union (was) not a Friendly Society but a Trades Union . . . the Government (had) no legal power to direct an investigation into its affairs.'[37]

Arch himself immediately wrote to Major Rasch, asking him to produce evidence of the alleged misappropriation. Rasch's only response was to refer Joseph 'to the statements of Mr. Mitchell' and to a meeting of union dissidents which had been held on 13th July. Arch pressed for something more definite than this, asking 'how and by whom this misappropriation occurred.' But he could obtain no satisfaction.[38]

Furthermore, this exchange did not prevent Major Rasch from returning to the Parliamentary attack in the following year, when he once more asked for investigation of the Union's affairs (and this time he mentioned Joseph Arch by name in connection with the matter).[39] Once again, however, the Government refused to act, but the repeated unfavourable press publicity to which these questions gave rise was obviously extremely damaging to Joseph's reputation. It also helped to account for the dramatic slump in Union membership which took place — to a level of only 4,254 by the end of 1889. Indeed, one group of labourers in Essex were so disturbed over the 'differences' which had arisen concerning the management of the N.A.L.U. that they wrote to the National Liberal Club in November, 1890, asking for help and advice. But the Club's Political Committee — to which their request had been referred — prudently declined to take any action in the matter.[40]

With these further attacks in progress even Joseph's tremendous self-confidence was affected, and it is possible to detect a note of weariness in his end-of-year message to the labourers in 1888: 'The Union coach is yours, the coachman is your servant. Dismiss your coachman if you will, but no man, no number of men, no number of enemies, however formidable, can smash your coach only yourselves. . . .'[41]

There is, in fact, little doubt that the charges of deliberate corruption levelled at him were 'largely untrue or exaggerated,' as *The Times* pointed out in its obituary notice on him, published many years later. It seems likely that political rivalry and a personality clash between Arch and Mitchell were more important in giving rise to the allegations than were any positive acts of corruption and mismanagement in themselves. Support for this view is given by the fact that in his pamphlet, issued in 1887, Mitchell declared, in the middle of a long tirade against Union mismanagement, and quite out of context, 'But what do I get from the Liberals for doing my duty, excepting the most cruel treatment? . . .'[42] This sentence indicates, at the very least, a preoccupation with his own apparent rejection by Liberal Party leaders — an experience in marked contrast to the reception given to Arch after his success in the 1885 general election.

Unfortunately, too, the difficulties of the Union's financial position were aggravated by the unsatisfactory position of the Sick Benefit Society. This had originally been established without any real thought being given to its long-term progress or future stability. Consequently by the end of the 1880's the outgoings of this section of the N.A.L.U.'s work were dramatically exceeding its income; even at the 1886 Annual Council of the Union, 'The exceptional sickness which (had) prevailed during the past year' was blamed for the fact that expenditure on sickness claims had exceeded contributions by "about £1,000", and only a donation of £423 from an unnamed 'friend' had partly saved the situation in that year. Regrettably, the following months showed no improvement, and at the 1888 Annual Conference it was disclosed that the demands on the Sick Fund had been such that withdrawals to the tune of about £500 had had to be made from the reserves. To combat this damaging trend, a levy of 1s 6d. per member was proposed However, as Joseph and the other members of the Executive Committee were to discover, it was one thing to impose a levy and quite another to collect it. Many members refused to pay, and as Arch admitted in his 1889 presidential address to the Annual Conference, even its imposition had caused 'great dissatisfaction.' Nevertheless, he went on to state, rather bitterly, that 'other societies had had to impose levies, but . . .there was no other society in the kingdom which had been subjected to the attacks that this society had experienced.'[43] During the financial year to April, 1889, the position had if anything deteriorated; income from sick benefit contributions amounted to £2,840 19s 8½d. — outgoings to £4,816 17s 9d.!

Clearly something had to be done and so from 1st October, 1889, reductions in benefits were proposed. Yet, still the outflow of cash continued, and all of the remaining younger or healthy members who could join more stable societies did so. Only the aged or infirm remained members of the N.A.L.U. scheme. By May, 1890 there were said to be altogether 838 members of the Sick Benefit Society in thirteen districts — of whom 448 had received benefit of one sort or another during the course of the preceding year!

The next reform was proposed in December, 1890, when payment of doctor's fees was suspended and funeral benefits were reduced. Then, in February of the following year, it was finally decided to to give up the unequal struggle. Payments out of the Sick Benefit fund ceased entirely and about a year later, it was decided that the whole business must be wound up. As Joseph had feared, therefore, the Sick Benefit Society came to an unsatisfactory conclusion. In 1893, when new N.A.L.U. rules were registered, all mention of the Sick Benefit Society was carefully omitted.

Yet, if there was much to worry and depress Joseph in these years of the later 1880's — when even the Liberals seem to have had less need of his services as a speaker or organiser[44] — there were at least a few bright spots, including his election as a County Councillor.

Following the passage of the 1888 Local Government Act, setting up County Councils, he had agreed to offer himself for election to the first Warwickshire County Council. He stood as a Radical for the Wellesbourne Division, and in his Address to the electors he declared that he did not 'intend to canvass' for votes and therefore 'each Elector (would be) free to use his or her own judgment at the poll.' His main message was on the need for more allotments, and he pointed out that, 'as one who knows personally the benefit of a good Allotment to a working man's family, I shall advocate and support the Allotment system, and will do my best to see it carried out in every parish where the men require land. . .'[45]

Joseph's electioneering was organised on a very low key and he only addressed three meetings during the entire campaign — one being at Barford and another at Wellesbourne. There are no accounts of the labourers flocking to his support as they had done nearly seventeen years earlier. Indeed, all the evidence points the other way. Clearly the first great phase of hero-worship had disappeared — apparently for ever.

Joseph's opponent at Wellesbourne was a landowner and county magistrate from the village of Loxley, named Mr J. Cove Jones, and when the election was held on 24th January, 1889, its outcome was by no means certain. In the event, Joseph *was* elected — but by the narrow majority of 34. He secured 423 votes as opposed to Mr Jones's 389.

The *English Labourers' Chronicle* naturally hailed it as a 'famous victory;' 'Mr. Arch fought the contest almost single handed. A few tried and faithful friends stood by his side. But so far as regards organisation, Committees, conveyances and wealth, all the odds were against Mr. Arch. . . .'[46] The significant part of the statement is, however, the reference to a 'few' tried and trusted friends. Even in his home area, many former supporters had deserted him.

Joseph was to serve on the County Council until 1892. Although he was a fairly good attender, being present at seventeen out of a possible twenty Council meetings, and twenty-one out of thirty-eight meetings of the Roads and Bridges Committee, to which he was appointed, he took no very energetic role in Council affairs. He did not stand for re-election in 1892, being obviously dissatisfied with its rather limited sphere of influence. He made this very clear at a Liberal meeting at Rougham in Norfolk at the end of February, 1892, when he declared: 'It had been his privilege to sit on Warwick County Council for three years and a greater farce he never knew. The Local Government Act was from first to last a Tory Bill. With one hand it gave them two things, and took four from them with the other . . .'[47] (A similar lack of enthusiasm for local affairs was, incidentally, displayed by him when he was appointed Highway Surveyor for Barford at a meeting of the parish vestry in March, 1889. After some discussion, his name was put forward by a Mr Baker, the local poor law guardian, and Joseph reluctantly accepted the office, on the grounds that the County Council would 'take over the roads of the county on the 31st of March, 1890, and he hoped that, as a member of that body he should be able to do something towards improving the state of the roads — now in a bad condition . . .')

On the other hand, Union affairs were taking up less of his time as well, at this stage. During the six-month period from January to June, 1889, he addressed only twenty-seven N.A.L.U. gatherings, according to reports given in the *English Labourers' Chronicle* at the time. All of them were held in Norfolk and Suffolk, save for the Union's Annual Council, which was organised at Leamington, at the end of May. In the old days he would have addressed more meetings in six weeks than he now did in six months. In addition, he addressed eleven meetings for local Liberal Associations — again all, except one, in Norfolk and Suffolk. Most of these were indeed in the North-West Norfolk area, in which he still had a political interest. It is, no doubt, a sign of his fading fortunes that he no longer received invitations to address Liberal gatherings of national significance.

By the end of the 1880's, therefore, Arch's round of activities had narrowed very considerably, with much of his time now being spent quietly at home, working in the garden or around the house. When a correspondent from the *North Devon Journal* called on him at the beginning of January, 1889, for example, he was busy in his small workshop. The reporter noted that 'with his knitted jacket and soft round hat, he (looked) the part of a well-to-do artisan who (had) settled down to enjoy the residue of his days.' But Joseph had certainly not retired; he was still being paid £2 10s. per week as N.A.L.U. President and he was merely biding his time, waiting for a chance to return to public life. Meanwhile, he was keeping himself as fully occupied as possible. With the aid of his carpentering skills he had 'made new furniture' for the house. and in his small green house cultivated several 'rare ferns and some nice plants.' He had still retained his old-fashioned country hospitality too, for he invited the reporter to stay to lunch and to share with himself and Mrs Arch 'a pig's chunk' and some Savoy cabbages which he had grown in the garden![48]

And about three years later, when Mr Roger C. Richards, an Assistant Commissioner in connection with the Royal Commission on Labour called on him, he was similarly at work — this time in the garden. Although his hair had now turned grey and had thinned considerably, and the hazel eyes had lost some of their old keenness (for he now had to wear glasses to read or for close work), in most other respects he carried his sixty-five years very lightly — save only that like most hedgecutters he was a martyr to rheumatism.

To any impartial observer, it must have seemed, then, that by the latter part of 1889 the N.A.L.U. had almost reached the end of its life. Membership was down to just over 4,000 and it only looked a matter of time before the whole organisation folded up. Even Joseph's perennial optimism and self-confidence had by now been sadly shaken. It is significant that in the spring of 1890, for example, he was trying to increase the circulation of the Union newspaper, the *English Labourers' Chronicle*, by seeking to establish links with the Tyneside and National Labour Union, an urban union centred around Newcastle-on-Tyne. The negotiations do not seem to have been very successful, but the mere fact that Joseph had embarked upon them shows that he was obviously willing to try almost anything to bolster up the N.A.L.U. Then, suddenly, the whole picture changed, and his flagging hopes were revived.

Following the successful London dock strike in August, 1889, and a brief upturn of the trade cycle, there was a resurgence of interest in trade unionism among many unskilled or poorly-paid workers — including the agricultural labourers. From the beginning of 1890 reports of more hopeful recruitment trends began to be received from Norfolk in particular. Here the N.A.L.U. was fortunate in having as its district organiser Zacharias Walker, a Methodist local preacher and former tailor, who was devoted to the Union cause. Nevertheless, Arch himself, realising that every chance to revive the movement must be taken, quickly stepped in, too, to give all the help he could. At the beginning of January, despite the bad weather, he paid a brief visit to the county, and then, about a fortnight later, returned again, this time for a week's tour.

As his train drew into Thorpe Railway Station at the beginning of this second visit, Joseph saw the faithful Walker waiting for him with a face wreathed in smiles. The cause of his joy was the large increase in letters written to him asking him to come and help in the formation of new branches, or to address village meetings. Joseph naturally shared his happiness, and on his return to Barford enthusiastically wrote: 'I haven't paid a visit to Norfolk for a long time that has so delighted me as that of last week. . . .'[49] For the first time in years he had encountered some of the old enthusiasm and fervour for the Union. At the village of Bale, for example, despite the inclement weather, the meeting had been so large that it had overflowed outside the Methodist Chapel in which it was to be held and there were nearly as many people standing outside as there were in. Altogether, as Joseph jubilantly reported, 'There were labourers from twelve villages around present . . .' He went on to claim: 'The outlook for the Union is brighter now than it has been for several years. The enemies of the Union have about had their day. They can scatter broadcast their villainous falsehoods, but the labourers, especially in Norfolk and Suffolk, are not going to be gulled by professed friends, and I don't think were I to go into Oxfordshire again, 1 out of every 100 would condemn me.'

In the event, Arch's optimism proved to be justified at least in the short run. By the middle of February, Walker had organised 1,000 new members in Norfolk alone. However, if a revival did occur to some degree, it is important to note that it was confined primarily to Norfolk, with Suffolk, Essex, and in a very modest way, Oxfordshire, involved to a far smaller extent; elsewhere the labourers seem to have been unaffected.[50]

By the end of 1891, therefore, total membership had risen to about 15,000 — of whom over 12,000 had been recruited in Norfolk and 1,360 in Essex, under the eye of the enthusiastic Norfolk-born district organiser, David Sage. The role of Norfolk was thus clearly pre-eminent, and it is to Zacharias Walker especially that most of the success must be attributed. He worked tirelessly for the Union and Joseph fully appreciated this, for he later paid generous tribute to Walker's 'indefatigable' efforts.[51]

At the same time of course, Arch himself gave all the help and encouragement he could. Even in the 1890's, he was still an effective speaker, as one former Union member recalled many years afterwards: 'Young as I was, I was simply captivated by Arch's personality, for Arch's was a personality that, once he was seen and heard, you never could forget him. . . . Arch became my hero and my ideal in life, and when I was old enough I joined Arch's Union, and proud I was that I was able to do my little part to assist somewhat in his noble ideals.'[52]

By the end of 1891, then, the future of the Union looked more cheerful than it had done for many a long day — and from the N.A. L.U. President's own point of view the revival could scarcely have been better timed. For in 1892 there was to be another general election, and Joseph was again to have an opportunity to enter Parliament as the Member for North-West Norfolk. Although some of the fire and vigour of earlier years had gone, he was still a formidable opponent and an extremely determined one. He had weathered the fierce storms of the 1880's — perhaps in the 1890's he might hope for calmer waters and for a more favourable turn of the wheel of fortune.

[1] Sir P. Magnus, op.cit., p.337.

[2] *English Labourers' Chronicle* — 9th January, 1886.

[3] *Vanity Fair* cartoon No. 921, 1886. The waxwork model went on display from the end of April, 1886 at Madame Tussaud's. According to the *English Labourers' Chronicle* of 1st May, 1886, it was clad 'in a plain suit of tweed, . . .' and the cost of its production was 'some hundreds of pounds'.

[4] *English Labourers' Chronicle* — 16th January, 1886.

[5] Joseph Arch, op.cit., p.357.

[6] *English Labourers' Chronicle* — 23rd January, 1886.

[7] *English Labourers' Chronicle* — 30th January, 1886.

[8] Jesse Collings — *Rural Reform* (London, 1906), p.182.

[9] Ibid.

[9a] Sir P. Magnus, pp.353–354. See also Peter Fraser — *Joseph Chamberlain* — (London 1966), Chapter 3.

[10] Sir P. Magnus, op.cit., pp.363–364.

[11] Hansard, 3rd Series, Vol. CCCIV — 14th April, 1886, pp.1603–1606.

[12] Hansard, 3rd Series, Vol. CCCV — 21st May, 1886, pp.1786–1789.

[13] *Norfolk News* — 2nd July, 1892.

[14] Sir P. Magnus, op.cit., p.357 and Peter Fraser, op.cit., p.110.

[15] Sir P. Magnus, op.cit., p.358. See however, M. Hurst — *Joseph Chamberlain and Liberal Reunion* (London, 1967) for details of an abortive attempt to heal the breach early in 1887.

[16] Joseph Arch, op.cit., p.380.

[17] *English Labourers' Chronicle* — 19th June, 1886.

[18] *Norfolk News* — 19th June, 1886.

[19] *Norfolk News* — 26th June, 1886.

[20] *English Labourers' Chronicle* — 3rd July, 1886.

[21] Joseph Arch, op.cit., p.363.

[22] *Norfolk News* — 24th July, 1886.

[23] Ibid.

[24] *Norfolk News* — 2nd July, 1892.

[25] *English Labourers' Chronicle* — 25th December, 1886. J.P.D. Dunbabin in 'Parliamentary Elections in Great Britain 1868–1900 — A Psephological Note' observes,'It was in the countryside (where the full effects of the franchise were felt) that the landslide came (in 1885); and in 1886 the swing from the Liberals was more marked there than elsewhere; . . . Between 1885 and 1900 the Liberal share of the electorate was at best

stagnant.' In *English Historical Review*, Vol.LXXXI, 1966 pp.87 and 96.

[26] *English Labourers' Chronicle* — 14th August, 1886.

[27] *English Labourers' Chronicle* — 15th January, 1887.

[28] *The Times* — 6th April, 1887.

[29] *English Labourers' Chronicle* — 9th April, 1887.

[30] *The Times* — 6th April, 1887.

[31] *English Labourers' Chronicle* — 18th April, 1887.

[32] Report of the Twentieth Trades Union Congress — 1887. (Howell Collection.)

[33] *English Labourers' Chronicle* — 1st December, 1888.

[34] Howell Collection — Note attached in MS. to pamphlet issued by Mitchell and Ball in 1887.

[35] *Leamington Spa Courier* — 19th November, 1887.

[36] *English Labourers' Chronicle* — 31st May, 1890. Report of the N.A.L.U. Annual Council Meeting at Norwich.

[37] Hansard, 3rd Series, Vol. CCCXXIX, p.328.

[38] Joseph Arch, op.cit., p.374 and *English Labourers' Chronicle* — 25th August,1887.

[39] Hansard, 3rd Series, Vol. CCCXXXVIII, pp.1432–33.

[40] Minute Book of the Political Committee of the National Liberal Club — Meeting on 3rd December, 1890.

[41] *English Labourers' Chronicle* — 29th December, 1888.

[42] Mitchell and Ball pamphlet, p.13.

[43] *English Labourers' Chronicle* — 8th June, 1889. Another Union which imposed such levies — in 1884 and again in 1898, — to stablise its Sick Benefit Fund was the National Union of Boot and Shoe Operatives. — See A. Fox — *A History of the National Union of Boot and Shoe Operatives, 1874–1957* (Oxford, 1958). For information on the 1886 Annual Council see *English Labourers' Chronicle* — 5th June, 1886.

[44] In a leading article written in the *English Labourers' Chronicle* of 25th January, 1890, for example, he asked whether the Liberals were 'going to help the Labourers' Union by subscribing a few thousands to their funds to help to push on the work of organisation? If not, at the next election, I am afraid the Liberals in the counties will be behind in the swim . . . The Labourers' Union would be the backbone of the Liberal Party in the counties if they would only help us to establish it in every village . . .' Clearly he was trying to revive flagging Liberal Party interest in the Union; at the same time, the union newspaper contained fewer accounts of speeches made by him to Liberal gatherings.

[45] See Address in Appendix 4.

[46] *English Labourers' Chronicle* — 2nd February, 1889.

[47] *English Labourers' Chronicle* — 5th March, 1892.

[48] *English Labourers' Chronicle* — 12th January, 1889.

[49] *English Labourers' Chronicle* — 1st February, 1890.

[50] See P. L. R. Horn — 'The Farm Workers, the Dockers and Oxford University' in *Oxoniensia*, Vol. XXXII, 1967, for information on union recruitment in Oxfordshire.

[51] Joseph Arch, op.cit., p.385. 'In 1890 the Union, largely owing to the indefatigable efforts of Mr. Walker — he pushed it hard and fast, and never spared himself — began to look up once more.'

[52] *Memoirs of Josiah Sage* (London, 1951), p.48. Josiah Sage was a second cousin of David Sage, the Essex union organiser.

CHAPTER TWELVE

The Final Years: 1892-1919

For Joseph, the beginning of the year 1892 was a time of new hope. It seemed that the dark clouds which had overshadowed the late 1880's had finally rolled away and a more optimistic view could now be taken of the future, On the previous 10th December he had been invited to take part in a Rural Conference organised in London by the Liberal Party and had grasped the opportunity of assuring his fellow delegates that he would do his 'best to show the agricultural labourers who (were) their friends and who (were) their foes.' Shortly afterwards a pamphlet written by him and entitled *Joseph Arch's Advice to the Labourers* was issued as Liberal Leaflet No. 1568. In this he called upon the labourers to: 'Unite together and claim your freedom while you have the greatest of living statesmen to champion your just and righteous demands.' On the political front, therefore, Joseph was clearly well in the swing of Liberal Party affairs once more, after his spell of being rather out of favour only three or four years earlier. Perhaps not surprisingly, he celebrated this by noticeably hardening his attitude towards his former friends, Chamberlain and Collings — and indeed towards the Liberal Unionists generally. Early in 1892 he told an appreciative audience in Thetford that the Liberal Unionists were 'neither fish, flesh, or (sic) fowl, nor a good red herring . . .(They) were like a lot of political marauders going up and down the country without any visible means of subsistence.'[1]

As regards the Union, too, the situation appeared quite satisfactory; in a new year message Arch noted that 1891 had been a 'year of unparalleled success to the National Agricultural Labourers' Union . . . The coming year will be brighter . . . if you only keep combined.' Recruitment in Norfolk was especially heartening, and during a tour of that county early in February he was given an enthusiastic welcome by his labourer audiences. In addition, the members of the Stoke Horley Cross, Eaton and Swardestone branches clubbed together to buy him a 'beautiful walking stick, mounted with a silver top and bearing . . . the inscription 'Joseph Arch, President, N.A.L.U.'

This was presented to him as a memento of the twentieth anniversary of the establishment of the Union at Wellesbourne, on 7th February, 1872.[2]

The remainder of February and the beginning of March were spent in tours of Essex, Norfolk and Suffolk and it was whilst addressing a meeting at Brettenham in Suffolk on 8th March that Joseph caught a chill. As his diary records, on the next day he was too ill to carry out his programme,[3] and for a brief period he was forced to remain in bed. But, being anxious to keep up the momentum of Union revival, he would not allow himself sufficient rest to permit a proper recovery. Instead, he decided to go ahead as planned with a tour of Essex early in April. Unfortunately, the chill had brought on a bad attack of rheumatism and sciatica and on Thursday, 14th April, when due to address a meeting at High Easter in Essex, he was in so much pain that he could hardly stand. The members who attended the meeting were shocked at his changed appearance. 'He was wearing a pair of blue spectacles and walked with a stout stick.' He seemed suddenly to have become an old man. Nevertheless, he refused to allow his illness to prevent him from speaking, and a report in the *English Labourers' Chronicle* noted that he had lost 'none of his old declamatory powers.'[4]

Yet even Joseph could not carry on in this fashion with impunity. The following night (Good Friday, 15th April), after he had addressed an outdoor meeting at Patiswick, he became quite seriously ill. He was staying in lodgings with David Sage, the Essex district organiser, and the latter became very concerned at the severe pain he was enduring. Although Arch managed to make his way home to Barford after the weekend, he was forced to stay in bed for three weeks, and not until 6th May was he again able to go outside. Then he could only walk slowly round his garden with the aid of a stick. This seems to have been the most severe illness Joseph suffered during his entire career as a Union organiser, and although his candidature for the North-West Norfolk Division had been announced, it was not until after the middle of June that he was well enough to go into the county again to begin electioneering.

Indeed, his first Union engagement came only on 18th May, when he went to Yarmouth to preside at the N.A.L.U.'s Annual Council meeting. The warm welcome he received there from everyone he met — 'railway porters and guards; fishermen and labourers' — helped to raise his morale and, it was claimed, assisted his recovery.

Meanwhile, the faithful Zacharias Walker, in a letter to the *English Labourers' Chronicle* of 30th April, had already suggested the establishment of an election fund to help to meet Joseph's expenses, 'being as the General Election (was) fast approaching and may be upon us just after Whitsuntide or July . . .'[5]

In the event, the dissolution came on 29th June, and Joseph soon found himself in the thick of electioneering. He had already issued his Address, and in this had called first and foremost for Home Rule for Ireland, and then for the establishment of elected parish councils, a reform of the poor law, the abolition of the 'Hereditary Principle in the House of Lords' and such old favourites as the establishment of the 'fullest possible religious equality' and 'a complete repeal of the Game Laws.' (See Appendix 4).

As at both the 1885 and 1886 elections, Arch's opponent was to be Lord Henry Bentinck, and the poll in the North-West Norfolk constituency was fixed for 15th July. Great was the excitement of Joseph's labourer supporters as the appointed day at last drew near. When it eventually dawned, it proved ideal for him, at least as regards the weather. As the Liberal *Norfolk News* noted with satisfaction: 'Although very little rain fell during the hours of polling, enough had fallen overnight to render work in the hay fields almost an impossibility. To a purely agricultural constituency such as the North-West Division of the county this circumstance was of immense benefit to the candidature of Joseph Arch . . .' It meant that his supporters would be able to get to the poll in time to vote and would not be kept haymaking until late in the evening; the labourers, for their part, certainly seem to have taken advantage of this opportunity.

Although, as in 1886, Joseph was poorly placed in the matter of carriages, his supporters were quite prepared to walk to the polling stations, and in some cases the 'old women lent their donkey carts' to help bring people in. The poll proved, in fact, to be an extremely heavy one, especially in the most rural parts of the constituency. At South Creake, for example, 300 out of the total electorate of 370 had voted by as early as 5.30 p.m. and at Sculthorpe, Snoring, and Toftrees, it was proudly claimed by the Liberals that only 'two available voters remained unpolled'; the high turn-out in these three latter villages was, however, partly due to the fact that a brake had been secured to carry the voters to their polling station.

And everywhere that Joseph himself went on that day, there were cheers and welcoming smiles. At Hunstanton a large crowd of supporters stood applauding loudly on the railway station as he left by train to return to King's Lynn, and at South Creake the villagers stretched four large banners across the road with the inscription 'Welcome to Joseph Arch.'[6] (Even on the walls of some of the schoolrooms, posters were stuck bearing the words 'Vote for Joseph Arch'[7]) If he had claimed that one of the reasons for his defeat in 1886 had been 'abstentions,' certainly no such charge could be sustained in respect of the 1892 election. In the event, no excuse was necessary. When the result was announced at King's Lynn Town Hall on the following day,

Joseph was the winner — by the handsome margin of 1,089 votes. (His success had been achieved, too, with a total election expenditure of £949 9s. 1d. — a sum which was met by friends in the Liberal Party.[8] Lord Henry Bentinck, on the other hand, had spent £1,336 8s. 1d. — see Appendix 8).

Arch himself was, of course, jubilant at his victory, but his Conservative opponents naturally felt very differently. Indeed, according to his own account, 'When the High Sheriff saw the figures, he was so much annoyed that he refused to declare the poll, and the under Sheriff had to do it. I then went up to the High Sheriff, held out my hand and thanked him for the very able way in which he had conducted the count. He shook hands with me, then deliberately pulled his handkerchief out of his pocket and wiped his hand. After that I just went up, shook hands with him again, and told him I was perfectly satisfied with the state of the poll, if he was!'[9]

When Joseph left the Town Hall there was a tremendous crowd outside waiting to congratulate him and as he later recalled: 'I noticed five big, burly fishermen walking behind me, and when I got to the first donkey cart they laid hold of me and lifted me in and started hurrahing, and the crowd took it up, and then the donkey was started off and I was carted round the place, the people cheering all the time . . .' This rather strange procession finally ended up at the local Liberal Club.[10] And, as in 1885, Mary Ann Arch, too, was present to witness her husband's triumph — despite her steadily deteriorating health.

Nor was this all. In his native Warwickshire great celebrations were likewise prepared for the new M.P. When he and Mrs Arch arrived in Warwick on 19th July, a large crowd was there to greet them. They were first collected from Milverton railway station in a brougham and then, as they entered Warwick itself, the Town Band struck up, playing 'The Conquering Hero,' while behind them a mass of people marched, carrying banners with such devices as 'Welcome to Joseph Arch' and 'Civil and Religious Liberty Restored.'[11] The horses were unharnessed from Joseph's carriage, and it was pulled along instead by a group of his supporters. The whole thing was, to him, an unforgettable experience; as he later wrote, 'it was a reception to uplift a man.'

Joseph's success in North-West Norfolk was a reflection of the national picture. Once more, the Liberals had been returned to power; they and the Irish Nationalists together (plus one Labour member) had a total majority of 45 over their Unionist opponents. And given both the important role of the Irish Nationalists, with their 81 seats, and Mr Gladstone's own preoccupation with Ireland, it is not surprising that Irish Home Rule once again assumed a prominent position in Liberal Party deliberations. Yet, despite Mr Gladstone's efforts in introducing a Second Home Rule Bill on 13th February, 1893, and despite its successful passage through the Commons, it was rejected by the Lords on 8th September. Gladstone was too old to fight on any longer and the members of his Party lacked his enthusiasm for the cause — and so the whole question died, for a time at least.

If Gladstone's last ministry had little solid achievement to its credit, therefore, the same must unfortunately be said of Arch's own final stint in Parliament. Although he was to remain in the House until 1900, he added little to his reputation. He became more an ornament for the Liberal Party than a true representative of his class (even if, in the matter of clothing, he still continued to preserve his old independence, wearing a rough grey tweed suit and matching billy-cock hat, rather as he had in 1886). Furthermore, he was now beginning to drink heavily, despite his earlier strongly pro-temperance views; it will be remembered that even in 1874 allegations were being made, that he was too fond of alcohol, and despite denials, the rumours continued to grow. Perhaps the habit had, to some degree, been encouraged by his practice of staying at village public houses whilst he was on his speaking tours as Union President. As one friend, Sir Richard Winfrey, M.P. later recalled: ' . . . he used to hold a court function in the bar parlour first and then go into the kitchen so that all might converse with him.' The publicans naturally welcomed the practice, for their premises were 'always crowded until closing time with those who wanted to shake hands with Mr. Arch.'[12] Nevertheless, whether this link with public houses was influential or not, by the 1890's it is clear that Joseph's drinking habits were well established. Clegg, Fox and Thompson, in their *History of British Trade Unions Since* 1889, Vol. I, rather unkindly note: 'Joseph Arch a loyal Liberal satellite, sat in the House from 1892 to 1900, drinking his bottle of whisky a day but hardly opening his mouth for any other purpose.'[13]

Interestingly enough, however, this fact did not prevent him, in 1896, from condemning the then Conservative Government to Thomas Bayliss, an old Oxford agricultural trade unionist, as a 'parson, publican and brewer Government' opposed to the Sunday closing of public houses![14]

During his second spell in Parliament, Joseph made only twelve speeches, and all but three of these related to the Local Government (England and Wales) Bill of 1893–94, which set up parish councils. It will be remembered that in his 1892 election address he had called for the establishment of such councils, and he therefore took a personal interest in this legislation, which was concerned, in large measure, with the village life he knew and understood. In particular, he was anxious that the Bill should ensure that parish meetings were held in the evening, so that working men might attend: 'His father died at the age of 70, and never attended a parish meeting in his life, and he (Mr Arch) himself was turned 60 before he had the opportunity of attending such a meeting. Why? Because those meetings were held at eleven o'clock in the morning, when the working classes could not possibly attend. Fortunately, in a great many villages he had been the humble instrument of getting the labourers to go and change the hour of meeting from eleven o'clock in the morning to seven in the evening. . . . If the council were allowed when elected to fix the hour for meeting he felt sure that in too many instances the hour would be fixed for the morning . . . To say that men would not attend a meeting after six o'clock in the evening was to say that men took no interest in matters going on around them, and this was contrary to fact.'[15]

In the major political issues of the day, however, Joseph played no part. After the end of May, 1894, he never again made a speech in Parliament, and on his retirement even a friendly newspaper remarked that he 'was seldom seen in the legislative chamber itself, but he was a familiar figure in the lobbies and corridors,' where he always 'had a pleasant word for everybody, members, officials, and policemen alike.'[16] This relative neglect was undoubtedly due to the fact that he found the long hours and late sittings customary in the Commons extremely irksome. He came to the House too late in life to change his mode of living. This is demonstrated, for example, by the fact that on occasion even when walking along the streets of London, he would stride briskly 'down the middle' of the road, 'just as if he were marching along a Warwickshire lane,' as a friend later recalled.[17] Fortunately for him, the London traffic seems to have borne with his idiosyncrasies, for he does not appear to have been involved in any accident![18]

Yet, despite his indifference to the legislative processes of the House, Arch was honoured, in 1893, by being asked to serve on the Royal Commission on the Aged Poor, 1893–94. Once again, he played no particularly active role, although he did attend thirty-four out of the forty-eight days of the Commission's deliberations. Such questions as he did ask witnesses appearing before the Commission were, in the main, concerned with the position of the aged poor in the rural areas. He displayed little interest in the plight of the urban aged, and in many cases he put no questions at all.[19] One of his fellow Commissioners was, however, the Prince of Wales, and Joseph was pathetically proud of this link with the heir to the throne and also of the fact that, as Sandringham lay within his division, the Prince might be considered one of his constituents. The Prince himself, in his good humoured fashion, seems to have had some affection for the old man, too, for in 1893 he sent him two tickets for the opening of the Imperial Institute by the Queen, and a few years later, in 1898, even paid a brief visit to Arch's Barford cottage whilst he was staying at Warwick Castle. Indeed, according to Henry Broadhurst, another trade unionist M.P.

and fellow member of the Royal Commission on the Aged Poor:
'There was no member of the Commission with whom the Prince
seemed to enjoy a chat or a joke more than with the representative of
the agricultural labourers,' and within Arch's Norfolk constituency,
'no estate . . . offered less opposition to his candidature than Sandringham did'[20]

Needless to say, Joseph's own admiration for the Prince soon
called forth malicious comments from a number of observers, including the Fabian social reformers, Sidney and Beatrice Webb, who
wrote of him at this time: 'Glorified farm labourer, shrewd, suspicious,
narrow, with oratorical gift, courage, persistency. Now overcome
with honour of acquaintance with P(rince) of Wales whom he mentions
at every turn.'[21] Joseph's own view of the Webbs would probably
have been equally uncomplimentary, for he felt little sympathy towards
the Socialism of his own day. In his autobiography he wrote — like a
true son of the nineteenth century — 'Self-help and liberty, order and
progress — these are what I advocate . . . Present-day Socialism will
die a natural death sooner or later. To my mind the Socialism of the
future will consist in the improvement and upward tendency of the
strength . . . of the rural and urban population of England.'[22]

In addition to his appointment on the Royal Commision on the
Aged Poor, Arch was also offered a place on the Royal Commission
on Agricultural Distress which was set up in 1893, but this he declined
to accept, stating firmly that: 'Such an inquiry cannot yield any
useful results. The only remedy is in replacing seventy per cent of the
existing tenant occupiers of the soil by practical men, not afraid of
toil or seeing the sun rise.'[23]

Nevertheless, if these final years of the century were in some
respects attended with success, Joseph was at the same time, often
in financial difficulties. Even in 1892 his diary reveals that he frequently
owed sums of money to his daughter Annie — perhaps for housekeeping expenses. For example, an entry for 7th October, 1892,
states: 'Owe Annie 7 weeks. Paid 10/-', and for 30th December of the
same year: 'Owe Annie 11 weeks'. Other small debts to unnamed
persons — of £5 or so — are also recorded.[24] At this time his salary
as Union President was paid irregularly — sometimes every three
weeks and sometimes more frequently. This undoubtedly contributed
to his problems. But worse was to come. In 1893-94, he blamed the
ill-health of his wife, and the consequently heavy doctor's bills he had
to meet, for his failure to visit his constituency as frequently as he
should.

Mrs. Arch had been ailing for many years, having suffered 'two
paralytic seizures' already (in 1878 and 1885). For a long time she
had only been able to move about with the aid of a 'stick and stilt',

because of the paralysis in her left side and the effects of rheumatism, and she was too ill to live in London with her husband after his 1892 success, as she had in 1886. Then, towards the end of 1893, she became seriously ill with a liver disease and was forced to remain in bed, nursed by her elder daughter, Hannah Bray. There seems little doubt, therefore, that Joseph's financial resources were extremely strained at this stage, and often he was 'walking the streets of London, as an M.P. with scarcely a penny in his pocket.'[25] In Februrary, 1894, the N.A.L.U. general secretary even suggested that branch secretaries might appeal to their members to make a donation of 1d. each to help to solve Joseph's monetary problems. But, since there were only about 1,000 members in the Union at that time, it is difficult to see how such a levy, yielding about £4 or £5, would have helped him very significantly, even if the suggestion had been adopted — which it was not.

Perhaps rather unwisely, Joseph did not attempt to hide his contempt for the labourers in permitting him to remain in this predicament. At a meeting at New Buckenham, Norfolk, towards the end of July, 1894, he berated his audience bitterly: 'They had sent him to the House of Commons and now they wanted to starve him. For nine weeks he had not had a single penny out of the Union in wages...' He then went on: 'You poor, craven, milk-and-water fellows, ... Why, you button up your pockets at the thought of paying 2¼d, a week when you are told by a lot of lying scampery and scandalism that I have run away with your money...'[26]

Eventually, his wife's long illness came to an end on 15th March 1894, at the age of 69. The wrench caused by her death was naturally a particularly painful one for him to bear after forty-seven years of married life. Many letters of sympathy were sent to him by his friends in the Union movement and outside, but perhaps the one he valued the most came from the Prince of Wales. Joseph's only slight consolation can have been the easing of his financial problems which this sad event brought about.

The death of his wife was not the only blow he had to bear in 1894. In September of that same year the Union newspaper was compelled to cease publication, because of a shortage of funds. By the end of the year N.A.L.U. membership had slumped to a mere 1,100, from the figure of about 15,000 obtained in the revival of 1890-91. The financial situation of the Union had become equally desperate. Even in 1893, expenditure at £2,521 (including £1,822 'working and other expenses') exceeded the total income of £1,549; but in 1894 the deterioration became very much more severe. As might be expected, in view of the low membership figures, total income had fallen to a mere £488, while expenditure stood at £958 (of which £877 had been absorbed by 'working and other expenses'). This deficit almost completely wiped out the Union's previous reserves, and the year 1894 ended with the total funds in hand fixed at a derisory £2! (See Appendix 2). It was obvious that things could not continue for much longer in this fashion.[27] Finally, in October, 1896, the Union was dissolved; hardly surprisingly, Joseph felt that final rejection keenly.

Yet, it is interesting to note that the decline in the Union did not prevent Arch from retaining his seat in North-West Norfolk at the snap general election called in the summer of 1895 by Lord Rosebery, who had replaced Gladstone as Liberal Prime Minister about fifteen months earlier. Although the Liberals lost power as a result of this election, Joseph was returned with an increase in his majority, to 1,297. Clearly the Norfolk labourers were prepared to trust him with their votes if not their pennies! But he was perhaps helped by the fact that his opponent on this occasion was an Irish landowner from Kilkenny, Mr. E K B Tighe, who had no personal links with the area.

The Conservatives, for their part, had quite legitimately spared no effort in trying to bring Joseph down. Perhaps most resented was the way in which, on the eve of the poll, bills were posted up, giving information on the unsatisfactory financial position of the Union in 1894 and on its great loss of membership. In the end, though, this apparently had little damaging effect. The Liberal *Norfolk News* wrote happily of the triumphal arches and the streets festooned in Liberal colours, in honour of Joseph, which could be seen on polling day — 26th July. The newspapers recorded that: 'The Liberals centred their hopes on the huge purely rural district lying between Fakenham, Hunstanton, and Creake, where there are miles upon miles of villages in which the name of Arch is a household word. In many of these places it is literally true that the electors turned out and voted for him by the cartload. One of the vans lent for the occasion . . . brought to the Fakenham polling station at a single journey nearly forty perspiring rustics, who were hanging on to the vehicle in every conceivable attitude.'[28] Joseph's arrival at Hunstanton was greeted with cheers from a large crowd of supporters, but one feels that his committee room here must have been rather cramped, as, according to the *Norfolk News*, it was only 'a bathing machine!'

Feelings nevertheless ran high among some of the electors. As the *Norfolk News* noted, when Arch had left Hunstanton, 'some rather rough play followed . . . the opposing sides being drawn up on either side of the road. A man from Heacham started stone-throwing. At another time a few blows were struck, but the police were able to quell the disturbance and persuade those taking part in it to desist.'[29] Again, at Fakenham, when Mr Tighe and his wife appeared, they were attacked by a mob, and only 'four or five . . . burly constables' prevented Tighe from being pushed to the ground. This conduct was condemned strongly by the *Norfolk News* as 'a disgraceful exhibition of rowdyism.'

However, when the result was finally announced, these unfortunate scenes could be forgotten. Arch was 'almost carried' through the streets of Lynn by his rejoicing supporters, and he, for his part, was obviously proud of the continued allegiance of the Norfolk labourers in the political field, if not in the Union one. Yet, at the same time, his re-election carried with it the old financial embarrassment, which was made even more acute by the final collapse of the Union in 1896. He had been almost completely dependent on the £4 to £5 per week salary and expense allowance from this source, and although the Union's collapse was by no means unexpected, he obviously did not now know where to turn for a regular income. (Apart from his own food and clothing there was his Barford cottage to maintain as well as his rented accommodation in a London apartment house, no. 6 Barton Street, which was situated in Westminster, about five minutes away from Parliament itself.)[30] Consequently, just before the Union's dissolution, in the summer of 1896, a fund was set up by friends in the Liberal Party, to help him out of his difficulties. Ultimately, about £1,200 was collected, with which an annuity of £157 was purchased and presented to him early in 1897. Among those who contributed were Lord Rosebery, Sir George Trevelyan and the Countess of Warwick, who in August, 1896, forwarded a donation of £10, with a note saying: 'I am anxious to add even such a trifle to the sum being raised on behalf of the man who first taught the agricultural labourer to see light on the mountain.'[31]

The Countess indeed began to take an interest in the old trade unionist who lived so near to Warwick Castle, and whose grandparents and mother had been servants at the Castle in years gone by. To the disgust of many of her 'society' friends, she decided to edit his life story, and approached him on the matter towards the beginning of 1897. The book, entitled *Joseph Arch — The Story of His Life Told by Himself*, was eventually accepted by Hutchinson & Co. for publication early in 1898. The Countess soon became involved in her work as editor, and near the end of 1897 sent an advance copy of the book to her journalist friend, W. T. Stead. He, quite disregarding publishing etiquette, wrote an article based on this for the *Contemporary Review* of January, 1898. The article appeared more than a week before the book's official release date, which had been fixed for 15th January, and the tone of Stead's remarks, bitterly critical of the Church of England as they were, did little to endear either him or the book to the better-off sectors of the community. Stead, a convinced Nonconformist, called upon the Church of England to reform itself if 'in the future (it wished) to avoid losing men like Joseph Arch,' whom he praised as 'self-sufficient, self-reliant, dogged, good-natured.'[32] Naturally, he was scarcely regarded as an impartial critic, and Hutchinsons, for their part, wrote hastily to *The Times* of 8th January, disclaiming all knowledge or permission for this breach of accepted practice.

When the book did officially appear, it had, as might be expected, a rather mixed reception. *The Times* was somewhat condescending in its approach, declaring that it was 'full of artless and, on the whole, inoffensive egotism; it is marred here and there by needless acrimony of tone; . . . certainly the narrative would have been more pleasing if some crude invectives as to the country clergy, "Squarsons" and Squires generally had been omitted . . . Towards the close of the book are discernible signs of a kindlier spirit, a more mellow judgment as to men and affairs. . . .'[33] The *Manchester Guardian* called it 'full of interest from every point of view,' and the *Daily Chronicle* considered it 'a notable book, the story of a great career.,

Others were less restrained in their views. Not unexpectedly, members of the clergy in particular showed their displeasure. One Staffordshire parson described Joseph as a 'humbug,' while 'A Midland Vicar' declared: 'Joseph Arch is a successful demagogue, and nothing more; . . . it is much to be regretted that one in the position of the Countess of Warwick should take up and pat on the back, such a man as Joseph Arch, who, if he had his way, would very soon make short work of her and such as she. . . .' Landowners were in some cases equally strong in their condemnations — for Joseph had so often made clear his hatred of these 'Lords of Brobdignag,' as he called them.[34] The owner of Burbage Hall in Leicestershire, for example, complained of Arch's attitude, and asked why the labourers should not show humility towards their 'betters' anyway.[35] Once more, therefore, as in the 1870's, the walls of parsonages and country houses echoed to loud denunciations of Arch and all he stood for.

Nevertheless, the controversy may have benefited Joseph financially, in so far as his book quickly ran into three editions. The second edition was published only about a month after the first, in February, 1898, and like its predecessor, was priced at 12s. The third edition was a cheap one, which appeared in November, 1898, at a price of 6s.; Hutchinsons in the Christmas edition of the *Bookseller* for that year described it as a 'cheap edition of a notable biography,' and there is little doubt that royalties from the book's sales would provide a very welcome addition to Arch's slender financial resources. (Unfortunately the exact amount of the royalties cannot now be calculated as Messrs. Hutchinsons records for this period were destroyed by the blitz of World War II.)[36]

As for the Countess of Warwick, she was quite unrepentant regarding her role in the affair. Indeed, in the summer of 1898, she even took the Prince of Wales to visit Joseph at Barford. On this occasion, however, the old man was rather overwhelmed by the importance of his visitor, and as the Prince sat before the fire in the small sitting room, Joseph harangued him about the wrongs of his class, instead of 'telling his story in the interesting way Lady Warwick had anticipated.'[37]

But of Joseph's admiration for the Countess herself, there can be no doubt. Shortly after his book was published he warmly wrote of her as 'an admirable and energetic lady,' and in the autobiography itself he praised her as 'noble' and 'unprejudiced.'[38]

Nevertheless, despite the measure of success clearly achieved by the end of the 1890's, it was becoming increasingly apparent that Arch (now in his seventies) could not continue in public life very much longer. In May, 1899, he recognised this fact for himself, when, following a severe chill in the early spring of that year, he announced his retirement from Parliament at the next General Election.[39] That the decision was justified is illustrated by a quotation from *The Times* of 24th May; this spoke of him as being 'exceedingly feeble and aged,' when he was present at Sutton Bridge, Lincolnshire, at the laying of the foundation-stone of the Liberal Club there. Arch himself characteristically spoke of his retirement in rural terms: 'I am going to back my wagon into the shed and put it up . . .' At the same time, he voiced his sincere regrets that he had not been able to accomplish more to improve the position of the labourers, especially with regard to cottage accommodation and sanitation.

But 1899 was of more significance than the mere announcement of his retirement from Parliament. It was on 27th December in that year that Joseph married again. His bride was Miss Miriam Blomfield, the daughter of a Norfolk sadler (although she herself had been born in London). Miriam was about fifteen years her husband's junior, and had been acting as his housekeeper for some time before the wedding. Nevertheless, the decision to marry seems to have been a fairly sudden one, for Arch only wrote to the Barford rector, the Rev. Cecil Mills, on 19th December, to make arrangements for the ceremony, which was held in the parish church. It was a very quiet affair as Arch's health was still poor, and his second son and namesake, Joseph, acted as best man. (This younger Joseph had spent most of the 1880's in the United States of America, where he had gone shortly after his marriage in about 1883. After his return he had for a short time in 1893 been Manager of the National Liberal Club in London, but by the end of the century had left this and was apparently employed as a licensed victualler in the city.)[40]

209

In 1900, following the dissolution of Parliament in the late summer of that year, Mr and Mrs Arch finally returned from London to Barford. There they continued to live until the old man's death on 12th February, 1919, at the great age of ninety-two. After his retirement, his days passed peacefully enough. He had a secure income of £157 per annum, his well-loved books to read, his pipe of tobacco to enjoy, and the garden in which to potter. Mr George Worrall and Mr R. K. Hemmings of Barford, who both remember him at this time, say that he was rarely seen away from his plot of land, which he continued to look after himself as long as possible. The only exception to this was that every fortnight he would hire a brougham from Mr Hemming's father (who was a baker and carriage contractor) and would be driven in to Warwick to do his shopping — including the collection of a supply of whisky from the Woolpack Inn in the town. When, on one occasion, the brougham was not ready for him, he soon made his annoyance known in no uncertain terms!

Often, one feels, his mind must have turned back in these declining years to the heady days of the 1870's and 1880's, when fame and adulation were his for the asking.[41] Indeed, just two years before he died, even though his memory was beginning to fail, he could still remember, according to at least one friend, the time when he had formed part of a torchlight procession into the town of March, in Cambridgeshire, during the late 1880's. Lord Lincolnshire had shared a processional carriage with Arch, and 'at the close both of them were well sprinkled with tar, so close had the torches been to the carriage. It entailed a new suit of clothes for the labour leader, at the expense of the enlightened Liberal landowner.'[42] And always pre-eminent in his recollections, of course, would be the memory of that fateful day on 7th February, 1872, when his career as a trade union leader had really begun, beneath the famous Wellesbourne chestnut tree.

After his retirement from Parliament, Joseph apparently took little part in local politics, although he did, it seems, make an unsuccessful attempt to establish a local co-operative society.[43] Neither did he appear to take any further interest in agricultural trade unionism, even when a new Union — the forerunner of the present National Union of Agricultural and Allied Workers — was established in Norfolk in 1906. Indeed, his attitude in regard to this was made clear when a member of the Union, Tom Higdon, made a special trip to interview him, in 1909. Although the old man received him warmly, offering him beer and tobacco, there was a sad finality about his statement that his work was 'all done now.'[44] There could be no new role for him to play — he was too old. Nevertheless, on this occasion, and in fact earlier on, too, Joseph showed himself somewhat embittered and disillusioned even with his own career as a union leader. As early as

1895, for example, he had warned a Norfolk agricultural trade unionist, George Edwards (who was to be the founding father of the new Union, in 1906): ' . . . never trust our class again. I am getting old I have given all the best years of my life in their interest, and now in my old age they have forsaken me.'[45] No doubt, some part of the blame for this alienation lay at his own doorstep, for he had frequently been unwilling to accept advice or help from other members of the N.A.L.U. in earlier days. Jealousy of his apparent worldly success, too, possibly played some part in driving away former friends and supporters, like Henry Taylor and George Mitchell.

And if Joseph had lost most of his concern for politics and for trade unionism, in the matter of religion, too, there had been a change as compared with his attitude in years gone by. Despite the fact that his son-in-law, John Leuty, was still a Primitive Methodist Minister and that he, himself, had been such an enthusiastic local preacher once upon a time, his connection with the Barford Primitive Methodist Chapel had become seriously weakened during the last years of the nineteenth century. In March, 1890, his name was also removed from the list of Trustees of the Wesleyan Chapel in the village, and when he married for the second time it was the local parish Church that he chose for the ceremony, rather than a Methodist Chapel. After his retirement, the Barford rectors and their curates paid regular visits to him and he seems to have become quite friendly with at least one of the curates, the Rev. Douglas Long, who was at Barford from 1899 to 1901. Mr Long had assisted at Arch's wedding in 1899 and called to see him quite frequently thereafter.

When Long left Barford to go to a living at Pershore in Worcestershire, Joseph expressed his regret in a friendly letter, dated 8th December, 1901:

'Dear Mr. Long,
'I was so pleased you had got a Charge w(h)ere there were (sic) plenty to do. I daresay you miss some of our old faces.
'You will be pleased to hear Mr. Parker is moving among the people, have received a very nice visit from him, and was very pleased with his manner. I think he will make his way very well. Have spoken to several of your leaving Barford, and there's only one remark — we liked him very much, sorry he is gone away.
'Well my Dear Long, as a Father of 4 Sons, I sincerely hope and pray God will cause the sun of health and prosperity to shine on your path through Life making your Life a useful one with all and to all you are called upon to minister.
'As Ever Faithfully Yours,
Joseph Arch'[46]

It is significant that when Arch died in 1919, the Superintendent Minister of the Leamington Circuit noted that he had not been identified with the Primitive Methodist Church 'for many years'.[47]

Within the village itself, Joseph was well respected — being usually addressed formally as 'Mr. Arch', for example, and not 'Joseph'. However, he was not always popular. He sometimes showed an arrogance which other Barford inhabitants resented! He was apparently especially hard on the small boys. Mr. Hemmings remembers even after sixty years, how as a lad he was reprimanded by the old man for delivering the milk late, because he had become involved in some boyish games. Joseph wearing a large, floppy Panama hat, was in the garden, picking raspberries, when the sheepish lad appeared before him. It was soon made abundantly clear that he had no time for young boys who indulged in fun and games when they should have been doing their duty! However, with some of the older people his relations were a little happier, and he would often gossip with the passers-by on a summer evening as he sat out on an old wooden chair under his small front porch.

Then, too, there were friends from earlier years who would visit him from time to time. Although members of his family apparently only came rarely, this was not true of some of the others. In particular, the Countess of Warwick would call, driving up in a phaeton, dressed in fashionable attire; she would go inside the small cottage and would talk to the old man for a little while.

The Rev. Douglas Long, on the other hand, came only once — in 1916, when he was visiting Barford to conduct a service. At that time, when Arch was almost ninety, he could see that the old man had become very feeble, and there is the sadness of declining powers in his description of Arch during this final phase of his life:

'I last visited Joseph Arch on Sunday, 5th Nov., 1916, when I preached in Barford Church after nearly 18 years . . . He was vigorous in body but had lost all recollection of me at the time . . . He was sitting in the little cottage room wh. was most untidy, in front of a roaring fire . . . He had a coat on but no collar or waistcoat only a strange flat black necktie round his neck . . .' His powers of concentration had diminished, and his memory had become very poor. Then, too, Mrs. Arch herself — now in her mid-seventies — was obviously having difficulty in coping with the ordinary household chores, and Mr. Long regretfully noted that the surroundings lacked their old order and neatness, and presented a very different picture 'from the days when (he) knew them best.'[48]

There is no doubt that in his prime Joseph had displayed many faults of character, being both autocratic and vain. Yet, despite this he was a remarkable man. His self-confidence was almost boundless and he did not hesitate to speak out even in the face of formidable opposition; the Countess of Warwick called him 'one of the bravest men (she) ever knew.'[49] Even in his eighties, as Tom Higdon discovered during his visit in 1909, 'some glimpse of the power, the fervour and the personality of Joseph Arch as he had been' was still apparent in his manner and conversation. As the years passed many of the old quarrels and conflicts which had formerly beset him, became softened by the influence of Time, the great healer; and in numerous country cottages his 'strong bearded face (looked) down from the walls in faded photograph or print,' while he himself was remembered with respect.[50]

When he died on 12th February, 1919, Arch's important contribution to the emancipation of the farm worker was recognised. His funeral service was conducted at Barford by the Bishop of Coventry, while a message from Mr Lloyd George, then Prime Minister, was read at the graveside by the Liberal candidate for the Rugby constituency, Mr O. F. Maclagan. In it, Lloyd George spoke of the old trade unionist's 'sterling qualities.' However, perhaps most notable of all was the fact that when Joseph had his final stroke, the King (George V) sent a message to him, regretting to hear of his illness; Joseph had always been deeply proud of the fact that Sandringham was in his Parliamentary constituency.

At his death, the press, too, paid generous tribute to Joseph's past career. The *Birmingham Daily Post* in a 'Special Memoir' on 13th February, declared that: 'As an agitator he was a more commanding figure than any industrial agitator of recent times . . .' The *Manchester Guardian* of the same date called him 'one of the most remarkable leaders that the English village labourers ever produced,' and *The Times* praised the way in which he had sought to improve the lot of his fellow workers.

However, perhaps the most unexpected tribute came from the *Church Times* of 14th February, 1919 — in an article displaying very different sentiments from the earlier Church of England hostility towards the trade union leader: 'Times have indeed changed since the the name of Joseph Arch used to arouse storms of invective in the Press, on the platform and, we are ashamed to add, even in the pulpit. There must be very few now who will not hear with sorrow of the death of this veteran champion of the agricultural labourers . . . Alike on the platform and in Parliament during the years that he held a seat, from 1892 to 1900, he devoted all his powers to the cause which he had at heart, and, at the age of ninety-three (sic), he has died full of honour. It is regrettable, when we look back to the early days of the agitation he led, to recall the loss of a great opportunity by the country clergy. They might have won the labourers to the Church, but, largely ranging themselves on the side of the squirearchy, they alienated, in too many instances, their struggling parishioners. Since then a more enlightened spirit has prevailed but there remains much leeway to be made up.'[51]

Yet, if Arch's leadership had done much to raise the morale of the farm worker, it had certainly not made him a wealthy man. When he died his estate was valued at £349 13s. 11d. gross, and the net value was a mere £237 13s. 11d. Most of this estate, including the Barford cottage, was left to Miriam Arch for use during her life time, and was then to pass to his granddaughter, Daisy Isabella, the child of his fourth son, Thomas (and the adopted daughter of Annie Leuty — née Arch).[52] Nevertheless, Joseph's Will did contain at least two echoes from the past. The first came in the words: 'I give unto my son Joseph Arch . . . my silver watch given to me by the late Sir John Bennett . . .' Sir John had been a prominent Liberal politician — and watchmaker — during the final quarter of the nineteenth century. In the far-off days of the 1880's he and Arch had travelled together in a processional coach during the famous political demonstration in honour of John Bright, which was held at Birmingham in June, 1883. Prominent in the procession had been two hundred N.A.L.U. members carrying a large loaf and a banner on which were inscribed the words: 'We demand the vote as our right.' To the war-weary world of 1919 in which Arch died, events such as these must indeed have seemed to belong to a very different — now almost forgotten — era.

The second reminder of Arch's past came in the person of John William Sleath, a Warwick boot manufacturer, whom he had appointed as executor and trustee. In 1892, he had collected Joseph and Mary Ann Arch from Milverton Railway Station on their triumphal return from the victory in North-West Norfolk and had also organised the public reception for them in Warwick. That joyous day had been one which Joseph had declared that he would 'never forget.' We can be sure that he never did!

[1] *English Labourers' Chronicle* — 13th February, 1892.
[2] *English Labourers' Chronicle* — 13th February, 1892.
[3] Joseph Arch's Diary for 1892 — entry for 9th March, 1892. The Diary is preserved at the Museum of English Rural Life, University of Reading.
[4] *English Labourers' Chronicle* — 22nd April, 1892.
[5] *English Labourers' Chronicle* — 30th April, 1892.
[6] *Norfolk News* — 16th July, 1892. On the matter of transport, the newspaper reported also: 'The Tories worked their very hardest for his lordship in every polling district, village, and bye-lane in the constituency. Four wheelers, dog-carts, and vehicles, sporting orange and purple favours, careered in scores from one end of the constituency to the other. . . . The Liberals had scarcely a conveyance, except at Fakenham, where they were pretty well off in this respect (Mr J.J. Colman, M.P., sending a wagonette and horses from Norwich).'
[7] Letter from Mr J.C. Purser to Thomas Bayliss, dated 3rd February, 1931, in the Cole Collection, Nuffield College. Of course, schoolrooms were on occasion used for election

meetings, as at South Creake and Thornham during the 1892 campaign.

[8] See Joseph Arch's Diary for 1892 — entry for 16th July, 1892, however, where he notes election expenses (excluding returning Officer's charges) as £648 16s. 7d. This was clearly a slight under-estimate — see Appendix 8.

[9] Joseph Arch, op.cit., p.387. Arch, with 4,911 votes, had about 56% of the votes cast.

[10] Ibid. and also entry in Arch's Diary for 16th July.

[11] *Warwick Advertiser* — 23rd July, 1892.

[12] *Land Worker* — 18th September, 1919. Winfrey recollected that on one occasion when they were stopping at a south Norfolk village inn, the landlady refused to accept any payment for Joseph's lodgings, saying: 'Mr Arch is my honoured guest — he is, and always will be welcome in my house.' — Ibid. . .

[13] H.A. Clegg, Alan Fox and A.F. Thompson — *History of British Trade Unions since 1889*, Vol. I (Oxford, 1964), p.248. See also *The Guardian* — 11th April, 1960. As will be seen, Joseph's second son, Joseph junior, later became a licensed victualler in London, according to an entry made at the time of the burial of his infant son, Percy, in September,1900. — See death certificate issued at Warwick.

[14] Letter written to Thomas Bayliss, dated 5th May, 1896 — Cole Collection, Nuffield College.

[15] Hansard (4th Series) Vol. XVIII, p.1500.

[16] *Leamington Chronicle* — 23rd May, 1899, quoting from the *Daily Chronicle*.

[17] *Leamington Chronicle* — 20th February, 1919.

[18] Arch was, however, rather less fortunate on one occasion in June, 1897. Whilst he was walking in St. James's Park, he was suddenly attacked and beaten up by a complete stranger, who was later judged insane; luckily, he was not seriously hurt. — *Midland Free Press* — 19th June, 1897.

[19] *Royal Commission on the Aged Poor* — Parliamentary Papers, 1895, Vol. XV. Arch's preoccupation with the practical problems of the labourer's life was shown, for example, when he pointed out to Robert Elcock, builder and auctioneer, who was a poor law guardian of the Wimborne and Cranborne Union in Dorset, the difficulty farm workers experienced in aiding their parents with monetary support. They were, on the other hand always ready to help with 'gifts in kind' — such as vegetables from the garden, or assistance in cleaning the house or in doing the washing. — Q.4,784.

[20] Henry Broadhurst, M.P. — *The Story of his life from a Stonemason's Bench to the Treasury Bench Told by Himself* (London, 1901), p.157.

[21] Webb Collection, London School of Economics — MS. Coll. E.Sect.A.XLII.

[22] Joseph Arch, op.cit., p.404. See also F.E. Green, op.cit., p.176, where it was noted that Arch was 'strongly opposed to Socialism'. He was 'simply a Liberal of moderate John Bright views taken more or less secondhand'.

[23] *Midland Free Press* — 29th July, 1893.

[24] Diary for 1892 at Museum of English Rural Life. Examples of other small debts can be found in entries for 15th July and 16th December, for instance.

[25] *Memoirs of Josiah Sage*, p.50.

[26] *Leamington Chronicle* — 28th July, 1894.

[27] *Seventh Report of the Board of Trade Labour Department on Trade Unions for* 1893 — Parliamentary Papers, 1895, Vol.CVII and *Eighth Report of the Board of Trade Labour Department on Trade Unions for* 1894 — Parliamentary Papers, 1896, Vol. XCIII.

[28] *Norfolk News* — 3rd August, 1895.

[29] Ibid.

[30] Kelly's Directory for Warwickshire — 1896 and Post Office London Directory — 1895, which records that a Mr John Leach kept the apartments at No. 6 Barton Street.

[31] *Midland Free Press* — 8th August, 1896.

[32] Stead had first met Lady Warwick in the spring of 1892, when he was editor of a new

weekly magazine, the *Review of Reviews*. Although a convinced Radical, his approach to journalism was frequently of the sensational variety. He died in 1912 in the Titanic disaster. For an account of his life see, for example, F. Whyte — *Life of W. T. Stead* (London, 1925). His article on Arch's book was entitled 'How Joseph Arch was Driven from the State Church' — *Contemporary Review* — January, 1898.

[33] *The Times* — 15th January, 1898.

[34] See, for example, Joseph Arch — 'Lords and Labourers' in the *New Review*, February, 1893, p.129.

[35] *Midland Free Press* — 22nd January, 1898.

[36] *The English Catalogue* 1898–1900 (London, 1901) and *The Bookseller* — 4th March 1898. See also letter from the Hutchinson Publishing Group Ltd. to the author, dated 23rd March, 1970.

[37] M. Blunden — *The Countess of Warwick* (London, 1967), p.127, and Frances, Countess of Warwick — *Life's Ebb and Flow* (London, 1929), pp.124–128.

[38] Joseph's comments appeared in an article written in the *Land Magazine*, Vol. I, No. 10, January, 1898, in which he discussed favourably the Countess's ideas for establishing an agricultural training college for women. It was indeed, under the Countess's influence that the Studley Agricultural College for Women was later set up in Warwickshire.

[39] *Norfolk News* — 27th May, 1899.

[40] *Warwick Advertiser* — 30th December, 1899. For information on Joseph junior's visit to the United States of America, see a letter from Joseph senior to the American Consulate in Birmingham, dated 24th June, 1888 — Birmingham City Reference Library, 67419A7. In this letter Arch senior wrote: 'My Son Joseph Arch was married some 5 yrs. ago as far as I can remember. None of his own family were at the wedding soon after his marriage he went to the States. What he did there I don't know. We have not seen him for years.' — *Warwick Advertiser* — 3rd June, 1893, mentions that young Arch was the Manager of the National Liberal Club.

[41] For information on Arch's later years I am very much indebted to the help given to me by Mr R. K. Hemmings and Mr George Worrall of Barford, who knew Arch at that time.

[42] *The Land Worker* — 18th September, 1919 — Sir Richard Winfrey, M.P. — 'Some Reminiscences of Joseph Arch'

[43] F. E. Green, op.cit., p.175.

[44] Reg Groves, op.cit., pp.90–92.

[45] George Edwards — *From Crow Scaring to Westminster* (London, 1922), p.90.

[46] Letter in the possession of Mr R. Moore. Nevertheless, this friendship did not prevent him from condeming some of his Barford neighbours, earlier in that same year, as 'squire-ridden and parson-ridden, no man dare call his soul his own!' — *Leamington Spa Courier* — 3rd May, 1901.

[47] *Leamington Chronicle* — 20th February, 1919. See also F. E. Green, op.cit., pp. 175–176.

[48] MS. notes in the possession of Mr R. Moore, who has kindly allowed me to reproduce them.

[49] Frances, Countess of Warwick, op.cit., p.124.

[50] Reg Groves, op.cit., p.92.

[51] A similar change of attitude was also displayed in 1921, when the then Bishop of Peterborough wrote to the Socialist, R. H. Tawney, on 22nd June in that year, supporting the agricultural minimum wage and ending his letter: 'I am indeed anxious that the Church should not display the same apathy as she did in the days of Joseph Arch.' — Quoted by A. Peacock — *The Revolt of the Fields in East Anglia* (pamphlet, 1968), p.8.

[52] Thomas Arch, who worked as a compositor in Leamington, was apparently rather

given to drinking too much. For example, on 7th November, 1895, he was fined 10s. 6d. including costs, at Leamington Borough Police Court, for being 'drunk and disorderly in the Theatre Royal', Leamington, on 28th October.Perhaps for this reason and because she herself had no children Annie Leuty (née Arch), Joseph's second daughter, had adopted Daisy and had brought her up as her own child.

CHAPTER THIRTEEN

Epilogue: 'His Soul Goes Marching On'

'Time was is past
Thou canst not it recall
Time is Thou hast,
Employ the portion small,
Time future is not
And may never be,
The present is the only time for thee.'

JOSEPH ARCH wrote these lines in the copy of his autobiography owned by the Rev. Douglas Long, a former Barford curate and a friend of his. They perhaps sum up his philosophy in life. Certainly, he had seized his opportunities as they came, and when he died it was secure in the knowledge that he had helped to raise the agricultural labourer from a position of almost complete subservience to one where the first hesitant steps had been taken towards independence and self-respect.

Indeed, even by the last years of the nineteenth century (when Arch's political career came to an end) the farm worker had clearly progressed a long way, both economically and socially, from his position in the 1860's. And although a considerable amount of the credit for this improvement must be given to economic forces outside the labourer's own immediate control, nevertheless a proportion at least stemmed from the work of the agricultural trade unions. It is in this connection that Arch's strong and dynamic personality was so valuable.

It may be argued that the rise in wages which occurred in the early 1870's would have come anyway, as agriculture was prosperous and the demand for labour buoyant at a time when employment in urban industry was at a high level; but against this argument must be set the fact that such prosperity had existed before, without the labourers deriving any great benefit from it.[1] Under Arch's leadership the Union agitation pinpointed the need for some redistribution of agricultural income in favour of the farm worker.

Furthermore, although a part of the gain in money wages achieved in the early 1870's was lost in the 'depressed' years at the end of that decade, not all of the benefit was sacrificed. In almost every case, agricultural wage rates at the end of the century were higher than they had been before Joseph commenced his agitation — while workers had gained from the decline in food prices which characterised the last quarter of the nineteenth century. Nevertheless, despite these improvements, agricultural wages still remained low as compared with those of other categories of workers, and many rural labourers showed their realisation of this fact by leaving the land. It was indeed unfortunate for the ultimate success of Joseph's Union that its establishment should coincide with the start of a long period of falling prices for British arable agriculture. This fact stiffened farmers' opposition to the N.A.L.U. and its demands, and thereby eroded the confidence of members in the effectiveness of their organisation.

At the same time, the process of decline was nurtured by the repeated clashes within the leadership of the movement. These clashes undoubtedly owed something to Joseph's own self-willed personality, for he was a difficult colleague to work with — and yet without him it is unlikely that the Union would ever have got under way at all.

However, perhaps Joseph's most important contribution to the welfare of his class was the way in which he inspired in farm workers feelings of self-confidence which they had so obviously lacked in earlier years. After 1872 neither landowner nor farmer could forget that the labourer was a human being — not an ignorant 'chaw bacon' or 'Johnny Raw' whose views could be dismissed out of hand, but a man prepared, if necessary, to demand the rights and privileges which were his due. Ten years after the demise of the N.A.L.U., in 1906, it is significant that stirrings of independence showed themselves again, when the Norfolk labourers once more began to organise into a trade union. It was Joseph Arch, with his fierce self-reliance and strong determination, who had helped to bring about this change of attitude in a class formerly so subservient to those in authority. Certainly Sir Richard Winfrey, M.P., a Liberal who was a supporter of both Joseph and the new Union established in 1906, was quite positive as to the debt owed to the old man. In an article in the *Land Worker* of 18th September, 1919, he wrote: '(Arch's) name must always stand out in history as the pioneer of Trades Unionism in rural England. It is upon the foundation which he laid that the present success has been attained; for it was he who trained George Edwards and the other men who re-started the Union under brighter auspices in 1906.'

But perhaps the most fitting epitaph has been provided by a fellow agricultural worker and unionist, Josiah Sage, who remembered Arch in the 1890's, when he himself was a young man. Sage declared in 1951: 'Never before the days of Arch, nor yet since, have the ranks of the agricultural labourers produced such a man.'[2]

The present National Union of Agricultural and Allied Workers acknowledged its debt to Arch in 1922, when it arranged for the erection of a memorial in his honour at Barford Churchyard. The memorial (a Cornish granite obelisk) was unveiled on the 25th March 1922 — almost exactly fifty years after the original Warwickshire Agricultural Trade Union had been established under Joseph's leadership at the first Good Friday demonstration at Leamington. Among those present at the unveiling were George Edwards, the founder of the new agricultural workers' union, who was at that time Labour M.P. for South Norfolk, and Walter Smith, the President of the Union, who was Labour M.P. for Wellingborough. Joseph's son-in-law, the Rev. J E Leuty, and the latter's adopted daughter, Daisy, were also in attendance. In a moving speech, Edwards paid tribute to Arch as a man who had given 'his life in the interests of the people, and devoted his energies to the uplifting of the class to which he belonged.'[3]

It was perhaps fitting that not until the day following this ceremony Miriam Arch, Joseph's second wife, should die, at the age of 80. She had been lying seriously ill for some time, in the small cottage almost directly opposite to the Churchyard; for the last few years, since Joseph's death, she had been living quietly alone in Barford. Nevertheless, it is interesting to note that her death did not pass unnoticed. Arch would certainly have been proud to know that the Royal Family had forgotten neither him nor his, for when Mrs. Arch died Queen Alexandra's private secretary sent a message on behalf of the Queen to Daisy Leuty, regretting to hear of the death and sending 'her sincere sympathy' to the family.[4]

Nor was this all. Joseph's memory has lingered on through the years into a world very different from that which he knew and in which his life was spent. In recent times additional steps have been taken to preserve his name for posterity, and in April, 1960, the name of the *Red Lion Public House* in Barford was changed to that of the *Joseph Arch*. Joseph is thus one of a small band of Englishmen who have had a public house named after them!

The National Union of Agricultural and Allied Workers was represented at this ceremony, and its interest in Joseph's birthplace has continued since with, for example, annual mass rallies held every summer from 1967 onwards. The rallies, which are held in the local cricket ground, are attended by the present-day leaders of the agricultural trade union movement. At the rally in 1968 one of Joseph's American granddaughters, Mrs. M A Fabyan of Massachusetts, the eldest daughter of Edward Arch, was present, to provide a link with the family. On this occasion, as on others, a procession was formed and marched, headed by band and banners, to the Churchyard where a simple ceremony was held. Mrs. Fabyan was asked to lay a wreath of white flowers and for her it was, quite naturally, a 'red letter day'.[5]

Although Joseph Arch has now been dead for over fifty years, therefore, the memory of his dogmatic, vain — but above all courageous — character lives on. Through both the good times and the bad, Joseph showed his powers of endurance and his belief in the rectitude of his cause. He stood firm against the onslaughts of his enemies, and in the end, even if his Union did not survive, its spirit did, to be revived in 1906, while he himself won through, to secure an honoured place in the gallery of British labour leaders.

[1] There had, admittedly, been *some* rise in basic agricultural wage rates during the later 1860's — estimates indicate an increase in the basic rate in certain Midland counties (including Warwickshire) from about 9s. 6d. per week in 1860–61 to 10s. 6d. by 1867–71, for example — but these 'meagre' gains rather had the effect of whetting the appetite of the labourers for more substantial rewards, than of satisfying them. See E. L. Jones — *The Development of English Agriculture* 1815–73 (1968), pp.33–34.

[2] *Memoirs of Josiah Sage,* p.50.

[3] *The Land Worker* — May, 1922. (This is the journal of the National Union of Agricultural and Allied Workers.) Some of the Barford villagers also attended the ceremony and one who did remembers that after the speeches had been made, all those present repaired to the local school room, where cups of tea were served. For the present day visitor to the quiet country Churchyard at Barford there is also another link with the early days of the N.A.L.U., for buried very close to Joseph is Benjamin Herring, who had chaired that second meeting held at Wellesbourne in 1872, at which the real foundations of the Warwickshire movement had been laid. Herring outlived Arch, dying on 31st May, 1920, at the age of 89. He, too, had been a Primitive Methodist preacher, but unlike Arch, had maintained his loyalty right to the end of his life. Rather surprisingly his other main claim to fame in Barford in these later years was his activity as a herbalist and 'quack' doctor! (Information kindly provided by Mr George Worrall of Barford.)

[4] *Warwick Advertiser* — 1st April, 1922. On 19th April, 1922, Daisy married a Mr John Taylor at Normanton, Yorkshire, and shortly afterwards the Arch cottage at Barford was sold.

[5] Letters written to the author by Mrs M. A. Fabyan.

Appendix I

(a)

TOTAL MEMBERSHIP OF THE NATIONAL AGRICULTURAL LABOURERS' UNION

(Information derived from Returns submitted to the Chief Registrar of Friendly Societies, unless otherwise indicated. The Registrar observes that the figures are 'not always exact, being stated approximately only in the returns'; they relate to the end of each year in question.)

Year	Membership	Year	Membership
1873	71,835*	1885	10,700
1874	86,214*	1886	10,366
1875	40,000	1887	5,300
1876	55,000	1888	4,660
1877	30,000	1889	4,254
1878	24,000	1890	8,500
1879	20,000	1891	15,000
1880	20,000	1892	15,000
1881	15,000	1893	14,746
1882	15,000	1894	1,100
1883	15,000	1895	None given
1884	18,000	1896	Dissolved — October,1896

* Information derived from Press at the time of the Annual Council meeting held in May or June of the year in question.

(b)

CONSTITUTION AND RULES OF THE NATIONAL AGRICULTURAL LABOURERS' UNION
(1872)

Central Offices: Balm Cottage, Forfield Place, Leamington.

To the Members of the National Agricultural Labourers' Union.

In submitting to their brethren the Rules of the 'National Agricultural Labourers' Union,' the Members of the 'National Executive Committee' have added certain Supplementary Rules, for the use of Districts and Branches, These Rules are not regarded by the National Executive as exhaustive, but simply as fundamental. It is felt that

Districts and Branches should have perfect liberty to frame such laws for their own guidance as their own special circumstances may suggest; that liberty is freely accorded, and the National Executive hope it will be exercised on the basis of the Rules for Districts and Branches, and in harmony with the General Rules of the National. The National Executive hope soon to see a Branch Union in every parish, and a District Union — that is, a combination of Branches — in every county or division, all communicating with a common centre, all observing the same principles, and all working for the same end. In the early stages of our movement, let the Branch and District Meetings be frequent, that enthusiasm may be kept alive, information be dispersed, and the Union be perfected. We must have no local jealousies, no self-seeking, no isolation. Unity of action is above all things necessary, and this can be secured only as all the Branches and Districts work through a common Representative and Executive Committee. We must have money, and we must have it in one central fund, to which all shall contribute, and from which, in time of need, all shall in turn be aided. The strength of the great trade societies is in their central funds. If we have a balance here and another there, it will be simply impossible to support a number of men in any emergency that may arise. We must have a common treasury large enough, through the payments of all, to support the demands that may be made in the interest of all.

The funds of a Branch or District would soon be exhausted if a number of men were thrown upon them, but the National Fund — the fund of all — would be rich enough to meet any demands which the National Executive might entertain, and to support our Members through any crisis. Let it be clearly understood, then, that the Branch remits its funds to the District; that the Districts remit three-fourths of their receipts to the National, and that any Branch or District failing to do this, has no claim whatever on the general resources of the Union. The fourth, allowed to be retained by the Districts, can be disbursed at the discretion of the District Committee in meeting current expenditure and in promoting the general objects of the Union. For the working expenses of Branches, an Incidental Fund is recommended which may easily be realized by a small payment from each Member. Our movement has begun well. Success is, under God, in our own hands. Let us cleave to and work for the Union. Let peace and moderation mark all our meetings. Let courtesy, fairness, and firmness characterize all our demands. Act cautiously and advisedly, that no act may have to be repented or repudiated. Do not strike unless all other means fail you. Try all other means; try them with firmness and patience; try them in the enforcement of only just claims, and if they all fail, then strike, and, having observed Rule 10, strike with a will. Fraternize,

Centralize! With brotherly feeling, with an united front, with every District welded into a great whole, with a common fund to which all shall pay, and on which all shall have the right to draw, the time will not be distant, when every Agricultural Labourer will have, what few, as yet, have enjoyed, a fair day's pay for a fair day's work. Nine and a half hours, exclusive of meal-times, as a day's work, and 16s. as a week's pay, are not extravagant demands. Society supports you in making them, and they will be met soon. Brothers, be united, and you will be strong; be temperate, and you will be respected; realize a central capital, and you will be able to act with firmness and independence. Many eyes are upon you; many tongues are ready to reproach you; your opponents say that your extra leisure will be passed in the public-house, and your extra pay be spent in beer. Show that their slander is untrue! Be united, be sober, and you will soon be free.

(Signed) JOSEPH ARCH,

Chairman of the National Executive Committee.

Rules and Constitution

NAME

1 The National Agricultural Labourers' Union.

OBJECT

2 (A) To improve the general condition of Agricultural Labourers in the United Kingdom.

(B) To encourage the formation of Branch and District Unions.

(C) To promote co-operation and communication between Unions already in existence.

COUNCIL

3 A Council, consisting of one Delegate from each District Union, shall meet at Leamington, or elsewhere, as may be determined by the preceding Council, on the third Tuesday of May in each year, for the following purposes:-

(A) To elect an Executive Committee, together with a Treasurer, Secretary, and four Trustees.

(B) To receive a Financial Statement, with a Balance Sheet for the previous year, duly audited by a public accountant.

(C) To consider the General Report to be submitted by Affiliated Districts for the year ending 31st March preceding.

(D) To confer and decide on the general business and interests of the Union.

4 The National Executive Committee shall consist of a Chairman, who shall have a second or casting vote, and of twelve Agricultural Labourers, seven of whom shall form a quorum.

5 The National Executive Committee shall seek the counsel and co-operation of gentlemen favourable to the principles of the Union, and shall invite them to attend its meetings, without power to vote.

6 The National Executive Committee shall meet each alternate Monday, and oftener, if necessary — all meetings to be convened by the Secretary.

7 The National Executive Committee shall be entrusted with the expenditure of all moneys contributed by the public, by the Affiliated Districts, or otherwise; and shall employ the same in furthering the objects specified in Rule 2; it shall also adopt such general means as it may think desirable to carry on the work of the Union, and shall appoint paid agents and officers at discretion.

8 The National Executive Committee shall make the necessary arrangements for each Annual Council, and submit a programme of the business to be considered to the Secretary of each Affiliated District, at least fourteen days before the third Tuesday in May. Should any important and unforeseen circumstances arise to necessitate such a course, the National Executive Committee may at any time convoke a Special Council, upon giving the usual notice, and shall do so forthwith on the written request of six District Committees.

9 The National Executive Committee shall communicate to the Secretary of each District Union, any proposals or suggestions that may seem advisable in the general interests of the Union as a whole.

SETTLEMENT OF DISPUTES

10 All cases of dispute between the Members of the National Agricultural Union and their Employers, must be laid before the Branch Committee to which such Members may belong; and, should the Branch Committee be unable to arrange the question to the mutual satisfaction of the parties interested, in conjunction with the District Committee, recourse shall be had to arbitration. Should the District Committee be unable to arrange for such arbitration, an appeal shall be made to the National Executive Committee for its decision. Any award made by arbitration or by decision of the National Executive, shall be binding upon all Members of the Union; and in no case shall a strike be resorted to, until the above means have been tried and failed.

FINANCIAL

11 The funds of the National Agricultural Labourers' Union shall be invested in the names of the following gentlemen as Trustees:–Mr A.

Arnold, Hampton-in-Arden; Mr Jesse Collings, Birmingham; Mr W. G. Ward, Periston Towers, Ross; Mr. E. Jenkins, London.

12 The Treasurer shall make no disbursements except on receipt of a resolution of the National Executive Committee, signed by the Chairman and Secretary; at the first Meeting in each month he shall present a Cash Statement to the National Executive, and shall deposit, at interest, in the names of the Trustees, with Lloyds Bank at Leamington, any sum in his hands exceeding £50.

DISTRICT COMMITTEES

13 District Committees shall bear the name of the County or Division embracing them, as the 'Kent District', or the 'West Berks District of the National Agricultural Labourers' Union.' District Committees shall be composed of Delegates from the various Branches of the District; and each District Committee shall elect an Executive of seven Members, together with a Chairman, Secretary, and Treasurer, who shall meet monthly, and oftener when necessary.

14 Each District Committee shall regulate its own affairs in conformity with the general principals laid down in the preceding Rules; but no Rules drawn up by any Branch shall be accepted by the National Agricultural Labourers' Union, unless they shall first have been ratified by the District Committee to which such Branch belongs.

15 District Committees shall do their utmost to prevent men who may migrate to another locality from underbidding their fellow Labourers already at work there.

16 Each District Committee shall be required at its own cost to send a Delegate to the Meetings of the Council.

17 Each District Committee shall send to the National Committee on or before the fourteenth of every month, a brief Report of its proceedings; and on the third Friday in April, July, October, and January, under a penalty of 10s. for neglect, a Financial Statement, with the balance due on the quarter.

18 Each District Committee must inform the National Executive Committee of any important action contemplated within its jurisdiction; and, should any proceedings be taken by a District without the sanction of the National Executive Committee, and be persisted in after the National Executive has signified its disapproval, such District shall not be assisted in its action by the funds of the National Agricultural Labourers' Union.

19 All Districts wishing to be affiliated with the National Agricultural Labourers' Union must remit three-fourths of the entrance fees and of the weekly contributions to the National Executive Committee, to be invested and employed in accordance with previous Rules.

226

20 Cards of Membership, bearing the device of the National Agricultural Labourers' Union, shall be issued to the District Committees, to be supplied by them to their several Branches.

BRANCHES

21 Each Branch shall bear the name of the village or parish in which its business is transacted.

22 Branches shall consist of the Agricultural Labourers of one or more parishes in the same locality, who shall pay an entrance fee of 6d. and a weekly contribution of 2d.

23 Branches, as soon as practicable, shall unite in forming themselves into Districts.

24 Each Branch shall annually elect a Chairman, Treasurer, Secretary, and a Committee of seven Members, for the management of its business, to communicate with the District Executive, and, through it, with the National Executive.

25 Branches shall meet fortnightly for the payment of contributions and other business.

26 The Chairman shall preside at each Meeting of the Branch; he shall preserve order, promote the interests and repute of the Union to the best of his power, and sign all reports, minutes, etc. The Secretary shall keep the accounts of the Branch, record the minutes of all the Meetings, and pay all funds to the Treasurer without loss of time. The Treasurer shall receive all monies, and under a penalty of 2s. for neglect, shall, in conjunction with the Secretary, remit them to the District Executive on the first Thursday in every month, together with an audited account.

27 Each Branch shall raise an incidental fund to meet its own working expenses.

28 Branches shall be at liberty to frame any bye-laws they may think necessary — regard being had to Rule 15.

29 These Rules shall be subject to additions or alterations only by the Annual or a Special Council. One month's notice of any Amendment must be given to the Secretary in writing, and such Amendment shall not be adopted unless two-thirds of the Delegates present approve it by vote.

During the course of the succeeding years these Rules were amended on a number of occasions; for example, the weekly contributions were increased from 2d. per member to $2\frac{1}{4}$d., the $\frac{1}{4}$d. being retained by the Branches for administrative expenses, etc. With the establishment of the National Sick Benefit Society in 1877, further Rules were incorporated to deal with this, and among other changes apparent in the 1879 Rule Book, for example, were:

Rule 2

To improve the condition of Agricultural and other labourers in the United Kingdom, Members of the Union, by:–

1 Increasing their wages, and lessening their hours of labour.

2 Protecting their trade interests, and securing them legal redress against oppression.

3 Assisting them to migrate from one part of the Kingdom to another, or to emigrate to other Countries.

4 Providing for all those Members who shall pay the Benefit contributions hereinafter mentioned, a weekly allowance during sickness and the payment of a sum of money at death.

Rule 21

ARREARS, EXPULSION AND RE-ADMISSION OF MEMBERS

1 Any member whose contributions shall be more than three months in arrears, shall not be entitled to relief, and if they are six months in arrears he shall be considered as excluded from the B(ranch).

2 An excluded Member may be re-admitted, upon payment of an entrance fee of one shilling, but shall not, until six months after his re-admission, be entitled to relief.

Rule 22

MISCONDUCT OF MEMBERS

Any Member losing his employment through drunkenness or any other misconduct, or who shall remain wilfully idle, or who shall wilfully neglect to provide for his family, shall not be entitled to relief, but shall be liable to expulsion.

These are but a sample of the relatively minor changes and additions which were made by the Union in the light of its experience.

Appendix 2

FINANCES OF NATIONAL AGRICULTURAL LABOURERS' UNION — 1875-95

(All details given below have been obtained from the 4th to 8th Annual Reports of the Board of Trade Labour Department on Trade Unions. — Parliamentary Papers: 1890-91, Vol. XCII; 1893-94, Vol. CII; 1894, Vol. XCIV; 1985, Vol. CVII; 1896, Vol. XCIII.

Year	TOTAL Yearly Income (a)			Income from Contributions, included in (a)			TOTAL Yearly Expenditure (b)			Expenditure on 'working and other expenses', included in (b)			TOTAL BALANCE in hand at end of each year (c)		
	£	s.	d.	£	s.	d.	£	s.	d.	£	s.	d.	£	s.	d.
1875	12,625	0	0	Not available			10,050	0	0	Not available			6,843	18	3
1876	8,648	17	2	8,411	17	5	6,587	14	9	2,075	19	0	8,905	0	8
1877	11,501	13	8	11,283	4	2	14,048	8	2½	6,114	11	6½*	6,358	6	1½
1878	11,226	0	3	11,063	0	3	11,536	19	10½	5,364	9	1½	6,047	6	6
1879	9,331	16	2	9,201	15	10	8,936	14	11	3,021	12	10	6,142	7	9**
1880	8,737	11	9	8,572	1	1	8,272	16	11½	3,252	1	2½	6,607	2	6½
1881	7,781	16	4½	7,615	1	10½	7,776	2	10½	3,882	0	8½	6,612	16	0½
1882	7,176	10	6	6,958	12	11	6,723	1	1½	3,399	11	4½	7,066	5	5
1883	6,931	9	8½	6,685	3	1	7,033	3	6	3,393	0	10	6,964	11	7½
1884	7,430	7	9½	7,008	11	5	7,309	18	3	1,376	3	7	7,685	1	2***
1885	8,133	10	5½	7,885	5	6½	8,597	11	4½	2,473	15	10½	6,621	0	3
1886	6,886	14	2	6,311	17	0	7,314	0	9½	1,548	1	7½	6,193	13	7½
1887	4,285	0	0	Not available			4,738	10	2	Not available			5,740	3	5½
1888	4,558	7	7½	4,241	0	5½	6,834	10	4	1,428	7	0	3,464	3	9
1889	3,018	4	9	2,914	10	5	5,173	12	5	1,390	7	7	1,308	13	1
1890	Not available			Not available			Not available			Not available			421	0	0

229

	£	s.	d.	£	s.	d.	£	s.	d.	£	s.	d.	£	s.	d.
1891	3,675	0	0	3,562	0	0	2,950	0	0	1,680	0	0	1,146	0	0
1892	3,196	0	0	3,178	0	0	2,891	0	0	1,868	0	0	1,451	0	0
1893	1,549	0	0	1,531	0	0	2,521	0	0	1,822	0	0	479	0	0
1894	488	0	0	441	0	0	958	0	0	877	0	0	2	2	0
1895	Not available			Not available			Not available			Not available			Not available		
1896															

The Notice of Dissolution was issued on 23rd September, 1896, and the form of dissolution was signed on the Union side by Joseph Arch and seven other members on 30th October, 1896. — See Public Record Office — F.S.7.4/154.

* The working and other expenses for 1877 include £2,829 3s. 3d. for 'Newspaper Account'; 1878, £472 9s. 0d.; 1879, £220; 1880, £457 8s. 0d.; 1881, £269 19s. 0d.; 1882, £7 7s. 0d.; and 1883, £150 for the same account; a total of £4,406 6s. 3d.

** There is a deficiency of £300 in this balance; the balance from the previous year being brought forward less this amount.

*** There is a surplus in this balance of £600 caused by entering value of stock and copyright to this amount, as funds, which do not appear in the accounts of the following year, causing there an apparent deficiency to this amount.

Appendix 3

COBDEN CLUB LEAFLET NO. XVIII

WOULD PROTECTION REMOVE THE PRESENT DISTRESS, AND BENEFIT
THE WORKING MAN?

by Joseph Arch

Some of the Tory party seem to have found a remedy for all the ills that afflict us as a nation.

That marvellous panacea is 'Protection.'

'Let us tax,' they say, 'the production of the foreigner when he sends it over to this country.'

Well, now, we will begin with bread. Suppose, by taxing our bread-stuff, the price of the quartern loaf were 7d. Let us take a family who consume fourteen loaves every week; that would cost 8s. 2d. per week for bread alone. At present we have a good quartern loaf for 5d. Take the same number of loaves, and the bread bill of the family is 5s. 10d.

'But,' the Protectionist says, 'the wages would be higher.'

Suppose a man is earning 12s. a week, and his bread bill is 5s. 10d., and his wages rise from 12s. to 14s. per week, but his bread bill goes up 2s. 4d., what advantage does he gain?

There are many other necessaries of life that are cheap, because the tax has been taken off.

I can remember 1846, when the quartern loaf was 10d. and, at one time, a shilling; tea, 4s. per lb; the commonest sugar, 5d. per lb; and the labourer's wages 8s., 9s., or, at the most, 10s. a week. More than double the number of men in our rural villages were out of employ than are out of employ to-day.

There need not be a single hand out of work to-day in rural England if the land were properly tilled.

Shall we, as working men, go back to the time when many of us had barley bread to eat? I think every sensible working man will say, No.

Then let us, at the next General Election, fight this bugbear of Fair Trade at the ballot-box; insist upon the land being properly cultivated;

and withdraw from our over-populous towns the thousands of men who have been driven there by our inhuman land system.

Till the Land, give the tiller security for his Capital, and we should soon see at least some of these dark clouds of depression disappear.

(This and other Cobden Club Leaflets were supplied in packets of 100, price 1s.)

Appendix 4

(From *English Labourers' Chronicle* of 27th March, 1880.)

ADDRESS TO THE INDEPENDENT ELECTORS OF THE BOROUGH OF
WILTON

Gentlemen,
Having been strongly urged by the Liberal Association of your borough to become your candidate at the forthcoming election, I most cordially accept your invitation. I need not trouble you with a lengthy address as my political opinions are so well known.

I am strongly opposed to the foreign policy of the present Government, as I consider such policy has lowered the standard of English freedom and justice in the eyes of the world, and created hatred and mistrust abroad, distress and poverty at home.

I am in favour of reform in our Land laws, being thoroughly convinced that those laws as they now stand are a great hindrance to the proper cultivation of the soil and are injurious to the best interests of the landlord, the tenant farmer, the labourers and the public at large.

I strongly advocate the abolition of the Game Laws, as I know them to be a source of evil which seriously affects the prosperity of agriculture in this country.

For seven years I have been advocating, to the best of my humble ability, the extension of the Franchise to the Counties. Living as I have done all my life amongst rural workmen, I am fully satisfied that it is unsafe, impolitic and unjust to a large and deserving class of our countrymen to deny them the right to vote.

To my mind a temperate, liberal and wise continuation of measures for improving the condition of the Irish peasantry is calculated to unite the two portions of the Empire by ties of mutual regard, and is the sure and only means of rendering the union of Ireland with England hearty and indissoluble.

Peace, Retrenchment, and Reform, have ever been the cardinal principles of the Liberal party, which I feel sure every true Liberal of your ancient borough is prepared to support.

There are many other questions which I hope to bring before you shortly, when I shall be able to state my views more fully.

Should you do me the honour to return me to Parliament, I shall feel it my duty to support such measures as are calculated to secure peace abroad and prosperity at home.

JOSEPH ARCH

Barford, Warwick.
17th March, 1880.

(From *English Labourers' Chronicle* of 21st November, 1885)

TO THE ELECTORS OF NORTH WEST NORFOLK

Gentlemen,

The duly elected Liberal Hundred for this division, on the 5th May last, did me the honour, almost unanimously, of inviting me to represent you in the Liberal interest in Parliament. I desire to inform you of the course in politics I intend to pursue, should I become your representative.

For the past thirteen years I have been advocating in every corner of the kingdom, the assimilation of the County with the Borough Franchise, I would, therefore, first join with you in hearty congratulation on your admission, by the strenuous exertion of the Liberal party, and its great leader — William Ewart Gladstone — to the right of free citizenship.

I would also warn you that with the acquisition and exercise of the Franchise is conferred the heavy responsibility of governing righteously this great country.

Should I obtain your suffrages, and be returned as your member to the next Parliament, the undermentioned are the measures which will receive my constant and unwearing support.

1 The extension of Free Trade to all articles of Food and Daily Consumption, rather than its restriction.

2 A measure for conferring Local Government by Local Boards, upon County districts throughout the kingdom, such Boards to be elected on the Parliamentary Franchise, one man, one vote, having full control of all local affairs, including Liquor Traffic; to such Boards to be committed the administration of the Poor Laws, the amendment of which I intend to advocate.

3 A complete Reform of the Land Laws, including abolition of the system of Primogeniture, Entail, and Settlement, Copyhold and Customary tenure, by a just measure

rendering its transfer more easy, its distribution more equitable, and its possession and occupancy more profitable

4 A further Reform in the Agricultural Holdings Acts, giving greater protection to tenant farmers for their capital expended in the land, security of tenure, and compensation for improvements to small holders and allotment occupiers, and the total abolition of the Law of Distress.

5 The power to Government or Local Boards to acquire land in every village, at reasonable purchase value, and and re-let or sell in small portions to any person requiring the same.

6 The disestablishment of the State Church, the entire separation of Religion from State control, and the application of State Tithes to the equal benefit of all classes of the community.

7 An Affirmation Bill, to permit a Solemn Affirmation, in all cases where desired, instead of an Oath.

8 The Reform of the House of Lords, securing an effective deprivation of its power to obstruct any measure that has received the approval of the People's House.

9 Free Secular Elementary Education.

10 The security of Cottage tenants in their occupation upon yearly tenancies, and greater regard to their health, comfort and well being.

11 The closing of Public-Houses on Sundays, except to bona-fide travellers.

12 The extension of the principle of proportional taxation beyond the present £400 limit.

13 A revision of the Laws affecting the preservation of Game.

14 The Abolition of Perpetual Pensions.

15 The Substitution of Arbitration for War, in all cases where practicable.

16 Equal laws for all parts of the United Kingdom.

I do not appeal to you as an experienced statesman, or qualified legislator, but I seek your suffrages that in the House of Commons, on behalf of the class in which I was born, and to which I belong, I may draw the attention of the People's representatives, with the authoritative voice of practical experience, to those measures which affect the welfare of the agricultural labouring class.

As an Agricultural Labourer, I am well aware that I should be considered unfit to stand on even terms with experienced men in the world, but years of travels in this and other countries, spent in constant observation of men and things in the interest and for the benefit of my fellow labourers, have given me a practical education and understanding of the wants and needs of the people, and an insight into the Remedies required for their alleviation.

In placing my services at your command, I respectfully, but earnestly, solicit the combined and active support of all classes who love a fair and good Liberal Government, to secure my return.

I have the honour to be gentlemen,

Your obedient Servant,

JOSEPH ARCH.

Barford, Warwickshire.

(From the *English Labourers' Chronicle* of 26th June, 1886)

TO THE ELECTORS OF NORTH-WEST NORFOLK

Gentlemen,

Some six months since you generously undertook to champion in your constituency the principle of direct representation for the Agricultural Labourer in the British Parliament.

The extraordinary interest which your late contest elicited throughout the kingdom, and the wide-spread enthusiasm with which your victory for that principle was received, together with the cordial reception given me in your name, as the first Agricultural Labourer who had become a Member of Parliament, only add to the obligation I owe you, in the name of the Agricultural Labourers of England, for the support you have rendered to their cause.

I trusted on entering Parliament that in the few years of honest legislation in which I should watch your interests before again appealing to you, many beneficial measures affecting the welfare of the community, and especially my fellow-labourers, would have become law.

My first duty in the House of Commons was to protest against the absolute indifference displayed by the Conservative Party in their Queen's Speech, to the claims and needs of the Agricultural Labourer. Upon that question the Conservative Government was defeated, and Mr Gladstone and a Liberal Government were placed in office.

Since then I have been enabled to bring prominently before

the House of Commons the views held by the Agricultural Labourer upon the subjects of Land and Poor Laws, and to place those views before any fellow-member from the stand-point of one who had himself felt the cruel and unjust pressure of those Laws upon the poor.

The decisive voice of the Irish Electors in returning eighty-six representatives to demand Home Rule, compelled the Liberal Party, as the truly Constitutional Party, to give their claims due consideration. I have vigorously supported Mr Gladstone in his grand effort to do justice to Ireland, and as your representative I should again support to the utmost of my power what I deem to be the cause of justice and freedom.

I sincerely regret the unavoidable delay in proceeding with the great questions of Local Government, Land Law Reform, Free Education, Religious Equality, and the other measures I advocated in my late address to you, but I feel confident that a just settlement of the Irish Question will greatly accelerate the course of British Legislation, and these great questions will in future receive much fuller attention at the hands of a Parliament freed from a continuous occupation on Irish affairs.

I now appeal to you once more in the name of Agricultural Labourers to enable me by your confidence and support to represent this great interest, directly and practically in the House of Commons, while my earnest support will always be given to every measure beneficially affecting my constituents generally.

I therefore trust that every true Liberal will do his utmost to support Mr Gladstone and his colleagues in the cause of progress, by returning me as the Liberal Member for North-West Norfolk.

I am, Gentlemen,

Your grateful Servant,

JOSEPH ARCH

Barford, Warwickshire.

(From the *English Labourers' Chronicle* — 25th June, 1892)

TO THE PARLIAMENTARY ELECTORS OF NORTH-WEST NORFOLK.

Gentlemen,

The opportunity has presented itself for me once more to offer myself as your candidate, and as a supporter of Mr Gladstone, in the coming Parliament, I need scarcely make any apology for now seeking your suffrages for as you are all aware I am one of yourselves.

I am strongly in favour of Home Rule for Ireland, thus giving the right to the Irish to manage their own local affairs, whilst preserving intact the supremacy of the Imperial Parliament and the much vaunted integrity of the Empire.

I would as strongly advocate Home Rule for England through the formation of Parish Councils, selected by ballot on the One Man One Vote principle. Such Councils to have power to deal with all matters that specially concern the everyday life of the residents within the Parish, including compulsory powers for acquiring land not only for Allotments, but for Small Holdings, Chapels, Recreation Grounds, New Roads, and also for the erection of Cottages and Village Public Halls, and also power to deal with Charities, Commons, Waste Lands, Rights of Way, Public Foot Paths, and all other objects which are necessary for the improvement and prosperity of the people.

I should consider it my duty to support a great reform of our Poor Law so that the honest worker after years of toil and privation may have something better to look forward to than the hateful Workhouse. The Administration should be placed in the hands of Parish Councils and in Boards of Guardians, and should include a wisely divided scheme of State-aided Insurance to assist the thrifty in providing for a comfortable old age. Any person in receipt of aid through these reforms should not be disfranchised or pauperised.

I WOULD ALSO ADVOCATE:–

[1] A complete repeal of the Game Laws.

[2] A thorough revision of the Registration Laws, establishing the principle of One Man One Vote, and that it should be as easy for a man to get on the Register as on the Rate Book.

[3] The fullest possible religious equality.

[4] The removal of all Taxes on Articles of Food.

[5] The Taxing of all Mining Royalties.

[6] The Shortening of the duration of Parliament.

[7] The entire Abolition of the Hereditary Principle in the House of Lords.

The toilers of the Country can only look to the Liberal Party for the achievement of all these great and beneficial Reforms.

Should you again do me the honour to return me as your Representative to Parliament, I shall esteem it a duty as well as a pleasure to serve your interests to the best of my ability.

I am, Gentlemen,
Your obedient Servant,
JOSEPH ARCH

Barford Warwickshire.

Election Address

(From the English Labourers' Chronicle — 15th December, 1888)

COUNTY OF WARWICK — LOCAL GOVERNMENT ACT, 1888

To the Electors of the Wellesbourne Division,

Ladies and Gentlemen,

Having been requested to become a Candidate for the New County Council to represent the above Division, I have consented to place my services at the disposal of the Electors.

I have spent nearly the whole of my life among you as a working man and am pretty well acquainted with the business the Council will have to take in hand.

It will not be possible for me to see every Elector personally, nor do I intend to canvass, the ballot is secret, therefore, I shall leave each Elector free to use his or her own judgment at the poll.

The Allotments Question will have to come before the Council, and as one who knows personally the benefit of a good Allotment to a working man's family, I shall advocate and support the Allotments system, and will do my best to see it carried out in every parish where the men require land.

I am deeply interested and anxious to see the working men with a good home, as many have not sufficient room to be healthy.

Having worked on the land nearly the whole of my life, I am naturally anxious to see all connected with the cultivation of the soil prosperous.

If anything can be done to reduce the rates and place the public burdens on a more equitable basis it will have my steady and constant support.

If elected I shall feel it my imperative duty to promote to the best of my ability the welfare and interest of all ratepayers irrespective of party.

I am, Ladies and Gentlemen,
Your obedient Servant,
JOSEPH ARCH

Barford, Warwick.
November 26th, 1888.

Appendix 5

Joseph Arch's Maiden Speech in Parliament, made on 26th January, 1886, during the debate on the Address at the opening of Parliament. It has been included in *Famous Speeches* ed. by Herbert Paul (1922)

Sir, — I have no intention of wasting the time of the House with a long speech; but I think I have a just right to address the House on this subject. I am, as you are aware, the representative of a class whose interest, whose happiness, and whose comfort I believe gentlemen on both sides of the House are anxious to improve. With regard to the allotments question, I can remember when it was one of the most difficult things in the world for a labourer in a village to obtain anything like a decent allotment; but during the past fourteen years I am happy to say that honourable gentlemen — both Liberal and Conservative— have, to some extent, seen their way clear to grant and extend these allotments. The right honourable member for Mid-Lincolnshire (Mr Chaplin), when speaking last night upon the Amendment of my honourable friend the member for Forfarshire (Mr J. W. Barclay), said that the small freeholders in Mid-Lincolnshire were in a very destitute condition. I have watched all my life the working of a freehold and the energy and contentment of a freeholder, and it is quite true that where a man has had a heavy mortgage on his little freehold he has had a difficulty to face. But I have been pleasantly surprised to find on both sides of the House the great anxiety there is now to improve the agricultural labourers' position. Fourteen years ago, when I was asked by my own brethren in the counties if I could institute something to improve their condition, my policy was denounced, my actions were condemned, and not a few labourers were 'Boycotted.' I know that there are good landlords and bad landlords, and the Amendment of the honourable member for Ipswich (Mr Jesse Collings), I think, does not in the least interfere with good landlords who are willing to grant land for their labourers; but are there not places in the country where labourers are almost landless? Where have the majority of the unemployed men in our towns to-day come from? They have been divorced from the soil, and they have been driven into our towns. To my mind, the object of the Amendment of the honourable member for Ipswich is not so much to cure agricultural depression as to cure the poverty of agricultural labourers. How can that poverty be arrested if, during certain portions of the year, the working men in our villages are thrown out of employment? My remedy for years has been this — that if you do not require the services of a workman to till the land of the tenant farmer, then, in the name of common justice and humanity, allow him some land to till for himself. I think the Amendment of the honourable member for Ipswich is quite opportune. When I read the speech of Her Most Gracious Majesty the Queen, which expressed sympathy with the distress that was prevalent not only in trade but in agriculture, I took it certainly to mean this — 'You are in a terribly poverty-stricken condition. Your lot in life is hard. You are without employment and without money, and consequently must be without food. I know your lot is hard, but I have no remedy.' It seems to me something like this — that supposing as an individual I were suffering intense bodily pain and I sent for a medical adviser, he looks at me, he sees me writhing in agony, and he says — 'I have not a single ingredient in my surgery that I could apply to assuage your pain.' Would it not be natural enough for me to seek the advice of some more skilled physician? If Her Majesty's Government have no remedy for this distress, then, I think, the country will very soon look out for another physician who has a practical remedy already at hand. The right honourable member for Mid-Lincolnshire blamed the honourable member for Ipswich because he had prescribed no remedy; but I confess that I have not yet found honourable gentlemen on that side of the House prescribing any remedy themselves. If honourable gentlemen on this side of the House have not prescribed the right sort of medicine, the Government at the present time have every opportunity of finding that medicine and relieving the distress. The right honourable gentleman the member for Mid-Lincolnshire said last night that wages had gone down in that county from 18s. to 12s. per week. He expressed great surprise and wonder how these poor people managed to live. Now, I think I shall be quite in place if I ask the right honourable gentleman to try to live upon that wage for three months himself — then he will be able to solve the problem. He further said that, while wages were low, numbers of men were out of employment. Well, if it is difficult for a man with 12s. a week to support himself, his wife, and, perhaps, three or four children, what a sorry plight those men must be in who are out of employment and have no wages at all. Honourable gentlemen have said that about a quarter of an acre is sufficient for a working man in a village. There may be some working men, such as shepherds and carters, who would, perhaps be contented with a rood of ground; but I venture to say that a very large number of the labourers in Norfolk — and I am speaking now from my own experience in that county — would only be too glad if they could rent an acre or two at a fair market price. On the other hand, I do not not find any human or Divine law which would confine me, as a skilled labourer, to one rood of God's earth. If I have energy, tact, and skill by which I could cultivate my acre or two, and buy my cow into the bargain, I do not see any just reason why my energies should be crippled and my forces held back, and why I should be content, as an agricultural labourer, with a rood of ground and my nose on the grindstone all the days of my life. We want to put an end to pauperism; and I am prepared to say that among my class there are hundreds and thousands of working men who hate pauperism, and who have a perfect horror of the workhouse. But if we are to be cut down to 12s. a week, which the right honourable gentleman acknowledged was a very small wage, and if these men by their energy can supplement these wages by another 10s. or 12s. into the bargain, I want to know why it should not be done, and the pauperism of the country lessened. The right honourable gentleman spoke of men in France having to work very hard, and appearing very old when they were almost young. He said they carried fodder to the cows, and went milking, and the rest of it; but the right hon. gentleman forgot to tell us that they were their own cows. I have seen the women in Somersetshire, Wiltshire, and Dorsetshire milking other people's cows, and having very little of the milk which they drew from them. I cannot understand for the life of me why, if an English workman can, by thrift and industry and care, manage to secure to himself and his family a cow, he should not have the opportunity of doing so. The Amendment of the honourable member for Ipswich means that. We do not ask for borrowed funds, or for the land to be given us, and we have no desire to steal it. What the Amendment asks, and what I ask honourable gentlemen on both sides of the House, is, whether the time has not come when these thousands of industrious and willing workers should no longer be shut out from the soil, and should have an opportunity of obtaining a fair freehold, and producing food for themselves and their families? Why are these men out of work? Is it because the land is so well cultivated that no more of their labour is required? I travel this country from one end to the other, and I have an idea I know when land is cultivated and when it is not as well as any gentlemen in this House. I say, fearless of contradiction, that there are tens of thousands of acres of land waiting for the hand of the workman; and what this House ought to consider and aim at is to use every legitimate means to bring the land that cries for labour to the labourer as soon as possible. I am addressing in this House large landed proprietors; and will any honourable gentleman attempt for one moment to deny that the best cultivated estate is the best for the landlord? When I look at this question I go almost out of the region of party politics. It is not a landlord's, a tenant farmer's, or a labourer's, question; it is the question of the people, and they will very soon make it their question. We are not Socialistic — not in the offensive meaning of the word; but to a certain extent we are Socialists, because we are social beings. We like social comforts and social society; but we have a great aversion to social society paid for out of the poor rates. An honourable gentleman said last night that it was beyond the power of the honourable member for North-West Norfolk to raise wages. I thought it was equally impossible for landlords in this country to force up rent. We have always been told that the price of labour would be regulated by what it is worth in the market. That is just what land has got to be. My idea of justice in land is this — that if I have to sell as a tenant farmer my produce extremely cheap, then I say the rent of my land should be extremely cheap. But the time has come for, and this Parliament has been elected very largely to carry out, some just and wise measure, not only for the improvement of the tenant farmers and Heaven knows they want something, some of them — but for the benefit of the labourers and for the benefit of the country. When I look around on this side of the House I see several honourable gentlemen — a fair number of Liberal members — who have been returned by the votes very largely of the agricultural labourers. They know that during the contests in various divisions the labourers expressed a very great desire for land to cultivate for themselves. They naturally concurred with that idea; but I have never heard any Liberal candidate promise the labourers three acres and a cow. For myself, I never made such a vain promise. Something which dropped from the right honourable and learned Lord Advocate last night somewhat grieved me. When he was speaking of the labourers of Scotland I think he called them hinds. I should like to inform the right honourable and learned gentleman that though our lot in life has been one of poverty, though we were born in humble cottages, at the same time we look upon ourselves as men. I think honourable gentlemen on the other side of the House would feel very much annoyed if we were to call them aristocratic goats. The labourers of this country know they are men. They have largely contributed to the constitution of this House; and I hope it will be able to show honestly and fairly to the labourers who have sent us here that, at least, we did our best to redress their grievances, to dry their tears, to wipe away their sorrows and to place them in the position of free men.

Appendix 6

Some of the Union songs sung at labourers' meetings in the 1870's and later; they emphasize the personal importance of Joseph Arch in the agricultural trade union movement.

1 *To see the thousands on Ham Hill* — Composed by a Mr Reader, a blind man, who lived in the Ham Hill area of Somerset. (Information kindly obtained from Mr D. Price, Stanchester County Secondary School, Stoke-sub-Hamdon, Somerset.)

> To see the thousands on Ham Hill
> It is a splendid sight.
> Our motto, 'Now or never'
> May God defend the fight.
> We are a host of honest men
> With good hard-working hands,
> The cause of England's Glory
> And the tillers of the land.
>
> Chorus:–
>
> The farmers want to keep us down
> Upon starvation wage.
> But they have found their losing ground
> In this enlightened age.
> And if they come they will see
> A band of men determined then
> To put down slavery.
>
> Chorus:–
>
> Through Yeovil and through Preston too
> We'll bands of music play.
> And through the village of Montacute
> To Ham Hill take our way.
> The stinging nettles on the top
> It's plain enough to say
> We mean to sting the farmers' backs
> Until we get fair play.

Chorus:–

Success to gallant Joseph Arch,
He is our Leader brave
And with him I am sure you'll march
Your liberties to save.
They told his poor old father
To the workhouse he must go.
They would have done the same with him
But he said, 'Not for Joe!'

Chorus:–

Chorus

So, here we go, all in a row,
Happy ploughboy, merry cowboy,
Toil and mow, reap and sow, and
Stick to the 'Labourers' Union 'O'.

2 *We'll all be Union Men* (Tune: 'A day's march nearer home')

Ye tillers of the soil,
    Assert your manhood then,
You get your living by hard toil,
    Then all be union men.

Chorus:–

We've been oppressed we know,
    By money-making elves,
But Arch and Co. have taught us how
    To rise and help ourselves.

Chorus:–

Now since we've learnt the plan,
    That Arch and Co. have taught,
The Union for the working men,
    We'll never give it up.

Chorus:–

No never give it up,
    Not when the victory's won,
For what we get by Union,
    Protect it just the same.

Chorus:-

There is a simple rule,
    A very short one too,
It's do to others as you would
    Have others do to you.

Chorus:-
Chorus
Joe Arch he raised his voice,
    'Twas for the working men,
Then let us all rejoice and say,
    We'll all be Union men.

3 *We Demand the Vote* (Tune: 'Stand like the brave')

Hark, hark to the call boys,
Sounding loud, long and shrill,
And voices re-echo
O'er ocean and hill;
        Chorus:-

We lift up our banner
In the cause that is right,
Determined to be valiant
In council or fight;
        Chorus:-

With Arch our commander
The strife is begun,
We have fought sharp engagements
And Victories have won

        Chorus:-

From the mines and the mills,
From the forest and field,
We march in bold order,
Resolved not to yield;

        Chorus:-

With strong bone and sinew
And true British heart,

Stand firm by your flag boys,
And play the man's part.

Chorus:–

March on thus brave comrades,
In the cause that is right,
Show wisdom in Council,
Show valour in fight.

Chorus:–

Chorus
We have now a great army, both loyal and brave,
We ask for the vote and the vote we will have.

Appendix 7

SPECIMENS OF JOSEPH ARCH'S TRAVELLING EXPENSES, ETC. — 1876
AND 1877 —

From Account Book at the Museum of English Rural Life,
University of Reading

(The details given below relate to five separate weeks in 1876 and 1877.)

1876	s.	d.
Week beginning 25th September		
To Peterborough	5	9
Refreshments	1	–
To Spalding	1	9
Refreshments at Spalding	2	–
To London	7	8
Metropolitan		8
Refreshments	1	4
To Blandford	10	5½
At Hinton	3	–
At Blandford	7	–
To Basingstoke	6	5½
At Basingstoke	1	2
To Leamington	7	6½
Week beginning 2nd October		
To Worcester	3	4
To Bredon	1	–
At Overbury	3	6
To Cheltenham		9½
At Barrington	3	6
At Lechlade	3	6
To Fairford		9
To Cirencester	1	6
At Cirencester	1	6

248

To Tetbury	1	6
Telegraph	1	–
At Tetbury	2	6
To Nailbridge	1	–
To Gloucester	1	2
To Cheltenham		6
At Cheltenham	1	2
To Worcester	1	9
Refreshments	1	–
To Warwick	3	4

Week beginning 9th October

To Leamington		2
To Kirtlington	2	$10\frac{1}{2}$
At Kirtlington	1	9
To Chipping Norton	3	$-\frac{1}{2}$
Refreshments	1	–
To Ascott (under Wychwood)		$3\frac{1}{2}$
At Leafield	2	–
To Oxford	1	$-\frac{1}{2}$
Refreshments		8
To Leamington	3	9
To Stratford-on-Avon	1	$2\frac{1}{2}$
To Warwick	1	$2\frac{1}{2}$
Refreshments	1	–

1877
Week beginning 16th January

To Basingstoke	7	$8\frac{1}{2}$
To Salisbury	5	3
To Blandford	3	9
To Basingstoke	5	$3\frac{1}{2}$
To Warwick	7	$8\frac{1}{2}$
At Basingstoke	1	3
At Blandford	2	8
At Wimborne	2	–
At Wimborne (bed)	3	–
At Basingstoke	1	–

Week beginning 23rd January

To London	8	6
Metropolitan	1	3

At London	3	–
Stamps, etc.	13	$4\frac{1}{2}$
Refreshments	1	1

(In addition, a fare to Manchester of 15s. 5½d. and bed, breakfast, etc. of 8s. were disallowed during the week beginning 23rd January, 1877. Presumably they were disallowed because Arch was attending Liberal Party meetings — See *English Labourer* — 10th February, 1877.)

Appendix 8

ELECTION EXPENSES OF JOSEPH ARCH AND OF HIS OPPONENTS — 1880–95

1880 Election — Wilton Constituency

	JOSEPH ARCH			HON.SIDNEY HERBERT		
Agents, including Clerks, Messengers	£	s.	d,	£	s.	d.
and Canvassers	290	7	3	427	4	7
Hire of Conveyances*	112	0	0	71	2	0
Printing and Advertising	55	13	9	120	2	3
All other Expenses	–			39	17	4
TOTAL EXPENSES, *excluding* Returning Officer's charges	458	1	0	658	6	2
TOTAL EXPENSES, *including* Returning Officer's charges	512	14	7	712	19	8

*Expenditure to convey electors to the poll was made illegal by the 1883 Corrupt and Illegal Practices Prevention Act.

(From: Elections — Parliamentary Papers, Vol. LVII — 1880).

1885 Election   North-West Norfolk Constituency

	JOSEPH ARCH			LORD HENRY BENTINCK		
	£	s.	d.	£	s.	d.
Agents, Clerks and Messengers	260	11	0	212	19	6
Printing and Advertising	220	14	8	116	2	8
Stationery, Messages, Postage and Telegrams	92	8	7	387	13	9

	£	s.	d.		£	s.	d.
Public Meetings	56	19	0		54	19	0
Committee Rooms	20	2	0		40	17	6
Miscellaneous Matters	17	18	4		86	11	11
Personal Expenses	72	15	7		100	0	0
TOTAL EXPENSES, *excluding* Returning Officer's charges	741	9	2		999	4	4
TOTAL EXPENSES, *including* Returning Officer's charges	991	16	2		1,290	7	0

(From: Elections — Parliamentary Papers, Vol. LII — 1886)

1886 Election   North-West Norfolk Constituency

	JOSEPH ARCH			LORD HENRY BENTINCK		
	£	s.	d.	£	s.	d.
Agents	232	8	6	185	6	6
Clerks and Messengers	27	2	0	49	8	6
Printing and Advertising, Stationery, Postage and Telegrams	261	18	6	322	11	2
Public Meetings	35	17	0	20	8	10
Committee Rooms	14	0	3	25	3	0
Miscellaneous Matters	8	17	2	118	12	7
Personal Expenses	18	4	6	85	0	0
TOTAL EXPENSES, *excluding* Returning Officer's charges	598	7	11	806	10	7
TOTAL EXPENSES, *including* Returning Officer's charges	845	6	2	1,053	8	10

(From: Elections — Parliamentary Papers, Vol, LII — 1886)

1892 Election   North-West Norfolk Constituency

	JOSEPH ARCH			LORD HENRY BENTINCK		
	£	s.	d.	£	s.	d.
Agents	188	3	6	289	2	6
Clerks and Messengers	83	5	11	59	11	7

	£	s.	d.		£	s.	d.
Printing, Advertising, Stationery, Postage and Telegrams	240	0	0		411	3	6
Public Meetings	30	9	6		34	12	6
Committee Rooms	33	6	6		32	4	6
Miscellaneous Matters	73	5	2		128	9	8
Personal Expenses	16	19	3		98	5	7
TOTAL EXPENSES, *excluding* Returning Officer's charges	665	9	10		1,053	9	10
TOTAL EXPENSES, *including* Returning Officer's charges	949	9	1		1,336	8	1

(From: Elections — Parliamentary Papers — Vol. LXX — 1893-94

1895 Election — North-West Norfolk Constituency

	JOSEPH ARCH			E. K. B. TIGHE		
	£	s.	d.	£	s.	d.
Agents	197	14	0	188	19	6
Clerks and Messengers	80	8	0	101	16	0
Printing, Advertising, Stationery, Postage and Telegrams	243	3	4	415	10	2
Public Meetings	22	10	0	14	18	0
Committee Rooms	33	11	6	31	17	0
Miscellaneous Matters	77	2	0	77	6	11
Personal Expenses	22	10	1	99	18	4
TOTAL EXPENSES, *excluding* Returning Officer's charges	676	18	11	930	5	11
TOTAL EXPENSES, *including* Returning Officer's charges	950	8	1	1,203	15	1

(From: Elections — Parliamentary Papers, Vol. LXVII — 1896)

Index